Secrets of Selling
Yourself to People

Secrets of Selling Yourself to People

by

James T. Mangan

CASTLE BOOKS ★ NEW YORK

Born in a Hamburger Stand

This book was born in a hamburger stand. The time was midnight. The year one of the meanest of the Terrible Thirties.

I plopped down on a stool for a quick hamburger after a long day's work and found myself sitting next to Slim Kane. Slim and I had gone to grammar school together, parted, and now met for the first time in many years. He was in a talkative mood.

"Y'know," he said, "our school, along with all the other schools in this land is a failure."

I remained silent, waiting for amplification.

"Because," continued Slim, "no school teaches what a man out in the world needs to know—HOW TO SELL HIMSELF! Look at me. I'm an assistant cattle buyer at the stockyards. What do they pay me? Forty dollars a week! What do they pay my boss, the chief cattle buyer? Twenty-five thousand dollars a year!"

"Maybe he's worth it," I interjected.

From Slim: "No, from the standpoint of ability, knowledge of his job, knowledge of cattle, he should be getting the forty a week. And I SHOULD BE GETTING THE TWENTY-FIVE THOUSAND A YEAR!"

This started to sound much like ordinary griping. I guess Slim read skepticism in my face. "Look, Jim," said Slim, "let me make myself clear. That boss of mine *deserves* the twenty five thousand only because *he knows how to sell himself*. And I deserve what I get because I don't know how!"

Slim had plenty of skill in dealing with cattle.

But he freely confessed he had no skill in selling his own talents to the people who counted—his superiors.

"You're so right," I said. "I don't know of any school that

v

offers ten minutes' instruction on this important subject. Yet thousands of human beings sell themselves daily. And thousands have sold themselves in the past. It's clear that natural ability alone won't get you across. And a college education isn't enough, either. Slim, *this calls for a book!"*

Since that night in the mid-thirties I have interviewed myriad salesmen, thousands of business owners, executives and department managers, thousands of professional men, money men, intelligent men. Also a goodly collection of nobodies, and even a few nitwits—asking all the sundry the direct, basic question: "What do you think is the best way to sell yourself to others?"

(Incidentally, I just mentioned "nitwits." The truth does not necessarily exist only in high places. Sometimes asking a nitwit a serious question brings forth an amazing truth, awfully fast!)

If you've ever felt like Slim Kane; if you've ever wondered why it was and how it was that other fellows no brighter or more qualified than you have gotten that key promotion, closed that "impossible" sale or have been a big hit with the people who really count, then this book is for you. For a man like you who is interested in improving himself, this book will provide a complete program for revitalizing your business and personal life and for achieving success in your chosen field.

This book will tell you how you can develop your latent potential into actual accomplishments which will guarantee personal success. No longer will you have to endure the effects of a limited vocabulary, or suffer the pangs of starting a conversation with strangers. No longer will you tremble at the thought of speaking in public or preparing a written report for the boss. Instead, this book will give you 15 ways to improve your vocabulary quickly; 16 ways to start a conversation and keep it exciting; 8 keys to establish yourself as a competent speaker; 10 sure-fire methods to acquire sound writing ability and 20 steps for improving that ability.

After reading this book, you'll possess 8 bold "avenues to audacity" by which you can seize the moment and make your own opportunities. You'll learn 10 proven ways to make lasting connections with the people who can help you most; you'll know 12 secrets of personal showmanship which master show-

men, Ziegfeld, Barnum, George M. Cohan and Winston Churchill, have used and which you can adapt in selling yourself.
You'll have a 12-step program for setting up your own publicity
campaign, and you'll know 15 ways to "merchandise" your new
personality.

Along with these outstanding features you'll discover several
ways to set yourself apart from the crowd. You'll be told the
six key factors for developing your leadership potential. You'll
learn 10 different ways to become a livewire. You'll know how
to use both "visible" and "invisible" finesse when dealing with
people who really count. You'll find how "dependability plus"
can transform you from Dependable Denny to Remarkable
Roger.

These are only some of the many means that can be yours
through the use of this book. In all, there are 18 valuable chapters which will provide you with a step-by-step program for
mastering the SECRETS OF SELLING YOURSELF TO
PEOPLE.

Contents

Section One

YOU

You are an individual.

Pretty small, you think, when you reflect on your ignorance, your lack of abilities, your defects.

But you are an IMMENSE UNIVERSE when you begin to consider your *experience*—and the possibilities that lie ahead.

Yes, you have plenty of GOODS FOR SALE.

And how you sell the STUFF OF WHICH YOU ARE MADE will determine whether you become a SOMEBODY or remain a nobody.

[1]

Decide Right Now That You Want to Be a "Somebody!"

THERE'S NO rime or reason in buying, or even opening up, a book like this, unless you're going to decide not only to make something out of your self but, more specifically, to be a "somebody."

A *somebody* is a man who has definitely sold himself to others; who enjoys a solid reputation in his community, in his industry, in his chosen line of work; who holds the respect of all people he has met; who more than once has gained their favorable attention and, magically, lingers in their memory for months and years.

A "somebody" is a human being who, by his performance and example, stands head and shoulders above the motley throng of individual "nobodies."

I don't care if you're a nobody now. I don't care if you honestly believe and concede you're a nobody. All the big names of history, all the big names of today, were once names of nobodies. But these nobodies early in life, by instinct or artificial plan, decided that the quickest way to success was by selling themselves to others.

Neither success nor sparkling fame are necessarily earned by brilliant natural gifts, extraordinary talent, or *prodigious labor*. There are many short cuts, many ingenious efficiencies, an il-

3

limitable number of choices and "how-to's." But the ways and means that you can adopt must be suitable and practical for your own special individuality.

Jim O. did not want to be a civic leader, or a famous man in his own industry—banking.

What he wanted specifically was the same thing nearly all of us want—more money. Studying his chances for promotion to a higher salary, Jim saw a trend or policy in his own bank which was worth studying. Many promotions were in the form of titles —a better desk in a better position, a new name plate with the new fancy title, but very, very little extra money.

Jim decided to play the game, but with an ulterior and (we may as well admit) quite selfish motive. He announced to his superiors he was going out for the next higher job (with a nice title: Assistant Cashier). Eventually through industrious performance he got it. But no extra money. Now Jim began making contacts with other banks and bankers and eventually switched to another bank that needed a livewire assistant cashier—this time at considerably more money!

He more than made good at the new job in this big suburban bank. His great public relations ability and his hustling tactics in less than a year got him promoted to the big job of First Vice President. And though he did not live in the town in question, but rather in the nearby city, he was suddenly elected president of the Chamber of Commerce. These two big titles and honors should have gone to Jim's head, but didn't, because he saw only an infinitesmal increase in his own salary. So he kept his eye on the real ball—his *income,* not his honors. Old contacts congratulated him on his rise to fame, and Jim nourished these contacts into a new appreciation of his own size and ability.

So, again suddenly, it was announced in the big city paper that Jim again switched jobs, this time not to a bank, but to a financial firm not publicly related to activities like the Chamber of Commerce or community organizations. Jim stepped out on the spotlight of titles and honorary jobs (which had helped him sell himself) to go with a firm little known to the public but which was willing to pay him TWICE the salary he earned as the "big shot" vice president of the bank.

Let's Get Rid of that Cheap Idea You Have of Yourself

What we have to do at the start is knock out that cheap idea you have of yourself. You are not the only person in the world who is internally conscious of his own fears, his inabilities, his humble surroundings, and the million mean, crummy accents of day-to-day living. Practically *everyone* feels "crummy" most of the time. Shortage of laundry. Holes in the socks. Worn-out lining in the coat. Dirt under the fingernails. Rings around the washstand. Mistakes in grammar. Poverty-stricken vocabularies. Feeble ignorance on most subjects. These are universal *human* conditions.

In the act of being a somebody you do not lose this cheapness of living; but you do break its shackles. You build up a powerful self-esteem in spite of it. You suddenly realize *you* are more important than your minor traits and problems—that success is the property of any human being with enough boldness to *want* it.

What do you say? Shall we take that poor little you and make a great BIG YOU out of it? You not only have the right, but you definitely have the *duty,* of making *a name for yourself.*

I have known and worked with Frank Riley, the famous lettering artist and designer, for a long time.

Frank, inventor of Grayda and other printing types, always had every right to be known as one of the greatest letterers in the world. Even as a young artist he knew how good he was, but felt he needed the acclaim of others to prove his own ideas to himself.

So during the lush 1920's when his work went into great demand, he decided to show his nerve by charging more for his wares. Then, the impression seemed, the higher priced a man's lettering, the better the lettering. Frank finally got his scale of prices up to *$50 for one word of lettering*—the highest price scale ever attained in the lettering art. "I was simply raising my own self-regard," says Frank, "and confirming it through others." Of course, after proving himself capable of any standard, Frank's lettering prices are just as reasonable as those charged by comparable artists and his high craftsmanship goes into even the smallest and lowest priced jobs he may handle. "Raising one's standards of craftsmanship to the highest level and keeping it there is another, and still better, way of certifying self-regard," says Frank Riley.

Don't Try to Pass the Duty for Success on to Your Children

Most parents try to pass the duty for success on to their children. You are already strong, experienced, and wise in the ways of the world. Your children are weak, soft, unremarkable clay.

Yet you insist they are going to get a better chance than you got, a better education than you, and a good chance at the fine things in life that you have missed. You want them to make something of themselves, meanwhile resigning yourself to an anonymous little pigeon hole in life, burying yourself in its darkness and its smallness.

Wrong! Wrong! Wrong! No matter how old you are, you can make a better education for yourself than your children can ever hope for! I have met in my life many university presidents, many doctors of philosophy and bearers of high college degrees.

But the best educated man I have ever known is a young sculptor in Altadena, California named David Green. Green was equipped with no more formal schooling than high school, but early in life he learned *how to read*, fed an egregious appetite for knowing the great men of all time and their great needs. He has lived his whole life for greatness, and recognizes greatness as every man's goal. He is a writer, a teacher, an artist; and little wonder he was recently voted one of the "Forty Foremost Californians!"

In the Pasadena area Green commenced to put the retained result of all his years of selective reading to work. Though he spoke quietly and measuredly, important people began to give solid attention to his critiques on historical figures and famous classical works. He gave definite help to fellow artists and students who had only a sketchy grasp of the classics. He became, in effect, a human classical "library," and his fame quickly spread all over California, with resulting commissions in sculpture, his first art love.

Your children are going to have a much better chance at success if *You* are successful; a much better education if *your education for success* surpasses any formal education they may receive. For you, by your example in making something out of your own life, will always be the best and greatest teacher they will ever meet.

How to Root Out the Genius Within You

Any modest person would be embarrassed by being told he was a genius—and you are no exception. Yet I tell you here and now, *you are a genius*. Maybe not an all-around genius, maybe not a person with a record-breaking I.Q., or a wizard of ability and versatility. But you are full of genius just the same, *special genius* that can be made to pay you big dividends.

Proof?

You are sure you are different from other people. Your thoughts are special, your feelings peculiar to you alone. You certainly have an individuality—and whether in your heart you consider it good, bad, or mediocre—it is *your* individuality. Properly wrapped up, attractively packaged and beribboned, it could easily appear to others as *something very fine*.

How to root out your own genius? Find someone to push you, open you up, make you do what you know you can do. It ought to be a man's wife, if he is married, or his parents if not. But alas, too often little practical help comes from these quarters. Ask the help of other close relatives, of tried and true friends, seeking the one man or woman who will care enough to talk "cold turkey" to you, give you a fresh shot of ambition, help you find a new goal, and keep pushing, goading, and reminding you that you have to work to reach it!

Accept the DUTY of GREATNESS! That constant, everyday remorseful pounding inside your personal conscience, is a message from you to yourself: "You ought to be great." Get on speaking terms with greatness. A great designer with whom I worked intimately idolized the late W. A. Dwiggins so intensely, he was afraid to meet Dwiggins face to face, though he had plenty of opportunities to do so. Another, of immense stature of his own, so idolized Norman Bel Geddes that he was afraid to speak to him though they belonged to the same club. Eventually I had the chance personally to tell both Dwiggins and Bel Geddes of this idolatry. Neither could believe it existed for each man was so human and down-to-earth he could never understand how another individual of depth and discernment could get so out-of-perspective that he would put any other individual on a pedestal. The moral is: when you find yourself able to recognize greatness in another, arrange to get on speaking terms with that other person—your recognition is your right!

You are often astonished at the brilliant vocabulary of a fellow who never went beyond high school. He may be a professional wrestler, a broker, a salesman but with words he can outshine many a college professor. The explanation? He has made a fetish of words, he has picked greatness in speech as a personal goal. And what a great and practical goal! For speech can be practiced every minute of the day, studied intensely in the laboratory of human intercourse without recourse to school or books!

Too many young men and women give all their worry and thought to "dating" and social activity—not a great and noble goal! You can only root out the genius within you by tackling things that are big and difficult—and WORTHY OF YOUR GENIUS.

H. C. Mattern by trade is a leather worker who renovates, restores and rebuilds old or damaged leather furniture and other pieces. But by avocation he is much more than that. He follows the leather trade for a very good reason: it takes him and his wife all around the country meeting new people every day, sorting out the interesting ones, and especially helping the two Matterns to find individuals who may need their help not in leather, but in life.

Wherever a good cause, or a good man, may be in the throes of slipping, Mattern and Wife suddenly appear on the scene. With high Christian charity, and wise human understanding, they have solved thousands of problems for those in need of real help.

Now here is a man and wife whose trade is really Christianity, and not leather working at all. Expert at leathercraft, they have made themselves much more expert at human relations and have found the ultimate joy their genius for helping people can deliver, without in any way disturbing their means or methods for earning a living.

Just how do Mattern and Wife help people? One activity (and quite a rare and unusual one)—they encourage young authors, especially of "first" books, by buying the books in large quantities and *giving* them to others. They visit prisons, talk to the wardens, try to render assistance they need from the "outside" world, and have helped many a released convict to get a good job and restore himself to a dignified status in society. They are both Bible experts, and do ceaseless apostolizing for the power of the Bible, and have helped many a young minister strengthen his vocation. In short, rather than falling in the category popularly known as "do-gooders" they have actually become "jacks-of-all-trades" at fixing up and re-oiling broken bits of human machinery.

One great gift of H. S. Mattern and his wife is this: they never linger long in any one place. They never stick around to bask in their own glory. They couldn't possibly bore anybody—not even an enemy.

You can do what you want or refrain. You can say "yes" or "no" to any contemplated action. You are always free to do the exact opposite of what others would do in any given situation.

When invited to give a speech, or be chairman of a program, or take on some special work that puts you in a prominent spot —in that very instant you can screw your courage up to the point of saying: "I am not completely and abjectly afraid, I will not run away—I ACCEPT!"

YOU ARE A UNIVERSE OF EXPERIENCE

Who are you? You are your own experience! Everything you have ever done, everything important, everything insignificant, is you. Every dream you have ever had is experience, and that experience is your exclusive property. Every action, mechanical or unconscious, forgotten or remembered, is yours—it is stored within you, it cannot get away.

Believe in your experience, believe in its immensity; even though you can remember only the smallest part of it, it is all there for you to use, to work modern wonders and miracles.

A head of gray hair turns black, its owner not knowing how or why. New teeth grow back into the gums of a man of eighty against all apparent rules of nature and science. A fat man goes on a reducing diet and takes off fifty pounds in two months. An incurable drunkard suddenly stops drinking for the rest of his life. A hopeless arthritic straightens up and his arthritis leaves him for good. A greenhorn salesman captures the biggest order in history. The miraculous event is often attributed to will power, seldom to experience; but buried, indescribable *experience,* called into action by *will* and a mighty *want,* should get the credit.

All his mature life Harry C. wanted to sell himself. He wanted people (neighbors and strangers especially) to know his true stature which he was proud of and which, incidentally, was truly great and good. After each long conversation with an acquaintance, he felt disappointed that he hadn't "gone over" as he should. He started to analyze himself at last and came to this conclusion: "I am not talking too much about myself but I may be talking too much about my children." So he stopped talking about his children and steered each conversation to the other fellow's children. A miracle followed. People who used to dodge Harry now sought him out as a man among men, ultimately recognizing him as a successful man of the world. Harry had used up too much of his experience (experience with his own family) in trying to sell himself and it did not work. But he transferred his knowledge of children to the field of others' children, and was instantly a surefire hit.

The inclination of everyone who tries to sell himself is to talk about himself. This inclination can easily give you the label of ego-maniac. Very often if the news about yourself is sheer news —unusual, remarkable—it will gain a respectful ear. But it is better to transfer your own experiences into the possible experiences of others in the same category, when you want to win their interest and approval.

No matter how colorless or unremarkable your past history, it is loaded with gems of experience that can be turned into money, publicity, and practical benefit. This is the genius within. It was not *born* into you. You made it yourself. Genius for the most part is the brave use of past experience.

Make the attainments varied enough, numerous enough and there you have your proof of genius. Perhaps you know a man who is a very good bowler, a very good golfer, a very good card player, all rolled in one. You marvel at the man because of his all-around ability. You may even call him a genius. Well, most geniuses are people who have learned how to use the findings (experience) gained in one field to carry over the efficiency and good form into any other field. They save time in communizing their own practicing, pool it formally, so that in each new activity they seek to do "the right thing" in the easiest and most natural way to accomplish their aims.

If You Want It You Can Have It. Attainment is one proof of genius. And to accomplish anything you must first have an *objective.* Get a definite objective. Know it. State it. Repeat it endlessly. Photograph it, visualize it. Make a manifesto to yourself and to the world—proclaim publicly that you are going to attain your objective.

Now *want* it. Don't just wish for it, don't just admit it is a "good thing." Want it with all your heart, soul and body. If necessary, go a little mad. Suffer. Beg the "Inner You" to come through, ask your universe of personal experience to join in your crusade. And as you start on the way toward achievement of your goal, carry yourself as if you already possessed the goal itself!

Bill Stormer, Pittsburgh restaurateur, in his youth was sparring partner for the late great Harry Greb. He estimates he fought at least a hundred times with Greb in the gym. Among the boxing world at large, everyone knows Greb and his greatness. Few have met Stormer. But Bill has seen to it that the big slice of his life spent in the gym with Greb was not wasted.

Hundreds of sports figures constantly pour into Bill's restaurant to ask him about Greb, who every day is becoming more and more of a legend in boxing history. Bill Stormer, by encouraging the interest and dispensing intimate information, has learned how to turn the apparently valueless past into a prosperous present. This is the genius of the smart use of experience.

How to Make Yourself into Saleable Merchandise

Every person must sell himself in the way the big firms do. Have a good product. Present it in the most favorable light. Make it hard for the public to refuse to take it.

Let's find out what *you* have to sell. You, just plain, little, unknown you, have a great deal more to you than you may suspect.

Your body—"humble" servant

You have a body. Your body may not be remarkable, but you can do many remarkable things with it, things that do not require skill, special ability or experience. You can command your body to move, to go places, and one of the finest ways to move it is to *visit the sick*. A call on a sick, bedridden friend presents a marvelous chance for selling yourself not only to him and his family, not only to other friends who may hear you have been there, but, most precious of all, in *selling yourself to yourself*, by performing a grand work of mercy entirely on your own power.

Let's leave out all considerations of good faith or questionable motive. The deed is a good deed simply because you have brought your body to the spot. Your reward is immediate uplift of the spirit, but the large reward is your new awareness that you can do marvelous things *with your body*.

The man who keeps on saying, "I can't do a darn thing!" is ridiculous. If all he ever did was regularly visit the sick, attend wakes and funerals and lavish his spare time in this kind of work, he would be a standout among all his fellow mortals.

Anthony "X", less than 5 feet tall, and weighing under 100 pounds, is now a successful and prospering jockey. He started work as a shoe clerk where his small size helped him get close to his work. "Many customers," relates Tony, "would look me over and exclaim: 'My but you are SMALL—you ought to be a jockey!' Such remarks would tend to infuriate me, though I smiled outwardly. But one day a man came into the shoe store and said this: 'Do you like HORSES? You have the right BUILD for a jockey.' I told him I did like horses, but what impressed me most was his complimenting me on my BUILD instead of my smallness. With only that one word as a guide-post, I did, with help from him and others, learn to ride well. I had finally discovered that my body was an article of high value, though by normal standards it was inferior."

Just try a few experiments in moving your body around. Whether it's an humanitarian deed like visiting the sick, or a pragmatic act like attending a meeting of your industry or business, you will quickly learn that your body—your plain, uninspired carcass—is really a noble thing, capable of great service to society and to yourself.

Some how-to rules and suggestions: Help in a neighborhood or community event. Put up a flag pole. Patch up the cross-walks at streets and alleys so pedestrians do not have to step in puddles. Shovel off your sidewalk in winter, keep it neat. Keep a clean alley behind your own house. Open up sewers nearby when they are clogged with debris. Acts like these inevitably cause you to be seen working in public. You not only gain public respect but your good example invariably causes others to do likewise—the good work of your body sells them on you as well as on civic improvement.

Get those two hands working. You can sit in your chair and think with your brain. That is supposed to be lofty exercise. You can read a book with your eyes. That is supposed to be broadening and uplifting. You can talk with your mouth—oh, how you can talk!—and some of that chatter is supposed to be intelligent. You certainly give these familiar organs plenty of exercise.

But your hands are starved, hungry for action, crying to

express themselves and you in practical work. Sew a button on a coat, drive a nail with a hammer, change a broken shoelace for a new one. Perversely, we all seem to dread doing a job that requires special use of the hands. But after the job is done, no matter how minor its nature, we are thrilled.

After your face and head, your hands are usually the only uncovered part of your body. They can be much more visible than the face when they go into motion. One young singer has gone over, strictly with the use of his hands in interpreting the mood of his songs; another has missed hitting the top because his hands always seem to be in the way of his voice, actually obstructing the rendition of his songs. Kate Smith's hands are in a way as remarkable as her voice. You can use your hands in the whole gambit of self-expression. Practise interpreting abstract thought with the hands, for example: hope, despair, spirit, eagerness, appeal, skepticism, etc.

Willie Mosconi, pool and billiard champion, one day lost his job in a furniture factory. The skill in his hands determined him to find a more challenging activity than making furniture. Though he had played little or no pool in his early youth, his hand hunger drove him to the pool tables to learn and master the game. "Everyone's hands," says Willie, "have some special skill, and he who feeds his own hands when they are hungry will eventually find what he should do with his life."

Your heart—show it, use it. General Motors used to have a slogan "Making New Friends and Keeping the Old." A good slogan for a business and for human beings.

Keeping old friends is even more important than making new friends.

If you will now, this moment, call to mind the names of your real true blue friends and ask yourself how they were made, how the miracle of friendship came about, you will concede that it takes time, circumstance, sacrifice, trial, and a subtle, complicated network of sentiments to make a friend.

It cannot be done overnight, it cannot be done by intention or design. How important, then, to keep friendships alive! You may be separated by distance, but a local phone call is only ten cents and a long distance call only a couple of dollars. Isn't a true-blue friend worth a couple of dollars every once in a while?

Everything I have said about distributing your body generously applies to your heart in double measure. Don't let old friendships die! In your heart you think just as much of your old friend as you always did, perhaps you love him more than ever, but unless you let him see your love, hear and feel your affection once in a while, he may begin to doubt you and forget you.

Mental telepathy is no substitute for actual contact! If you can't do anything else, you can write him a letter, a letter for "no good reason," a spontaneous physical proof of your love.

The world knows your heart is there if you show it. It may be there but if you never show it, it's difficult for anyone to believe you have a heart at all. From a display of heart comes the love and affection not only of friends and acquaintances disposed to be friendly to you; total strangers are also attracted to you. Often out of a number of friendly strangers a new true friend appears.

Never be shocked or appalled at the disgrace, real or imaginary, that may fall on another individual. If you know him ever so slightly, call him up, drop in at his house, let him see that you are not afraid to be seen in his presence. Take him for a walk where scores of others may see you associating with him in his black hour. You have nothing to lose, and a whole world of everlasting gratitude to gain. And you cannot incriminate yourself in a single such act of charity.

If you have access to good news first, spread it fast. One worker sometimes hears of another's promotion before the promoted one himself. Tell him the good news—be the first with your heart. If you hear of a veterans' bonus that has just passed, tell other veterans quickly. The bearer of good news is liked almost as much as the originator of the benefaction. If you make the spreading of fresh good news a habit, people begin to regard you as a public benefactor, which indeed you are.

In the loss or misfortune of others, instead of merely offering to help, look around and find some specific way to actually help.

Your heart often works much faster than your mind. If you see a fallen article, your heart instantly says: "Pick it up." Your mind, however, begins to deliberate: "Whose is it? If I pick it up, will someone think I am a thief? Why not pretend I do not see it at all?" Follow your heart. If someone sees you, he can only admire your initiative, your spirit of service, your generosity.

You have a body, you have a pair of hands, you have a heart, you have an emotional system and a wealth of many other highly personal tools for making yourself liked, respected, honored. The fact that others have these same tools and rarely use them with real efficacy should make no difference to you. The defection of others is no excuse for your own conduct in the business and social world. Their unawareness of natural gifts makes your own, put to natural and practical use, shine by contrast.

Any *nobody* is instantly on his way to being a *somebody* the moment he decides to use the gifts God gave *everybody* the way they should be used!

Every Improvement Is a Big Improvement

There is no such thing as a "little" self-improvement. The tiniest, most insignificant act that improves you is a huge gain. It immediately puts you into the plus column. It fills you with elation and immeasurable self-respect. It puts you on intimate terms with self-progress, ambition. It gives you a new taste of success and *every taste of success* is a firm step toward your goal.

Study out the scores of little improvements at your fingertips; things you can do without consulting anyone else, without swaying or selling other people.

If your teeth need attention, you can go to the dentist. If your muscles are flabby, you can force yourself into some mild exercise. If you're fat, you can reduce at least five pounds. If you need a haircut and you're delaying for no good reason, hurry over to the barber. If your car needs washing, wash it or have it washed.

Did you ever in your whole life do one of these simple little things without feeling good, without knowing you were improved?

And then there's an assortment of many other little things that require a bit of daring. Are you game enough to try them? If you have never had a manicure in your whole life, go and get your first one. If you don't have a checking account at the bank and still have use for one, go and open one up.

Tackle the little things in the so-called "luxury" class, in the "first-time-for-you" class, and don't worry about anyone thinking you are trying to be a big shot.

Every successful person is a big shot. But no one ever became important overnight. You must condition yourself to the successful life by gradually and steadily getting a series of small accomplishments under your belt.

Many a full-grown man has yet to get his first manicure or massage. The longer you put off these "little things," the bigger and harder they become, but once—only once—accomplished, a feeling of great achievement results!

Are you *afraid* to be seen looking in a bookstore window? Are you actually *afraid to buy a book* you know you should read? If you are, break down the barrier by buying just one book as soon as you can.

A housewife expresses great surprise and some hurt on finding that her best pal, another housewife, is taking college night courses without having confided in her. You are not required to account to your friends for any self-improvement you engage in—it is all your own business and none of theirs.

Go to an art museum, though it's the first time in your life. Do it quietly, without a big to-do. If you have long felt like taking up a really fancy and "rare" sport like fencing or archery because these games have special class and atmosphere, go ahead and dive in. And you need not make a life-long hobby of them. Just being able to say that you undertook the sport once may be enough to gain you a little self-esteem and outside-esteem, too.

If you are studying French, don't be ordinary and tell it around. Let it be discovered accidentally as it surely will. It will make the news much more potent at selling you as a person on his way to success through self-improvement.

[2]

How to Turn Your Deficiencies and Fears into Great Personal Assets

THE LATE Augie Kieckhefer, national three-cushion champion, had only one eye. In a game where fine eyesight is demanded, he was especially noted for his ability to hit the object ball "thin", that is, barely touch it with his cue ball so as to preserve a long angle. Not many of his opponents even knew of his deficiency. To his intimates he confided that he had looked around to find a field where his defect might become an asset and discovered that in three-cushion billiards his one eye gave him more accuracy than two.

John Masefield, poet laureate of England, was a saloon porter for several years. He found inspiration even in cleaning spittoons. He used a low job as a means of studying humanity in the raw. All of his poems are of highest quality but their content has a down-to-earth quality and a great human compassion that few other famous poets have ever matched. Wouldn't you think that a saloon would be a poor place for the making of a great poet, especially in the face of the saying that "poets are born, not made"?

All through his later writings, we find that Masefield is on the side of the lowly, the underdog. In his greatest "manifesto" lyric poem he announced that while beauty, color and gold were for others, all he asked was a "handful of ashes and a mouthful of mold," and wished only to sing of the "maimed and the halt and the blind." Undoubtedly this alliance with the common and forgotten people did much to cause him to be selected poet laureate.

Your deficiencies are assets and your greatest fears can become your favorite hobbies.

How These "Greats"
Capitalized on Their Looks:

ILLUSTRATION: Abe Lincoln knew he was plain and homely.

TECHNIQUE: He often deliberately spoke in a plain and homely manner.

IDEA: Maybe, you can match your *words* to your *looks*.

Did you ever stop to consider the really large number of photographs you have seen of Lincoln? Photography was just coming in when Lincoln moved into the political spotlight, but he must have been willing to pose or sit for his photograph for practically any cameraman. And the pictures we have of Lincoln, all showing a plain and rugged man, reveal that he knew how to take a "good" picture in spite of his so-called homely looks.

Every published photo of Lincoln shows him to be a person of great public importance and a man of dignity.

Raymond Loewy, one of today's great industrial designers, speaks with a decided foreign accent. When he first came to this country, he had a great deal of trouble with his accent and with the English language. But he quickly mastered the language and now speaks with tremendous eloquence and persuasiveness. He could have changed his accent, too, but deliberately did not. He finds the foreign accent adds extra glamour to his personality and he is selling a glamourous Raymond Loewy just as surely as he is selling designing service!

Of course, Raymond carefully nourishes a complementary impression in distinctive appearance and a meticulous manner of dress.

ILLUSTRATION: Alice Longworth said of President Calvin Coolidge: "He looks like he'd been weaned on a pickle."

TECHNIQUE: Coolidge laughed at and enjoyed the description.

SCHEME: Knowing his looks matched his desire for New England thrift, he insisted on giving the people economy in government.

Coolidge apparently did not like to pose for "publicity" photos, he was "economical" in this as in nearly all other fields. If forced to put on an Indian headress, for instance, when meeting a group of Indian leaders, Coolidge playfully overdid his role and caused the picture to come out extra stiff and lifeless —probably because he did not want anyone to say he was trying to sell himself in public. But he had the sell-yourself spirit just the same and loved to play jokes on his secret service bodyguards, often sneaking out for walks on public sidewalks with no guard accompanying. Once the Presidential secret service men who had guarded different Presidents over a span of thirty years were polled to find out which President was most popular with them. Coolidge easily led the list as their all-time favorite President!

How often have we all been in the company of a person who has been pre-advertised as "a man of few words!" It's hard to resist trying to "open up" such a man, to get him to talk. When we do succeed, we give extra value to his every utterance, we regard him as a person of great wisdom. He not only sells himself by keeping his mouth shut, but constantly puts extra stress on the fact that he is a man who seldom indulges in copious conversation. In many cases, such a man is on occasion a loquacious speaker who can turn on a veritable torrent of words when necessary, but his reputation in word-economy is what gains him the attention and respect of his public and gives extra value to all his words.

ILLUSTRATION: Clark Gable had definite "loving-cup" ears.

TECHNIQUE: Gable decided he couldn't do anything about his ears, but could do a lot with the *rest* of his looks.

RESULT: Clark Gable has been called "the handsomest man in Hollywood."

After he got his first break, Gable dressed to kill in any situation which permitted richly tailored clothes. Any man's looks are immensely helped by an expensive, perfectly fitted suit of clothes.

ILLUSTRATION: Arthur Brisbane had an abnormally high brow.

TECHNIQUE: Brisbane wrote and dealt strictly in common ordinary horse sense.

STRATEGEM: His common sense was everywhere hailed as "classic thinking."

CONCLUSION: Your clumsy accent, your big nose, your moles and freckles can be turned into capital, if you will *use* them instead of merely *hating* them.

An Aside: The movies cannot use the most beautiful actress in the world if she is not PHOTOGENIC.

What does *photogenic* mean?

> It means: BIG MOUTH
> HEAVY CHEEKBONES
> STRONG SKIN

> And *not:* Pretty
> Dainty
> Feminine

Diogenes, the Greek philosopher, bore a different name up to the day a frank friend told him he looked like a dog. So he promptly changed his name Diogenes, meaning "dog-like."

TECHNIQUE: *Make a bad thing worse and it may change into something better.*

Diogenes got a lantern and went around town searching for an "honest man." He devoted his life to searching and preaching. His looks helped him cut an unforgettable figure in history.

Make up a list of everything you can't do and everything else you're afraid to try. Go into detail. Be honest. Get all the bad stuff down on paper.

Now stare at the list and ask yourself: "Am I really this helpless?" In the twinkling of an eye you will begin to reflect: "Some of these things I've confessed I can't do, I MIGHT ACTUALLY DO! And some of the things I fear, I admit I should have no need to fear."

If you have a definite handicap or deficiency, study it for its possible advantages. When handsome Franklin Roosevelt was stricken with infantile paralysis, all thought of his promising political career was finished. But, told he would never walk again, Roosevelt took stock of himself and meditated: "Most politicians are forever dashing around to meet other politicians and constituents and wasting valuable time in travelling. If I can make people come to me, with my immobility as a very good reason, then I can have better meetings and save an immense amount of time." And so the man who couldn't walk turned his handicap into an asset and was elected President four times!

A writer was recently asked to write a topical book in two weeks! Because the subject matter was so timely, the publisher insisted on having the first rough draft in that time. The author, being a fast writer, was not bothered too much by the deadline, but the day he started writing he came down with an agonizing backache. He could not even sit down to write, because if he sat, he would not be able to get up. In such straits, with acute pain crippling him, the writer had every right to turn down the job. But no, he took stock before conceding that all hope was lost. Finding he could stand up, he placed his typewriter on top of a high chest of drawers and bravely went about the task. His manuscript was not only finished on time but the writer also found that writing standing up is a good tonic for the brain. It brings the copy closer to the eyes. It allows one to walk around now and then while at the task. It is a lot easier to get started!

In every deficiency, there is a compensating asset. Before

surrendering to "disaster", be sure to examine the deficiency thoroughly for its potential success content.

A large percentage of history's greatest leaders were men of minor stature, *short*. But they always *stood up straight*. Standing up straight doesn't raise your physical height by much, but it does wonders for your moral height. It is hard to say *"I can't"* when you have *drawn yourself up to your full height*.

And consider the number of successful men who are *positively homely*. If you have a face that will stop a clock, *wait!* Don't retreat into your shell, that pan of yours has possibilities. It registers better than the average good-looking face, and is remembered longer. Perhaps it makes up into a better photograph, too, for homely men generally photograph well. Get some pictures taken of that face of yours and scatter them around boldly; everyone will be more impressed by your looks than you, because you are used to deprecating them.

Seven Solid Devices for Changing Bashfulness into Ammunition for Self-Advancement

Bashfulness is the big, unannounced beast lurking behind most "I can't's." If you're bashful, admit it. It's a universal disease, but it's the one malady that's boundlessly good for everybody. You say you can't be a boss because you're bashful; you can't be a public speaker, or a writer, or a salesman, or a political leader. You may give better, more rational excuses for your "I Can't's" but bashfulness still remains the real reason.

1. *X-ray your bashfulness*. Find what it is made of. Bashfulness is no deficiency, but really a tremendous asset. A good synonym for it is *super-sensitivity*. That means you feel things in a super-normal way; your thinking is excessive, exaggerated, prolonged. Nothing the matter with a quality that makes you feel and think deeply—it's an advantage! Your bashfulness with people gives you a rich understanding of them; your intense inquiries into every facet of your day-to-day problems delivers an amazing understanding of these problems.

2. *Put your bashfulness to work*. Dare to engage in conversation with the type of fellow who acts as if he "knows it all."

Argue a little. Deny a few of his dogmatic pronouncements. You may be able to stop him cold and make him look up to you with a new respect.

Take heart from the words of the gentle French essayist Montaigne, who said this about conversation: "The real secret of conversation is *contradiction*. I would rather sit down at a dinner table with a clumsy boor who contradicted everything I said than with the finest-mannered gentleman in the land."

3. *Bashfulness is courage germinating.* Bashfulness is not fear; it is courage in the germinating stage; it's a yeasty vat of millions of impressions and facts inside you ready to burst into bloom. Give it a chance, force it to work, and you're in for a wonderful surprise. A bashful man, springing into action, rises superior at once to the host of other men, nervy but insensitive, who are always trying to run things.

4. *Stop despising yourself for not speaking up.* Self-denunciation, according to Spinoza, is a perverted form of pride. What? You, bashful you, proud? Exactly! Every time you say things like "I haven't the guts," "I can't cope with others," "I'm no talker," you're indulging in a wild, foolish form of pride just as obnoxious as if you were boasting of your wealth, skill or accomplishments. Your duty is to be *great*. Your bashfulness is the basic equipment. You can never justify yourself with puny, little words of self-effacement.

5. *Force yourself and dare to do it!* Then examine yourself. Bust out of your shell of bashfulness the first time and you'll feel a permanent strength for keeping on with it, for using your sensitivity as a means of winning people to your views and selling yourself out loud.

6. *If loath to appear in public,* start attending meetings, especially those at which *you do not quite belong*.

No one will ask you for credentials, no one will throw you out.

Walk up to the front pew in church—just once in your life— to see how it feels.

At an association luncheon or dinner, where you think you're a "nobody", and seats are not reserved, get in early and grab a seat right next to the speaker's table.

7. *Invite the laugh.* If you can't dance, dance anyhow. They'll laugh. Let 'em.

Arthur Godfrey certainly is no prize virtuoso, and his vocal chords are not made of platinum, yet Arthur boldly sings to millions on TV and makes them like it.

My own father couldn't sing at all, couldn't hit a true note. But on occasion he would stand before an audience of a thousand or more and sing "Johnny Smoker" or "The Banks of the Wabash." His confidence was so paralyzing that no one could have laughed even if he wanted to.

Whatever you do—singing, acting, whispering, or shouting—*ring true!* Jenny Lind, "the Swedish Nightingale," COULD sing. But at her every concert, before the first song, she stood in the wings and prayed: *"Oh God, that I may ring true tonight!"*

Seven Easy Ways to Become a "Self-starter"

Successful business men agree that any young man going in business for himself must have a good stock of self-inspiration. Now you personally are going into the business of selling yourself to others. You're the chief investor in this business, the sole boss, and the only employee. To start the business isn't enough, you must keep it going, growing. Self-inspiration is the way.

1. *Show your pep.*

Everybody likes pep and a peppy man is a constant inspiration to all about him. Pep brings you instant prestige and a conscious sense of new power. Move briskly. Speed up your talk. Throw your chest out and pull your stomach in.

Vibrate *outwardly* instead of *inwardly.*

Jimmy Durante does it. You, too, can vibrate your eyes, your nose, your hands, your feet, your whole body.

Try it in private. Doesn't this extra shaking up give you new PEP *immediately!*

The most familiar expression of outward vibration may be a

"bounce" or "spring" in one's step. If you drag your heels, people put you down as an old man. How often has your deep regard gone out to a fellow, old or young, whom you have just seen run up a flight of stairs! If you do not feel like running up the whole flight, try to put a little extra spring into the last two steps at the top of the flight.

2. *Show a willing attitude.*

If someone asks for an undescribed favor, say "yes" even before you know what you are getting into. If you're faced with a task you despise, tackle it as if you loved it, devour it as delicious; pretend the loathsome thing is desirable and it *will be* desirable. Pin up this gem from Ben Franklin: "A task done willingly is a task done easily!"

3. *Increase the load.*

No job is too big or heavy when you're inspired. If you think it is, then deliberately *increase the load,* take on more than is required of you. Few of us ever do too much; most of us are inclined to do too little.

Ty Cobb, baseball great, was noted for the passion and ferocity with which he played the game. His speed on the bases allowed him to break all base-stealing records though he definitely was not the fastest man who ever ran the bases.

In the hour of practice before any game started, Cobb wore shoes *weighted down heavily with lead.* In the actual game, just as he came up to bat he swung three or four baseball bats. He deliberately increased the load! Later when in the throes of a bitter contest, he found that regulation equipment weighed practically nothing and allowed him to move with the speed of a panther.

If the boss tells you you have to make a five-minute talk, which you fear, insist on twenty minutes. Plan for twenty minutes. Prepare for the full twenty minutes. Then, when the time comes, reduce your talk to ten and it will be just as easy as the "five-minute" talk would have been!

4. Emulate the successful type.

You personally know, or have heard of, some man who is going places, powered by his own ambitions and wants. Copy him! Keep him in mind every minute. If you have learned he works longer hours than you, decide to put in more hours than he. If he squeezes more results out of his hours than you do, study his tactics, match his thinking, try to outdo him. The man in question may not know you exist. Doesn't matter. Use him as your goad, your whip. He's free!

Act as if you're successful. Ever notice how many male secretaries to big men end up as big men themselves?

Samuel Insull, utilities tycoon of the Twenties, as a young man was secretary to the financial wizard Tilden. Good at shorthand and typing, Insull could have been stuck in his secretarial job for life with its important aura, its frequent bonuses. It was a "good thing." But Insull, recognizing the "good thing" as a bad thing that could make him a prisoner for life, deliberately set out to copy Tilden. He copied his dress. His manner of speaking. His thinking. His wit and his strategy. To all intents he became "another Tilden." When a competitive organization began a search for a new leader, "as good as Tilden," they quickly found their man. Samuel Insull!

The list is endless. By intimate association they absorb the poise, the manners, the impressive gifts of the successful exemplars. They copy unconsciously.

You can do it consciously. Feel like a million, talk like a million, act like a million.

The old slogan went: "To be successful, look successful; wear diamonds." Diamonds don't apply to men today; but good clothes, fine grooming, cultivated language, and scores of other self-selling gems do.

5. Be a slave driver with yourself.

Take yourself seriously; you're here to make something of yourself and what could be more serious than that? Condone no laxity or self-indulgence, and *fine yourself* every time you say things like: "I'm tired," "Feel rotten!" This fine can consist of extra work, either obnoxious or inspiring, which you impose on yourself.

I once imposed a unique fine on myself. I had been feeling blue, due to my own self-consciousness that I was not doing enough creative writing. Then and there I imposed this fine: "For one hundred days you must write a five-hundred word inspirational essay each day. You may write more than one a day if you wish, but no day must pass without your writing *one*. After you have produced one hundred essays, the fine will be paid!"

Some days I would complete the essay early in the morning. Other times I would come home late, tired and exhausted, yearning for rest, but force the essay out through sheer will power. On many days, wanting to pay the fine up ahead of time, I wrote several essays; but no day went by without my writing at least one.

At the end of a single month, I had discovered I had completed my self-imposed sentence. What might have taken a hundred days was completed in thirty. I felt great, like a man released from prison. I stopped to look over what I had written under duress and found the stuff was free, sweet and thrilling.

In a little while I sold half the hundred essays for three thousand dollars! I had not fined myself at all but rather had pushed myself into an easy avenue for making money.

MORAL: When you become a "self" slave driver, you're working for the finest boss on earth!

6. *Experiment with your versatility.*

Your job, your trade has a name—and the label is pinned on you. But surely it is not the ONLY thing you can do.

Give all your other abilities a tryout.

John McCaffrey, president of International Harvester, was a truck pusher in the factory. But there were other things he could do better than push trucks. He could think. He could talk. He suspected he had "class." Now at the top of his organization, he is known not only as a great industrial magnate, but as a brilliant socialite. McCaffrey, being in the farm machinery business, latched on to as many good farm movements as he could, such as the 4-H Club, became a director on many committees which brought him into close contact with rich and powerful men who were members of the same committees.

What movements in your own industry can be noted as good for all in your line of business? Many committees are crying for new members to lend new action and fresh energy to their work.

There's nothing wrong with latching on to the hoi polloi, the uncountable hordes of ordinary people, but too often, unless we are out to become politicians or other leaders, we are absorbed by the masses and lost in anonymity.

Look around you for the "surefire" item, latch on to it. Carl Sandburg latched on to Abe Lincoln, and at the time Sandburg saw Lincoln as "free property." Right now, anyone would have a hard time disassociating Lincoln from Sandburg.

7. Get self-inspiration from others.

Practice at selling yourself to strangers. They are fair game. Practice at being convincing to strangers.

Strangers, you say, never convince you? You're too skeptical? Try believing *them*.

When they see you "believe" them, you become *convincing* to *them*. You'll probably never see the stranger again, so you have nothing to lose. Funny thing about this experiment—it makes you feel extremely elated and pure of heart.

In the preceding paragraph, notice that I have put "believe" in quotes. Actually, neither believe nor disbelieve, but *pretend* to believe. If a stranger is exaggerating or indulging in outright lying, he is pleased at seeing this surface belief though he cannot be sure you have been taken in. What can you lose by seeming to believe? Nothing! And all the while you are developing a ready knack for getting on with strange people.

For instance, a stranger in town asks where a certain street is. Or a remote employee in your concern wants to find a certain place or thing. Instead of giving hurried, complicated instructions which they can't understand, it's great fun to WALK WITH THEM to the street or place in question!

Come to Grips with "They Say"

You know a lot about what you fear. You have given it so much thought, have isolated and grasped so many reasons why you fear it; you are indeed an expert on the subject. Why, the very people who don't fear the thing at all know less about it than you!

Get close to what you fear.

Your main trouble consists in *fearing at a distance*. Move up close to the object of your fear, smell it, nudge it, take a swipe at it. Up close, fear is a very docile animal.

The fear of ridicule, the awful spectre of "They say", keeps more of us from trying to sell ourselves than any other fear. But, as Victor Hugo puts it, "People die every day without regard for opinions." Dying is probably the most serious act of a man's lifetime and yet when he comes to die, he doesn't give a whoop for what people may say. Don't hesitate to reveal your ambitions; *they* like ambition. Don't concern yourself with the outside opinions on your acts of self-promotion; *they* actually like promoters. Don't recoil from getting hurt. *Seek to get hurt;* invite pain or loss to enter your person and *they* dare not!

Insist on sampling every fear you have. Taste it. Probe it for its pragmatic possibilities; then use it to a fare-thee-well in your campaign for selling yourself.

TEN ROADS TO SUCCESS

Since you want success, Reason says: "Take the easiest and shortest route."

Sɪɴcᴇ childhood you have been given your choice of several different ways to attain success in life. Let's recap here the ten basic findings of all the success "experts."

1. *Hard work.*

Have a real goal, set your sights high. Keep your ambition in high gear, and your nose always to the grindstone. There is no substitute for industry and sweat.

2. *Passion.*

This requires a will-to-win so fierce it at times approaches violence. The traveller of this road never takes "no" for an answer. Obstacles mean nothing to him; he brushes them all aside and sparks fly as he passes by.

3. *Make your money work for you.*

You get your first money by saving it with miserly zeal. Then you spend it in order to make more money. Or invest it and let it work while you sleep. Or go in business for yourself and turn your money over as fast and as often as you can.

4. *Education.*

Prepare yourself for a special calling or career. Get all the schooling and self-development you can early in life.

5. *Connections.*

This highway is paved with the philosophic coating of: "It isn't what you know but who you know." Most people believe this is the very best road to success, even though there are comparatively few travellers to be found on it.

6. *Brains.*

By "brains" we mean talent, native ability, versatility. This is supposed to be a short-cut road to success, smooth and bumpless—very different from the road called "HARD WORK." Theory: the higher the brow, the less it sweats.

7. *Words.*

A sage has divided all men into just three classes: the money man, the working man, and the WORD MAN. The latter type believes words are the most powerful instrument available in life, so he speaks, writes, thinks, teaches, propagandizes his way to success.

8. *Inherit money.*

This is not a road you can select of your own volition. But if you set your mind to it, you may marry the boss's daughter or a rich widow. You can also associate with the wealthy in civic, charitable and patriotic enterprises, and some of their wealth may rub off on you.

9. *Luck.*

Of nearly every successful individual, the mob says: "This is the road he took." They try to follow by gambling, wishing, and dreaming.

10. *Sell yourself.*

This is the only road we are going to talk about in this book. Of course, the highway marked "SELL YOURSELF" merges here and there with most of the other roads to success, but it is a distinct highway all by itself and, all things considered, it delivers most speed with lots of joy and interest, and the scenery is delightful!

This road is available to everybody.

This road does not require a sensational supply of brains or a college education.

There is work to be done as you travel this road, but it is not "work" in the old-fashioned sense. When you do work at this, you scarcely realize you are working.

This highway has no road-blocks or detours in it; it is straight and true. And it takes you directly to the CITY OF SUCCESS.

If it were not for your fierce appetite for APPROVAL, there would be no need or urgency for your becoming a success in life.

Analyze your present discontent and you will probably rationalize thus:

> I am discontented because I haven't enjoyed all the good things in life, and that is because I haven't acquired enough MONEY!

Nearly everyone blames his discontent on lack of money. The real blame lies in *lack of approval*. Deep down few of us will ever *approve ourselves* (the ultimate in self-satisfaction) until we have secured the approval of the world outside us.

There is tremendous satisfaction in making a lot of money. But the money, and what it can do for you, is not the richest part of the prize. The great prize is this: your accomplishment in making a lot of money wins widespread approval of you as an individual.

Selling Yourself Is the FIRST Success

Selling yourself is the first success because it is a supreme natural need!

All the skill, all the ability, all the self-expansion you have achieved will not deliver to you their proper reward until you secure the approval of a large number of people—or of a number of important people—for your achievements.

Livewires may shy away from general publicity but they inexorably need the thick-rich, congested approval of a small band of worthy watchers, or they wouldn't be livewires. Politicians and show people need the O.K. of the millions because the very nature of their work calls for very widespread approval.

True worth has a lot to do with it, but true worth alone will not bring the kind of success that tells a man *he has made the grade*. Even the magic fluid of self-confidence will not deliver either complete self-approval or outside approval.

A sensible, well-managed campaign for selling yourself takes all the guesswork out of success. Nothing is left to chance or the wiles of Dame Fortune.

[3]

How to Pin Down
the Idea of Success

For the unsuccessful, success is a big idea; in fact, too big for comprehension or attainment. Success has been painted as a will-of-the-wisp, a pot of gold at the rainbow's end, a monstrous mountain to be moved, an impossible objective reached only by super-human effort.

The impression is wide-spread that success is only *for the few*.

Let me kill that impression here and now. Success is for everybody, especially for you. Success is waiting on your door-step, ready to follow you around like an obedient dog, if you'll just pick up the leash. To blazes with all the old impressions of success. I say *success is easy*.

It's all a matter of using your head. Break with the past. Leave the old-fogy preachments on success to those who like them. This is a new day, no fit place for old ideas. Let's stream-line the modern idea of success and do it so it seems simple and easy.

First, let's pick the idea of success to pieces and then put the pieces together.

STAND OUT!

To be a success, *you have to be a "standout."* Right off the bat, I'll admit that's frightening. All successful gents rise above those around them; metaphorically they become taller, broader, stronger. They are seen above the throng. They are recognized.

But being a standout does not demand that you be an ALL-AROUND standout, a super-man. A restaurateur serving gourmet food, charges the highest prices in town—boy, is he a standout! Yet sophisticates flock to him with their trade, thinking it is smart to pay premium prices for fine food.

Al Leach, a *Newsweek* editor, delivers lectures on journalism while doing astounding feats of magic with his hands.

Why, even a double-jointed girl who can throw her arm into an unnatural shape is a standout. A great salesman I know, half of whose face is covered with a disfiguring birthmark is a standout.

You don't have to talk fourteen languages or have read every worthwhile book to be a standout. If you're a male, bake your first loaf of bread and you're a standout. If you're a female, take a few puffs out of a cigar and you're a standout.

Do anything for the first time and you're a standout.

Any *little thing* which you can do better than those around you *makes you a standout*.

Make up a chart of "Who-AM-I's" and add to it voluminously. You haven't put enough little things in that chart. You can tie a strange knot—you're a standout. You know the longest word in the English language—you're a standout. You can wear a hat rakishly—you're a standout. If you're a woman and can park a car in one and a half times its length, you're a standout. If you're a man and can sew, you're a standout.

I'll go out on a limb and shout: It's downright impossible for anybody *not to be a standout* because he inevitably has several little things he can do which those around him can't, or can't do as well.

So you see, you're full of standout material. Make the most of it.

Get rid of that stodgy idea that to be a standout you have to be a "man among men." True, you have to be a standout to be a success. And you're going to be a success because you already are a standout. That's the first essential.

Kate Smith, "Songbird of the South", never took a music lesson in her life.

Ted Collins, her shrewd manager, was once asked why he didn't provide further instruction for his star. Ted's answer: "Her natural voice is her outstanding gift. SHOULD WE THROW THAT AWAY?"

Are *you* throwing away or neglecting any natural gift?

Ernest Thiele, noted atomic chemist for Standard Oil Company, is almost as well known in non-atomic circles for the excellent *verse* he writes, a skill he developed in his early youth and nurtured all through his highly successful career.

If you have kept up a certain skill through the years, it's time to cease regarding it merely as a *hobby*. Make it pay dividends in publicity, fame, or money!

Pick any little thing and develop it.

The little thing need not even be a *skill* or an *ability,* outstanding in itself, which you claim you own.

It can be an inanimate object, which anyone else could latch onto.

Harry Guilbert, of the Pullman Company, was one of the greatest industrial safety experts in history. Of course, he preached all-around safety. But he sought to point up his whole career with *a pair of safety goggles.*

"Save your eyesight—wear goggles" preached Guilbert relentlessly. Everywhere he went he had a pair of goggles with him, for dramatic demonstration. Naturally, he was known as "Goggles Guilbert."

You have a whole world of *things* to pick from. Give any little thing a ride, stick with it for good, and that little thing will become your best success-assistant.

Hedda Hopper, Hollywood columnist, originally made her fame as a motion picture actress. When movie jobs began to get scarcer, Hedda wondered if she were "through". Then, on analyzing her experience, she told herself that all the connections, the friends and acquaintances she had made in the past, constituted too valuable a property to throw away. She called a newspaper executive and told him: "I know everybody in the movie business. The whole country is avid for news of the movie colony. Let me do a column for your newspaper." With very little writing background, Hedda made her way to greater fame as a writer of a movie column than she ever had as an actress.

STAND OUT IN YOUR OWN CIRCLE

Operate in *your own circle*. The world is NOT your oyster. Where you are is the place to make good—at the unremarkable job you have, in the barren and uninspiring condition in which you find yourself, in your own plain bailiwick.

Don't seek new fields to conquer till you've conquered your own small circle. Nothing could be easier.

Decide to show 'em you're a standout in your own small circle.

That small circle is a soft touch because there's little or no *competition* there.

Somebody long ago balled up this idea of success by insinuating that you have to prove yourself in competition to be a success. Ridiculous. The smart bozo is the guy who ducks as much competition as he can. He doesn't like competition for it means violent work, heart strain, perhaps death.

If the spot you're in—your job, your career, your avocation—is a small one and a dull one, then we know this for sure: *there's no competition there*. *Competition* can stop you from being a success. The *difficulty* of mastering a given activity can stop you from being a success. You can stop *yourself* from being a success.

But that small circle in which you now find yourself cannot stop you! By being small, by being uninviting to a lot of competitors, it automatically throws the second essential to success right into your lap!

Am I urging you to remain a big frog in a little pond? No, I'm not saying you should not get out of this small pond—ever. But get your size established first, be a standout in your own circle, and take your first BIG BITE of success.

Once on speaking terms with success, you're no longer a frog. You're a lion! For all success is the same. The success thrill of being a standout in your own circle is exactly the same kind of meat as conquering the whole world single-handedly.

Ragnar Benson, big-time builder, recently treated 75 relatives to a free trip to Sweden.

Not too big a *circle*—just his own *kin*. But perfectly typical of a hundred *little* circles in which Ragnar likes to operate *big* because he has the funds for it.

Your circle need not be too expensive to operate in. Study it for ideas for bringing it to life, for inspiration, for new interest and surprise.

Lt. General "Slim Jim" Gavin, formerly in charge of U.S. Army weapon development, is a famed parachuter and soldier. Those *who remember* look up to him for his fearless exploits in World War II, but in his day *everyone* looked up to him as ONE OF THE BEST READ MEN IN THE PENTAGON!

Gavin says: "Reading is work, but it goes with rank."

Reading is a "must" in nearly all professions.

Most of the men in your given profession are well acquainted with a special list of "must's" for success. It's human not to embrace the "must," if one dislikes it. But embrace it anyhow, accept it completely, and go on to score higher than the other human beings in your circle who allow feeling to defeat reason.

Stand Out at a Special Activity

Be a standout in your own circle *at a special activity,* or specialty, or special alliance with a thing or project.

A young man asked Hillaire Belloc, famed English author, what a young fellow might do to attain sure success in the writing field. Belloc told him: "Spend all your time investigating and writing about the *earthworm*. That will assure you of everlasting fame!"

A "special activity" can sometimes be a single act, or a decision to team up with a single object for purposes of squeezing efficiency or special expediency from that object. When Andrew Carnegie was fourteen years old he took one hundred dollars—

almost all the money he had—went to a goldsmith and had him make a *solid gold shoehorn*. Young Andrew said to himself: "Every time I put on my shoes, I'll feel richer than a king!"

Ten million Americans every year think nothing of laying out three thousand dollars for a moderately priced automobile. But hardly one in a million would dare to spend $250 for a fine custom-made suit of clothes! The three thousand dollars makes each of us *just one in ten million*. But the rich, expensive suit, with the pride and luxury and exclusiveness one would feel every minute he wore it would make the individual owner superior to at least *a million* of his brethren!

One morning Dr. Richard Gamble, Chicago eye specialist, was operating to remove an annoying cyst from my eyelid. I sat in a small stiff chair and stared at the point of the sharp knife coming down into my eye.

"Doctor," I said calmly, "do you realize you're holding that knife in *your left hand?*"

"Oh that!" he replied just as calmly, "In handling your case, I find it's more convenient to use my left hand than my right!" He was ambidextrous! He was a *specialist*. He has as much courage and steadiness *at sticking knives into people's eyes* with his left hand as with his right! What patient could resist giving his full heart and his total confidence to such a surgeon?

When you take up a special activity in your rendezvous with success, do you become a *specialist?* Undoubtedly. You don't need a medical or an engineering degree to be a specialist. You have full power and authority at picking the field in which you are going to score. Make sure it's small enough, special enough! Make sure it's something you *can do well*. Make sure competition is missing. The smallness of the activity and the absence of competition mark the only difference between you and the big-name specialist.

J. Patrick Lannan, internationally famous financier, has "made his pile" and certainly is a success in the financial field, a top standout in a line where competition is always fierce, often ferocious.

But any successful person finds it hard to quit after reaching the top. So Lannan, still pursuing success (and being pretty sure of getting there), completely reverses his field and takes up *poetry* as his "next world to conquer. Not the *writing* of good poetry, for that is an activity probably more difficult than becoming a millionaire. But Lannan *sponsors* good poetry, sponsors it with a strong hand and a successful spirit that cannot be downed. He has taken on *Poetry Magazine* as his new love, encourages powerful friends to join with him in bringing more encouragement and more rewards to poets young and old.

And here J. Patrick Lannan, who should know what bitter competition is in business, has found something far *bigger than a hobby,* at which there is no competition to speak of! And his interest in poetry has sold him to a whole new world of friends and probably contributed as much to his lasting fame as all his financial exploits combined!

Ben Smith, "The Wolf of Wall Street", has made fortune after fortune by betting on the caliber of the men he picks to run his various enterprises.

He doesn't bet money AGAINST money, but ON *men.*

That's certainly something special, isn't it? But there's nothing so special about the activity that you yourself can't copy it on a smaller scale.

Your need to specialize is inescapable.

Every once in a while you hear of a truck driver, department store clerk, mail carrier who has a college degree in liberal arts. "Too bad he didn't specialize" is the consensus.

Take any field where talent is the call, where competition is greatest, and you'll find that the keenest, smartest people must specialize for success.

This book, therefore, seeks to point out for EVERYBODY the greatest specialty of all—the science of selling himself. This science is available to all people regardless of their occupations, their education or their background. It is the universal specialty that, once mastered, pays off best in wealth, personal influence and satisfaction.

Les Pope was purchasing agent for one of the largest business concerns in America. His job required his talking to hundreds of salesmen every month. A purchasing agent's job hasn't too much glamour in it, and purchasing agents as a class are only popular with the chosen few to whom they give business.

Though his work involved buying a tremendous variety of merchandise, Les felt the urge to *specialize*. Since he could not specialize on what he bought, he studied to see if he could do something further about the salesmen he *bought from,* and quickly found that the salesmen in most need of help, the ones who as individuals were most interesting to Les, were *young* salesmen just starting out.

Les Pope, the purchasing agent, soon became known "As the godfather of young salesmen." He arranged to see them all. Gave each a complete hearing. To a faltering soul, a small but encouraging order. To all, practical suggestions and personal help.

He turned a job, which seemingly admitted of no specializing, into a "human nature" specialty and sold himself not only to many young salesmen of America but, more important perhaps, to all his fellow employees and superiors, as a person of great heart and supreme fairness.

There are no ALL-AROUND movie stars.

You have dramatic stars, juvenile stars, star comedians, star heavy men.

Inevitably, when you think of the star you think of his or her specialty.

The stars in business, too, are pegged for their special abilities. In politics. In religion.

A saint is a saint for having been something special!

Now, if the most successful people in the universe have to follow this formula, what's wrong with your giving it a whirl?

Getting down to Brass Tacks on the Subject of Success

1. Separate your idea of success from your idea of greatness.

You can be a "Somebody", a man who sells himself to others, and can enjoy a fine reputation, without necessarily being

GREAT. You certainly need not be a prodigy, a phenomenon, a rare genius.

Separate your idea of success from wealth, honor, fame. Follow the rules and these things will come in their own way.

2. *Believe success to be plumb easy.*

We are wrongly educated to believe that success is only possible through prodigious work and bitter struggle.

A mistake. Every man born of woman is *entitled* to success. It is your birthright. Not to take it is folly.

Know for sure that "little success" and "big success" are one and the same thing. The smallest, most insignificant kind of success has the same rich and thrilling nature as the most sensational success.

Reversing the case of J. Patrick Lannan who occasionally moves from big competition to small, there is the case of young Thomas L. who moved from little competition to big. Tom was naturally gifted, his friends thought, a sort of a genius. Tom knew himself merely as a good student of life's activities and had early found the secret of success lying in the dark cave of *practice,* out of which, claimed Tom, comes any skill desired. He could do a lot of things extremely well. He felt he was a success, he believed success was *easy.* So Tom decided to invade the field which many say is the most competitive of all —*songwriting.* Tom could not sing or play. He could not read, write a note of music. "I can still write a hit," boasted Tom to himself, "because *I believe that success is easy,* though it is much smarter to be a success in a field where stiff competition is missing." He studied popular songs for their *surefire* elements. He asked himself, "What kind of a song is needed right now?" He looked around for every factor of percentage that could aid him.

He composed a tune in his head; the words were easy. He "sang" the song to himself inwardly and silently for weeks, making changes, refining, polishing. Finally, he hired an arranger and spent four hours one afternoon singing the song out loud to the arranger, and then demanding that the arranger sing the song back to him, over and over, line for line, changing and correcting till the arranger got down on paper exactly what was inside Tom's head.

"That part was easy," said Tom, "Now for a publisher." Using many of the principles detailed in this book, he sold himself to the publisher. "Easy again," smiled Tom, "Now for public acceptance." We will not go into detail concerning the thousand and one machinations Tom used in a field rife with politics, relationships, reciprocity, to get a great star to adopt the song as his theme. In one year it sold 500,000 records. It was sung over radio to audiences mounting into the billions. It became a "standard," reaching the music books that live on and on. "A great songwriter called it the *worst song ever written,*" confesses Tom, "and it probably was. But it was all I had to make good with in a field of the biggest competition imaginable. I merely wanted to prove that it was possible to be as great a success in tough going as in easy going. I wanted to sell myself to millions of people by the same processes I sold myself to hundreds. Natural talent has nothing whatever to do with it —it's all a matter of outlook and know-how."

3. Be a standout in just one small field.

Is your handwriting more beautiful than that of anyone you know? Hurrah! You're a success already. Find or develop just one special little thing at which you are better than those around you and you have shaken hands with Success!

The smallest taste of success is the *biggest kind of* success. The first real bite makes you hungry for more.

One of the top educators in this country was lucky one day while playing high school football. Believe it or not, he punted the ball for 84 yards in a hard-fought game between two teams of high standing. Over the years, as he proceeded in his vocation of teaching, a friend would occasionally recall the historic punt. It was some kind of a record! Our modest teacher would protest and murmur, "Forget it." He did not like publicity, especially publicity that connected him—now a sedate man of education—with the rough, brutal game of football. But friends, not so retiring, kept right on mentioning the famous punt. Slowly our educator opened his eyes. He was not adverse to success and he noticed that "the powers that be" were eyeing him not for his ability in education but rather for the memory of one kick of a lowly football! He decided to stop denying his feat, and began giving a few details of the game, the play, the actual kick.

Not only educators but politicians now gave him much extra notice. His ideas on education received a hearty welcome everywhere, not only because of the value of the ideas, but simply because their promulgator had once kicked a football 84 yards. Today this same educator, completely scholastic in appearance and looking nothing like an athlete, is superintendent of schools in a very large community!

4. Then find a bigger pond.

Master one small thing in one small area, and immediately you look for a deeper pond and a bigger one.

You seek a heavier and more challenging specialty.

You never need to force yourself on. Your first success is its own driving mechanism. It's automatic!

Bob Van Dee was a great success at selling office safes. But most of his prospects had use for only one safe and in a year he had sold nearly every customer he was allowed to sell. Policies of his company did not permit him to be given other's salesmen's territories. What should he do?

Quit, of course, and he did. He picked life insurance as a field which had no limit. He went through a four months course of training that did not pay him enough income to live on. But Bob had to get into a bigger field at any cost. Today his income is well over $50,000 a year. Proof that if you're frozen, though successful, you must not lie still and freeze to death in your own small success!

5. Sidestep competition.

Sidestep competition by picking a new field *real early* before competition shows up.

If definitive competition is there, avoid the human clash, the "who-is-the-better-man" type of showdown. Knocking people down and stepping on their faces is not success.

Always show good example to your competition. You will win their good will. You will learn from them just as they will learn from you.

And there's always a branch of any endeavor at which you can be superior without incurring the envy or hatred of others.

Most successful people have competitive spirit. They like a test of skill, a showdown of any kind. But the more seasoned the success, the more reason comes into play to subdue this competitive instinct.

One leader admits: "I'm smart and I know it. But do you think I'd ever be dumb enough to take an intelligence test? Why put myself on a spot where somebody—anybody—might grade and label me?

"Do you think I want to be Number One man in my company? Never! Number One has no place further to go. I'll settle for Number Three spot, where I am always in the running and everyone knows I have something on the ball, but no one knows exactly how much!"

6. And prompt yourself to sell yourself increasingly.

The best example of all is the very subject of this book: *winning success by selling yourself to others*. Little competition here because more than ninety-five percent of the people never acquire the knack of selling themselves. The right to sell yourself is a free right of man. The opportunities are boundless.

In the very nature of things, those who do are universally liked and respected, never hated.

[4]

How to Be a Livewire

Every man who sells himself is known as a livewire. He's a study in "success in action." He is known and looked up to far and wide. Thousands of people who have never met him in person are just as convinced he's a livewire as those who deal with him every day.

Livewires are individuals—men of action. They do not depend on other people or outside events to help them make a decision. As Frank Lloyd Wright said: "A man is more a man by being an individual than he is by being a committee-meeting." Charles Kettering of General Motors had capsuled this livewire principle in his pithy comment on Lindbergh's solo flight across the Atlantic: "A committee could never have done it."

Now I have nothing against committees, especially if they have livewires in the group and all the members are capable of recognizing the worth of a practical suggestion. But a just criticism of a good many committees is that they waste a lot of time and accomplish little. And it's a pity that livewires generally try to avoid service on committees. The reason? They believe they can do, as lone individuals, faster and better anything a committee can do.

How about you, little you? What are your chances of being a livewire? You may be a little too timid, too inexperienced, too unversed in all the ins and outs of fast dealing in the world. But if you are out to sell yourself to others, you know they will not "buy" you as a shy and slow thinking member of the human race. They want signs of life, of electricity. They want visible proof that you are a man on his way to success. How can you develop some of these external marks of a livewire?

A. THE SIMPLE APPROACH

On a day in June, 1958, I was in Washington, D.C., looking for a certain office building. Walking down an interesting street, I happened to spy a huge house that had some strange lettering on the door. It looked like Russian. "It might be the Russian Embassy," I guessed, "and with all this talk about Russia, right now I feel like talking to a Russian."

So I took the simple approach, walked up to the door and rang the bell. A guard answered. I said: "I am an American citizen and would like to talk to the Ambassador." I was told to wait a minute and soon a cheerful young man came out and invited me back to a private sitting room in the embassy. His name was Sergei A. Bogomolov and he announced he was Second Secretary in the Embassy. I wished to talk about the subject of space and the Russians' scientific advances in this field. He spoke perfect American—not merely English with an Oxford accent—but straight ordinary American with true American accent.

The conversation lasted for an hour and a half. We argued a great deal. We exchanged pleasantries, too. He was polite, but keen.

He was a *livewire!* In his late thirties, he felt he did not need to clear his talk with the Ambassador or with Premier Khrushchev. He was interested in me and I in him and it was with great reluctance I left because he wanted to talk still further.

The point of the story is this: I succeeded in having a good talk with a Russian diplomat in high standing, without resorting to introductions by mutual friends or political pull. I took the simple approach, which was very irregular. On the other hand, Bogomolov, seeing that I had used the simple approach, responded in kind. Livewires are always simple, direct, and do not like to use complicated methods for getting together.

B. To Be a Livewire, Increase Your Efficiency

Now "efficiency" sounds like a big word, but it really is not, if, again, you think of efficiency in simple terms.

If your right hand is injured, you quickly become conscious of how little work your left hand has been doing. Forced to use it in place of the right, you suddenly realize how thoroughly efficient the left hand can be in every process of living and working. If a sudden attack of "bad back" hits you, and it is painful to bend over or even walk, you quickly reorganize your movements to eliminate waste motion which means extra pain.

When Steinmetz first met Edison, he was not nonplussed by finding Edison totally deaf. He began to tap out his message on Edison's knee in the Morse code.

John L. McCaffrey of International Harvester when asked for his secret of fame and success replied: "Keep on doing what it took to get started." As you started on your way to achievement in your life activity, you did many efficient things. Recall some of these things and try doing them again, in the light of your added experience and wisdom.

C. Do Not Be Afraid to Dream

Contrary to general impression, livewires are never afraid of a dream, their own or someone else's.

Livewires grubstaked many a prospector in the days of the gold rush and made fortunes out of miners' dreams.

The livewire can quickly distinguish a practical dream from a "flight of fancy." Fisher was honeymooning on his yacht near Miami when one day he met a man named Collins who lived on a sand bar far removed from the mainland. Collins was a dreamer, with a flair for the practical. Fisher was a practical money man though never afraid of a dream. Each was a livewire in his own way. They got together. Miami Beach was the result.

Many people of means had met and talked with Collins before Fisher met him. They had listened to his dream and quickly joined the long list of scoffers who said, "It couldn't be done." It is only human and natural to join with the negative majority which vetoes any proposed project. But Fisher was different. He reasoned: "Why did I come here on my honeymoon? Because it is the garden spot of the country, especially in winter. One man, whose good sense I admire, has put a vast fortune into the development of other parts of Florida—Henry Flagler. Flagler has sunk millions into a strip of land compromising the whole state, so why can't I sink a few into a few miles of buried beach?"

A story in reverse should reinforce the point. A very wealthy man who "liked to stay out of the newspapers" called a university president one evening and invited him to dinner. This particular university was badly in need of funds and, in fact, was engaged in a fund-raising campaign at the time. But the university president who had never been educated to the need for knowing who the livewires are in one's own community, politely put his caller off and said he had no open date for dinner for at least a month ahead. In a week, the newspapers carried the story: "Mr. M. gives $35,000,000 to Rival University." Can we blame this university president for not knowing he was talking on the phone with a real livewire? Yes, and no. Sometime later I met, in Florida, a man who used to be personal masseur for the unpublicized philanthropist. I told him about the $35,000,000. "I never guessed he had that kind of money," said the ex-masseur. "All he paid me was $90 a month!" In one way the ignorance of the personal servant and the university president were excusable; in another way if either or both had especially attuned themselves to recognize a livewire by even the remotest means, two golden opportunities might not have been missed.

Perhaps you may say that stories like this happen only once in a generation. Actually it happens every day in a smaller way and on a smaller scale. How did you get the job you now hold? Someone must have thought you were a livewire when he hired you. There was a dream involved, at least on your employer's part. He had the hope—selfishly—that you would be worth more to him than your salary!

And every month in which you still prove you are worth

*more than your salary to your boss, he recognizes you as a real
livewire with right for increased salary and further promotion.*

Practice all the rules, suggestions, and devices detailed in this
book and you, too, will be a livewire who has won success by
selling himself to others. This chapter is not a complete study
of how to be a livewire. The whole book deals with the subject.

But a few extra tips are called for at this point, to help you
gather up added steam.

1. Open up your eyes.

Be alert. Observe! Rockne, the great football coach, said of
his quarterback, Harry Stuhldreier: "A hundred quarterbacks
can walk by a department store window, but after they get by,
Stuhldreier is the only one who can tell you what is in the
window!"

Maybe you think you're smart when you catch a typographi-
cal error in printing. But most anyone can do that. But do you
ever open up your eyes and look for other mistakes in printing
—black ink that is grey, colors that overlap at the edge, type
squeezed so hard that the impression comes through on the
other side of the sheet, and a hundred and one other imperfec-
tions which your eyes are ready to reveal to you if you will only
OPEN THEM UP?

I wanted a large leaf rake for cutting down work in the yard.
I knew what I wanted—a rake three times as wide as the ordinary one which most people use. After a two-week search I
found such a rake way out in a country store. People who
passed as I raked leaves, commented on the bother, the work,
the weather, everything or anything pertaining to leaves and
leaf raking. But only one little girl, aged four, noticed the extraordinary size of the rake. "That's three times as big as my
father's rake," she said.

Now if the adults who passed had had the observation power
of a four year old, they could have inquired about where I had
secured the rake, what it cost, how light it was, how it cut down
the work of raking.

Because their eyes were closed to a live opportunity and a great time saver, they go on working and slaving away hours that could be better used.

I've told this story so often all my friends and neighbors want to take a look at the phenomenal little girl. But she is not selling herself to them (she doesn't know they're interested—but I do) and hence I find myself unwittingly selling myself to others for my "keenness" in spotting this little girl observer!

Whether it is a significant inanimate action or an act of personal performance, people are inclined to marvel at you for your seeing something they have missed, especially if that something is worthwhile. Their enthusiasms for your special powers of observation produced endless boosting of your personal stock.

It should be stressed here that observation power is considerably different from "intellect." To be a livewire, you do not need to be a brilliant genius, an intellect with the highest I.Q. rating.

But you do need to keep your physical eyes open while awake. And your mental eyes should always stay open, too.

Television, especially live television performances, is another good medium for practicing observation. Look, scrutinize, inspect carefully—never assuming what the action will be—and the screen will present many odd little things never intended to be seen, things interesting and significant.

2. Learn how to listen.

All livewires are good listeners, and there seems to be a common agreement that if you keep your ears open and your mouth shut, you will learn a surprising amount.

Livewires listen but never entirely with their mouths shut. Sometimes you have to ask questions, questions which get at the heart of the matter. Sometimes you have to interrupt and guide the speaker back on the proper track, the track from which he may give you the information you need. Sometimes you may have to talk and listen at one and the same time—a real feat, but not impossible.

Roy Cohn, famed attorney for the late Senator McCarthy in a Senate committee, possessed the ability of "total recall." That means he could remember everything the other person said, even when two or more were talking, even when he apparently was paying no attention to the one speaking. Cohn could interrogate, interrupt, expostulate, talk at the same time as a witness, and later know every word that was said. Now the question is, did Roy Cohn merely have this gift of total recall and use it pragmatically in his law work, or did he develop it? I am inclined to believe the latter theory. If you put a real price on every word the other man says, even though most of these words are tripe, you can remember them no matter how many distractions tend to erase them.

FIRST MOVE: CARE. Project your brain inside the other person. Don't be reluctant to give him all of you, in the matter of attention.

SECOND MOVE: Read him as you would the printed page. Compare what he says with what you know is true. For every discrepancy make an extra impression on your own brain.

Listening is never a waste of time if you engage in it actively. This means *working on the speaker with your listening powers.* But if all you do is allow him to pour words into your ears, and nothing more, listening is just a routine way to kill time.

When you recall to another how the two of you first met on a very prosaic occasion some twenty years earlier, and elaborate on every plain and simple detail of the meeting, he is usually astonished into speechless wonder at your memory. And yet, if you work a little at this little "trick" (for all it consists in is superficially probing your mental recording of the meeting) you will not find it hard to do.

Or if you have the attention of a whole group of people and you can recall many of the little, surface details of a previous event in which they all participated, they will undoubtedly cry: "Bravo! What a man! What a memory!" All these little details are still inside everyone's brain, but the knack of calling them up out of the dim past makes you seem like the liveliest of livewires.

3. Don't deal in cheap things.

George S. May, business efficiency expert who ran the world's championship golf tournament as a sideline, is certainly a live-wire. Other tournaments have had more glamorous histories than May's, but none matches his first prize—$50,000 in cash with $50,000 more in extra emoluments.

Sam, the barber, meeting his "long lost friend" in a tavern, orders a seventy-five-cent bottle of beer for his old pal, instead of the customary thirty-five-cent brand. For an extra investment of forty cents he proves he isn't cheap. Sam, the same barber, owns his own shop and in no mistaken terms discourages his customers from giving him tips personally. Accepting a tip would seem to make the owner cheap and the barber shop a cheap barber shop, to Sam's way of thinking.

I observe an alert office boy treat his democratic boss to a needed pack of cigarettes. This is not subservience, this is the kind of richness that helps an office boy to go places.

4. Be efficient and practical in personal relations.

One mechanic judges another by his actions: how he works his hands, how he handles his body, the materials he work with, his tools. Just *being a member of the human race* requires that you too be a mechanic when you mix with others.

Don't get in the way of people. Don't block aisles and exits.

Don't go or remain where you are not wanted. If you go, don't be the last to leave.

Don't overdo your enjoyments. Leave something for the next time.

Use the best tools and equipment. The amateur paints his house with a one-dollar paint brush and wonders why he does such a poor job; the journeyman house painter, with much more skill and training, insists on using a twenty-five-dollar paint brush!

John Semerau ran the company print shop. Of course, the advertising department, the stationery department, and other departments had the final use or custody of the printing Semerau did. But often as the printing was used up and time

went by, there would be a sudden call by a lawyer or executive
for a particular piece of printing, the supply of which was now
"exhausted." Invariably we would turn to livewire Semerau,
who like a squirrel stored extra pieces for unseen emergencies,
and John would invariably deliver the wanted piece!

5. Don't seek honor or glory openly.

Thousands of livewires are unseen and unsung by the public
and known only to immediate associates. If there's honor or
great credit coming their way, they pass it around to others and
sidestep the glory.

They are seldom disturbed by unjust criticism. A segment of
the Chicago public criticizes Phil Wrigley, owner of the Cubs,
for not having night ball games. Wrigley has taken and smiled
at the criticism for years without offering a word of explanation.

His real reason is: he considers small home owners near his
park as his neighbors. He does not think they should be disturbed and lose sleep by fans milling around the neighborhood
late at night.

Yet he has never published the reason for his stand, a reason
that would stamp him as supremely considerate, humane, polite.

Everyone knows he's very much a livewire on this matter
without knowing why.

A wise high school lad pitches a no-hit, no-run game of
baseball. He rejects all congratulations, saying: "It was all on
account of those four sensational catches by the outfielders."
His public now stops but a moment to try to remember the
catches, but soon returns to acclaiming the modest pitcher as
the greatest man in town.

6. Be available.

William Wrigley, Jr., Phil's father, would see anybody who
came to his office asking to see him. He said this was his best
way for staying in touch with ordinary people. Most visitors
would ask the impossible or offer freak ideas.

Wrigley had a gift for quickly showing them the impracticability of their suggestions and pleasantly ushering them out. Yet he received so many bad ideas, he developed a phenomenal gift for recognizing a good idea by contrast.

Sam owns the barber shop, but Adam, his assistant, has the key and opens the shop nearly an hour early every morning. Adam likes to get up early, so he's available. Sam thinks Adam is the best assistant he ever had.

7. *Live in the present; the past is for deadheads.*

In a nearby small town I pay a visit to a bachelor friend, living in a great house all alone. He is a millionaire, but he is not interesting and certainly not a livewire.

All he wants to do is talk about the past. Thus he confesses he is an old man with nothing to offer me.

Livewires never talk about their "operations," ailments or sicknesses.

8. *Admit no catastrophe.*

Presidents Lincoln and Truman didn't ask for sympathy over their bankruptcies, and didn't consider bankruptcy the end of the world. An extraordinary number of livewires have been broke, or nearly so, several times. Some have been very close to death or suffered shocks that would ruin an ordinary man.

Regard each crisis as part of your education. Fear it if you must, but insist you can learn something from it. You will recover—you will live—and this crisis will help immensely in avoiding the next.

9. *Say "yes" fast.*

Be thinking about your decision in the seconds or minutes the other is asking for the favor. If you intend to say "yes," say it fast.

A fast "yes" always makes you seem overgenerous and sells you completely to the other.

Procrastinate with the "no." "I'll have to think it over because there are matters involved I can't explain to you" means "no," but hasn't its harsh sound.

10. Guard your time.

Kidnap extra hours from every day.

One man, in business for himself, and out to get ahead, often works three weeks in every week to make his success.

You're actually in business for yourself though you are an employee. Stop right here and think of a man in your own concern who definitely is a livewire. Seek him out and get him to tell what he does with "his spare time."

ASSOCIATE WITH LIVEWIRES!

Livewires are the elite of business, of society, of the professions and as such they should be hard to find and to meet. Not so. They are the most approachable of men.

Christopher Columbus as a small boy talked to all the captains when their boats drew into port. He spent all his time with the ones who knew their business. He gave no time at all to those who wanted to joke with him, make fun of him, or tell him grand lies.

Thucydides, Greek historian, shed tears when as a boy he heard Herodotus read part of his history of Olympia in public. He didn't have enough nerve to speak to the great Herodotus in person; but he made him the model of his life and wound up becoming a much better writer than his hero.

If you are in the audience when a great man speaks, go up and congratulate him after the speech. This is easy; others are doing it; your praise is more than welcome. I made the acquaintance of Bourke Cochran, William Jennings Bryan, Arthur Brisbane, Bruce Barton and many others in this way.

All celebrities are human beings. They are not too impressed with admiration and adulation. Meet them on common grounds, be a human being, kid around a bit. I was once on a committee meeting a group of movie stars at the railroad station. On the same committee was a shy fellow who kept muttering, "I just want one look at Greer Garson. She's a queen. I wouldn't dare to ask to meet her."

On the sly I told Greer about her worshipper and whispered: "Let's see you put on an act—give him a play!" Miss Garson gushed all over the man, got his life history in a few seconds, mesmerized him with her instant charm.

She even invited him to call at her house next time he was in California. Wonder of wonders he did exactly that (many of us thought he went out there just for that purpose) and Greer asked him to her home to have dinner with herself and husband. It was the highest point in that man's life. I often wondered if my shy friend knew the real explanation—his idol was a livewire, and livewires like people!

Even though you cannot meet the livewire in person, you can still know him and extract untold richness from him.

I saw Ty Cobb play *one hundred* games of ball. No one can take experience away from me. He was the best in a game that poses probably a greater challenge to skill, speed and brains than any other. I didn't need to meet him in person to use him as an inspiration. Every time *I think of him* I am moving in "faster company" and associating intimately with one of the greatest livewires in history.

There are several score of printers in this world who make fine books, I mean *really fine* books. If their printing were baseball, it would be the same kind of baseball that Cobb played.

Yet when I say to the ordinary printer: "Have you ever held between your fingers a page printed by Grabhorn, or a book designed by Dwiggins?" the answer is: "Never heard of those guys!" Imagine! This is the equivalent of a baseball fan of today saying: "Never heard of Williams or Musial!" Thousands of printers who make their bread and butter from printing do not even know who the livewires are in their business. Nor do they realize that a piece of printing is not a transient thing like a game or a show or a speech, but that it may be handled, studied, inspected with minute care for its excellence and craftsmanship.

You can associate with the livewires in your profession or

trade through their work, especially through their physical product.

Don't spend all your time marvelling at livewires and what makes them that way. Decide to be a livewire in your own right.

Try enacting a few of the livewire characteristics delineated above.

Meet as many as you can and ask any livewire to refer you to his livewire friends.

Connect yourself with modern movements:

Modern design: Try to understand it and appreciate it.

Abstract painting: Explore it, don't merely scoff at it.

Automation: Decide to cope with it, not fear it.

Rocketry, missiles and space: Inevitable!

ARRANGE TO LIVE A LIVEWIRE KIND OF LIFE

If you are a salesman, try to call on livewires. Separate the livewires from the time-wasters, the deadheads. Make a list of livewire prospects, and don't put a name on it unless you are sure the man is a livewire.

Livewires help your salesmanship. Their crisp, compact personalities furnish a fine model for you yourself to copy. They often give you valuable tips and references.

If you are an office worker, root out the real livewires in your organization. Get friendly, even intimate, if you can. The office livewire is seldom part of a political clique, and if you are already playing office politics, your attempt at friendship will be of little avail. He is strictly independent of cliques and combines; he's a lone wolf working for the good of the concern strictly in his own way. Study him. If your heart is pure, JOIN HIM, and cast petty politics aside. One such man can mean the successful re-making of your whole life.

If you are a factory worker, find the factory livewires. They are real mechanics, craftsmen. Not necessarily are they department heads or bearers of impressive titles. If you can make friends with them, they will help you, teach you, and in time hand over to you much of their ability and experience.

Attention! Policeman, postmen, sales clerks, clergymen, farmers, doctors, lawyers, school teachers, wayside merchants, and all who would have the world know you as livewires!

—If you have a rich fund of nervous energy, if you can stay on your feet, and in particular the balls of your feet, for many hours a day, and rush around showing your pep, your eagerness to work, and your willingness to serve, try to pick a field of operations where a large number of people can see you strutting your stuff!

Such a worker in a chain store supermarket or a bowling alley, for instance, is universally acclaimed a livewire. By showing people both your mental and your physical pep, you sell yourself to them and automatically earn the good title, livewire.

In what type of organization does one find the highest percentage of livewires? My answer is: *in any good advertising agency.* Here you find smart people, vibrant people; people who can reason, create, execute, and handle all form of contact with flair and finesse. The non-creative people in the average advertising agency very soon pick up the "livewireness" of the executives and the creative people. The stenographers, the typists, even the office boys soon become livewires.

Find the livewires! Meet them! Study them! Associate with them, and presto! you're a livewire yourself before you know it.

USING
SELF-TRANSFERENCE
(Part One)

Jesus Christ, founder of Christianity, is the world's best example of self-transference.

Christ had only three public years in which to serve His mission; He was still a young man, aged 33, when He died.

His "merchandise" was simple: salvation, kindness, brotherly love. He not only sold His "merchandise" well, but He sold Himself better than any person in history.

Though Christ is Divine, He offered Himself to us as a human example. In order to make His "merchandise" understandable to all people, He transferred everything He had in Himself to all the human beings outside Him.

During the three short years of His mission, He was a public speaker; He was a private speaker, too, and a very good one. He did not back away from self-publicity or say He was too good for it. He viewed "publicity" as a moral and natural way of getting Himself across.

He appointed the Twelve Apostles as His assistants and as His "press agents"; He educated them to the value of *words* and He equipped them to use words eloquently and effectively. Christ returned to God, but His "press agents" live on in the form of millions of priests, ministers and clergymen; in the

61

form of many more millions of laymen who are missionaries at heart and who spread the Word of God, the Bible, to hundreds of millions more.

The very success of Christianity wheels around the science which Christ instituted in "selling" Himself—*self-transference*.

Look on this business of selling yourself for success in life as an imitation of the hard work of Jesus Christ during His three active years and you will cease to regard selling yourself as a questionable or unworthy business. It is the most direct way to self-fulfillment. In a more inspired view, it is the way to doing more good in your lifetime by the simple act of being able to *reach* more people.

Self-transference asks that you take *everything inside yourself* and get it across to the multitude outside yourself! I have tried to prove to you that already you are a veritable universe of experience and ability, that you are much greater as a person than you suspect you are. You do not think highly enough of yourself and, in rebuttal, you may claim that if you did you would become an *egotist*. My opinion is that there aren't very many true egotists in this world; there should be millions more, for pure egotism is nothing but complete self-knowledge and self-faith. Nowhere in Christ's life can you show me where He doubted Himself or His "merchandise," or His methods of bringing men salvation. He picked the very best method—and He knew it, SELF-TRANSFERENCE.

For every *impression* you hope to make on those outside, you must pay out some *expression* of your own. This expression costs some effort. Smoothly executed, it calls for much practice and definite science. Language is your first means. You must be able to use words efficiently in:

> Private Speaking—Vocabulary and Conversation
> Public Speaking
> Writing

to proceed on your way to success. No successful man is a poor word-handler. No man ever got himself across without using words generously and smartly. Inside you are all the words you need. They represent your memories, your feelings, your thoughts, your education, your complete experience. It is up to you to transfer them to the world outside if that world is to know you, respect you, "buy" you.

[5]

How to Build a Successful Working Vocabulary

In your drive for success, you must never be at a loss for a word; in selling yourself, your chief means for expressing your thoughts and emotions to others is your vocabulary.

Accuracy in all things marks the successful man.

Samuel Johnson, who wrote a dictionary, never defined vocabulary as *a large supply* of words, or the possession of many *big words*. He said: "VOCABULARY IS ACCURACY WITH WORDS."

Every word you need *to think with* you already have.

Start with the words you already know. Use them exactly as you think them inside your head. You can't improve the thought by trying to redress it in words you did not use in thinking it. A good thought all by itself is fancy enough. Express it, and though people do not exclaim of you: "That man has a marvelous vocabulary!", they tender you this higher compliment: "I get what he means."

Use what you have properly and very soon new words, more accurate words, will come into your vocabulary. So-called "big words," when used appropriately, are nothing but the kind of words needed to give more accuracy, finer shades of meaning.

Accuracy with words suggests accuracy and dependability in

all your other actions. Personnel and employment managers, whether hiring for office or factory, are always anxious to find out what kind of a vocabulary you have.

If you're a factory hand, a good vocabulary makes you great material for promotion to assistant foreman, foreman, or a higher position. If you're an office man, an excellent vocabulary can land you in a top executive position.

If you're a salesman, an able vocabulary is of immense aid in explaining your product, making it attractive to buyer, and helps incalculaby in answering objections.

Most aptitude, intelligence, and personnel tests, given today by hundreds of thousands of concerns, center around vocabulary.

Johnson O'Connor, famed scientist in human analysis, says: *Vocabulary accompanies outstanding success more than any other characteristic I have been able to isolate scientifically.*

In his exhaustive tests this expert discovered that the majority of business executives (factory and office) have even better vocabularies than college professors! So, if you are not a college man, take heart. All the new words you will ever need to make you a success are available.

You pick up new words, first, from *other speakers.*

Second, from *books and teachers.*

Third, from *curiosity.* You hear a word misused; you look it up. Now it is yours to use properly.

Fourth, from *major experiences.* Undergo a serious operation and you'll come out with at least ONE new word—the name of the operation! Or you may be involved in extreme danger, or a political fight, or a stupendous assignment you have never faced before. Welcome the crisis, for *it's going to improve your vocabulary!*

Raymond C. was a sort of a fly-by-night young man, who never held a job for long, never secured anyone's respect. An only son, he did not know his own father very well, paid little attention to his father's career and its accompanying rigors. But suddenly his father became involved in a big political fight, needed help, and Raymond rushed to his aid. The young man gave two whole months of concentrated study and aid to his dad, digging into his problems, rooting out material and proofs for his father's defense.

I happened to meet Raymond in the middle of his campaign of paternal support. I was amazed! Raymond, who up till then had had the weakest, most careless vocabulary, had suddenly turned into a giant of word-power.

The enforced thinking and studying, the intensity needed for his father's defense, suddenly brought out in the young man material and resources no one knew he had. Forced to be comprehensive and exact, he rose to the occasion.

You can do the same any time you face a crisis or unusual situation. Welcome the unusual experience! It can deliver to you the equivalent of TWO COLLEGE EDUCATIONS in a few days of supreme personal effort.

How to Increase Your Word Power

Many new words come into your vocabulary unannounced, but the process ordinarily is too slow. Here are a few devices for bringing them in consciously, deliberately:

1. Ask the meaning of every good, new word you hear.

When you hear another using impressive words in conversation, you're inclined to admire the man and his words, and there let the matter rest.

But it's lost opportunity if you let the good words go by because you don't try to learn their meaning. Stop and ask the man what a certain word means. Confess out loud that you don't know. You'll find in one hundred per cent of the cases that a user of big words or special words is very happy to explain what they mean, and he *looks up to you* for confessing your ignorance and wanting to be informed.

This is much better than looking up the word in the dictionary, for you get not only the new word but a good instructor in its use, absolutely free.

2. Relate a special word to a special person.

My old philosophy instructor at college loved the word "germane." He used it freely, lovingly. When I first heard the word, I thought it meant "German," but soon learned its true meaning. When I hear the word today (some 40 years after college), I still connect it with the man I learned it from and think of him at once!

Sometimes a stranger or acquaintance uses a good word—gives it to you. Remember *the man, as well as the word,* and the word will be much easier to retain.

Similarly, try to put each new person you meet into a word, a particular, individual, extraordinary word:

John Jones may be "suave"; Fred Miller, "trenchant"; Sam Goodman, "obstreperous"—and so on. A word for every personality, and every personality in a word.

The word descriptions will help you remember the persons and the persons will help you remember the word and its meaning.

3. Make up a list of unusual words, each beginning with a letter from your own full name.

For example, "Jacob Byron Throckmorton":

> Jejune—sterile
> Annomination—pun
> Cerebrum—brain
> Obfuscate—confuse
> Bipartite—two parts
>
> Bon mot—witty remark
> Yaw—to zigzag
> Ratiocination—reasoning
> Osculate—to kiss
> Noxious—harmful
>
> Trauma—shock
> Heinous—hateful
> Resuscitate—return to life
> Ocular—visual
> Calescent—becoming warm
> Kaleidoscopic—changing,
>   many-colored pattern

Minutia—trifling detail
*O*btund—blunt, dull
*R*eplica—exact copy
*T*onitruous—thundering
*O*bloquy—abuse, disgrace
*N*ubilous—cloudy, vague

Take your own name, including middle name, and make up your own list of so called "big words." Pick adjectives or nouns that cover your good points so the list will be inspirational and on the plus side. You'll never forget your own name; neither will you forget the special list of words you have tied to it.

4. Memorize some lines with a lot of good words in them.

A Washington reporter was writing of the eagerness of Senators to attend social affairs even though the weather was very hot. He wrote: "This summer, sedate solons will sachez to any soiree at the drop of a sombrero."

When you meet up with a line that is pregnant with word power, memorize it and use it, if nothing more than to say you read it and repeat it.

5. Avoid the avoidable.

You can't carry in your pocket every word you would like to, but can certainly restrain yourself from using useless words and phrases.

Avoid the trite or threadbare expression, e.g., "ridiculously low."

Avoid the ungrammatical, e.g.:

Between you and I
One of these kind
Irregardless

Avoid childish exaggeration, like: "perfectly wonderful." If you want to say "fabulous," you might try "fabulistic" for a change.

6. Cross over your vocabulary from one field to another.

Suppose you are a carpenter. There are a lot of beautiful words and expressions in carpentry that can apply to many other activities of life:

"He planed down the rough spots in his speech"
"Mitered logic and toenailed arguments"

Consider all the expressions taken from the game of baseball (e.g. "something on the ball") and used in other fields. You can take words out of other games you know and put them into ordinary conversation. Think of the opportunities in "Hook," "Slice," "Jab," "Punt," "Foul," "Forty Love."

You can turn nouns into verbs, adjectives into nouns, even a little preposition of two letters can be made into a smashing "long" word. "The 'if' of the campaign," "the 'of' of fashion."

Yes, every little, plain word in your present vocabulary can be given a buzz and a zing by using it in a different yet appropriate way.

7. Eliminate swearing.

Swear off swearing and your vocabulary will be immensely improved. Cuss words are merely devices to prove you're a tough guy, hard-boiled, no sissy. (This is debatable for, as you well know, profanity makes you feel weak, not strong.) Anyhow, most swear words are so worn out by extravagant use, there is little meaning left in them. They impress nobody. They only publicize the fact that you have a poverty-stricken vocabulary. Cut out the rough stuff, and you will force more meaning into your ejaculations; eventually you will begin to create expressions that are entirely *your own,* full of force and subtlety.

8. Change your sentence.

As it stands now, you probably begin every sentence with the word "I"—"I think," "I mean," "I believe," et cetera! Put the "I" in a different place in the sentence—farther back. Try starting a sentence with a verb or an adjective, rather than a noun or pronoun. Mix your pitches. Start throwing curves.

9. Have fun with words.

Regard words as playthings rather than instruments. Experiment with your words. Try to originate a few slang phrases of your own. They may be clumsy and vague, but they will be *yours,* and no listener recoils at hearing words that are entirely your own!

Example: Father of several daughters in a one bathroom house complains: "I can't get a bath in edgewise."

10. Practice on your children—fun for you—a word of good for them.

Anything you can do to infect your children with a love for words is a direct contribution towards their future success. If you have a good vocabulary, do not hesitate to use it profusely in the presence of your children, no matter how young. If a big word is called for, use it on a two-year-old just as quickly as you would on a 22-year-old. The best way for anyone to broaden his vocabulary is to be associated with people possessing better vocabularies. If your present vocabulary is nothing to brag about, seize the chance to try out your new words on the kids. In teaching them, you will be teaching yourself.

If away from home and writing your children, do not hesitate to use words which they may not understand. In reading your letter they may have to ask Mama what you mean, or they may even have to go to the dictionary and find out—either method a good one. Whenever children hear a new word inserted into the scheme of practical living, they generally take pains to find out what it means and thereby make it their own property.

11. When you come across a new word in reading.

Should you stop and look up its meaning? Should you jot it down for future examination? Nothing wrong with the practice; it can't hurt. But to find the exact meaning of a strange new word will not guarantee that ever after it is part of your vocabulary.

A better trick is to *guess* at the meaning of the word. Next time you meet up with it, take another guess. Better to read the wrong meaning into it than to let your mind go blank. For the mistaken ideas you had about the word will help engrave the real meaning on your mind when you finally capture its significance.

Wait two days. Make some more guesses, try to derive meaning from the different syllables. Ask your friends if they know the word. Discuss it out in the open. A friend visited an Irish cemetery, copied the inscription on the monument to the martyrs of the famous "Easter" rebellion. One word seemed out of place. It was the word "indefeasible." We all discussed it and seemed to agree someone had made a mistake. But the dictionary proved the word one of supreme appropriateness, and because of all the discussion, objection and inquiry, I am sure we all will remember the true meaning of the word forever.

12. *Associate with the articulate.*

Try to associate with people of large vocabularies. You pick up new words from them without even knowing it is happening. Undoubtedly this is the best way of all to build a vocabulary.

Associate with people who speak clearly, whose communicative ability is superior. You may not pick up big words from them; but they will inspire you into greater clarity of expression on your own part.

The man of clarity sells himself so thoroughly that you favorably retain the memory of him months or years after you have met him.

I can never forget a priest reciting funeral prayers in Latin over a cemetery grave. He was so precise in pronunciation, so distinct and clear, I managed to understand every word *in Latin.*

I can never forget the vice president and chief engineer of a large industrial service concern whom I met only twice, and many years ago. His vocabularly was so clear and his thoughts were conveyed so perfectly to my mind that he made me realize that vocabularly can be a fine, clean-cut mechanism of a million parts all exact in measurement down to a ten thousandth of an inch, and each part working so beautifully with the others that *efficiency* was delivered, total and absolute.

I can never forget the talent scout for a great Midwest manufacturer who talked about machinery, engineering, invention, and patents with a clarity that was stunning and, then, at the drop of a hat moved over into subjects, personal, social, and confidential and was just as clear and exact in his communication.

No man alive, be he tycoon of business or common man on the street, can withhold his lasting admiration and respect from you, once you are able to reach him by conveying your exact thoughts from your mind to his!

13. Make your own definitions.

Nearly everyone refers to the dictionary for definitions and most frequently are disappointed by getting only a meaning, an explanation or identification. A complete definition is rarely to be found.

Perhaps the best ever created was by the Greek philosopher Aristotle who defined *man* thus:

"Man is a rational animal"

Try defining common ordinary things you are immensely familiar with, for instance: "Door," "Window," "Chair." So manage your definition that you include every kind of door, window, and chair, and at the same time exclude things that may come close to being these same objects as "gate," "screen," "stool."

Sample definition: "A pencil is an encased stick of solid writing or marking material."

Defining makes you think. Since you cannot think without words, defining makes you handle your words with extreme care.

14. Pronunciation is as important as meaning.

Mispronounce a big word and your best friend will laugh in your face.

Pronunciation is therefore as important as meaning, when you are speaking the word out loud. If in the slightest doubt, refer to the dictionary. Here the dictionary is indispensable. A large number of supposedly well-educated people may mispronounce a word, but that doesn't make it right.

For instance, the simple word *either* is now being pronounced by a large number of people as *eye-ther*. If you have a true Oxford accent, and if you pronounce a large number of other small words in the correct Oxford manner, eye-ther is correct. But eye-ther, all by itself is reprehensible, bad style; a tip to all and sundry that its user has a fake education.

Do not pronounce a long word *syllable by syllable*, even though you are following the exact pronunciation your dictionary gave you. Master the pronunciation syllable by syllable, yes; but in executing the pronunciation, *do it fast*, slur the syllables a little, join them quickly, and the sound of the word will be admirable.

15. Never drag a big word in by the ears.

You have met the fellow who has just picked up a new word and he kills it by dragging it in wherever he can. Someone has told him that the way to master a new word is to keep on using it as often as he can.

He makes you feel like the guinea pig of the experiment.

People who keep on using big words, even a lot of big words and in the proper places, may fail to impress *you* with their vocabulary. For though you grant they have the meaning of the words under control, their garish display of polysyllabic jewelry makes them seem poor rather than rich.

But when you hear a good talker who up to this point has been using familiar words suddenly utter an unusual word, which is the only word he can use now because it is the only one that fits, you are flattened with amazement and admiration.

The magic word came in, not because he dragged it in, but because *it had to come in*. And as he used it, he did not seem to know he was using it. Of such a man, you will say: "He truly has a great vocabulary!"

A SINGLE WORD MADE A PHENOMENAL SALE

One word from you—the right word in the right place—and you can sell yourself in a second.

I am thinking of a certain call my partner and I made one day. We were out to sell the designing of a complete line of labels to a big company. The project would run into tens of thousands of dollars. Other designers were competing for the business; it was a profitable account.

We had a good entree to the executive vice president in charge, though we did not know him personally. John, our friend inside the company, had arranged the meeting. John believed in us but the vice president was hostile, if not openly belligerent.

The meeting had gone on for half an hour. We had shown our wares as convincingly as possible, but the v.p. was clearly getting tired, and ready to quit the meeting. Finally he said:

"I don't know why we should choose you over any of the others. Could you put into a few words, or better still, ONE word, why we should pick you?"

Quickly, I replied: "Yes, I can do it. The word is CONSANGUINITY."

The v.p. reared up. "What did you say?"

I answered: "I said CONSANGUINITY. We intend to put consanguinity into your labels."

The big man stared as if in a trance. He had instantly realized my main selling point: to establish a "blood relationship" among all the separate labels, proving they were in the same family. Then he turned to his assistant. "John, give these fellows the business. Any outfit that will use a word like *consanguinity* in a business transaction has got something coming to them!"

The moral here, however, is that the mere boldness of the word or its unusualness did not account for the sale. *It was actually the only word that fitted the situation perfectly.*

Indicating that vocabulary does not mean having a lot of words in your pocket but rather having the ability to come up with the right word at the right time.

One new word accidentally dropped within your hearing can often start you going on the road to a fine vocabulary. Listen! Be on the lookout! The next man you meet may utter it.

Ten-year-old Mickey is helping me weed the lawn. As we

work together, I notice the extreme care he takes. "Mickey," I say, without thinking, "You're very *meticulous!*"

With alert interest he asks: "What does that mean?"

"What?"

"That word you just said."

"What do you think it means?" I counter.

"I don't know," said Mickey, "but it has a nice sound."

At intervals I repeated, "Mickey, you're very meticulous," and he would look at me quizically, each time.

The following day when he came to help me, I asked if he knew what "meticulous" meant. "It means I'm very particular," said Mickey, "and I found out by thinking about *the way you said it!*"

Mickey liked the new word enough to dwell on all its possible meanings overnight. Anyone who can fall in love with a word, with the wonder of language, and who will give enough time to ferreting out the meaning of a word without rushing to the dictionary, is bound to develop a great vocabulary as time goes by.

BASIC ENGLISH IS BASIC THINKING

Advocates of "Basic English" have developed their word system primarily for the purposes of helping foreigners or folks who speak broken English to improve their language by mastering simple words first.

The good theory is that Basic English is basic thinking. If you know the word, you can think the word, and your thinking will inevitably fit it in its proper place.

This is a good theory for everyone to follow, regardless of how well-versed in language he may be.

Don't monkey around with words you cannot "think" or "feel." Remain basic always.

And at this point it should be a good idea to review the words of Basic English you have already acquired. Then see how many more basic words and thoughts grow out of a review of this standard stock in trade.

THE 850 WORDS OF BASIC ENGLISH

OPERATIONS
100

Come	After	Of	But	Together
Get	Against	Till	Or	Well
Give	Among	Than	If	Almost
Go	At	A	Though	Enough
Keep	Before	The	While	Even
Let	Between	All	How	Little
Make	By	Any	When	Much
Put	Down	Every	Where	Not
Seem	From	No	Why	Only
Take	In	Other	Again	Quite
Be	Off	Some	Ever	So
Do	On	Such	Far	Very
Have	Over	That	Forward	Tomorrow
Say	Through	This	Here	Yesterday
See	To	I	Near	North
Send	Under	He	Now	South
May	Up	You	Out	East
Will	With	Who	Still	West
About	As	And	Then	Please
Across	For	Because	There	Yes

THINGS
400 General

Account	Back	Canvas	Cork	Design
Act	Balance	Care	Cotton	Desire
Addition	Base	Cause	Cough	Destruction
Adjustment	Behavior	Chalk	Country	Detail
Advertisement	Belief	Chance	Cover	Development
Agreement	Birth	Change	Crack	Digestion
Air	Bit	Cloth	Credit	Direction
Amount	Bile	Coal	Crime	Discovery
Amusement	Blood	Color	Crush	Discussion
Animal	Blow	Comfort	Cry	Disease
Answer	Body	Committee	Current	Disgust
Apparatus	Brass	Company	Curve	Distance
Approval	Bread	Comparison	Damage	Distribution
Argument	Breath	Competition	Danger	Division
Art	Brother	Condition	Daughter	Doubt
Attack	Building	Connection	Day	Drink
Attempt	Burn	Control	Death	Driving
Attention	Burst	Cook	Debt	Dust
Attraction	Business	Copper	Decision	Earth
Authority	Butter	Copy	Degree	Edge

THINGS

400 General

Education	History	Mark	Payment	River
Effect	Hole	Market	Peace	Road
End	Hope	Mass	Person	Roll
Error	Hour	Meal	Place	Room
Event	Humor	Measure	Plant	Rub
Example	Ice	Meat	Play	Rule
Exchange	Idea	Meeting	Pleasure	Run
Existence	Impulse	Memory	Point	Salt
Expansion	Increase	Metal	Poison	Sand
Experience	Industry	Middle	Polish	Scale
Export	Ink	Milk	Porter	Science
Fact	Insect	Mind	Position	Sea
Fall	Instrument	Mine	Powder	Seat
Family	Insurance	Minute	Power	Secretary
Father	Interest	Mist	Price	Selection
Fear	Invention	Money	Print	Self
Feeling	Iron	Month	Process	Sense
Fiction	Jelly	Morning	Produce	Servant
Field	Join	Mother	Profit	Sex
Fight	Journey	Motion	Property	Shade
Fire	Judge	Mountain	Prose	Shake
Flame	Jump	Move	Protest	Shame
Flight	Kick	Music	Pull	Shock
Flower	Kiss	Name	Punishment	Side
Fold	Knowledge	Nation	Purpose	Sign
Food	Land	Need	Push	Silk
Force	Language	News	Qualify	Silver
Form	Laugh	Night	Question	Sister
Friend	Law	Noise	Rain	Size
Front	Lead	Note	Range	Sky
Fruit	Learning	Number	Rate	Sleep
Glass	Leather	Observation	Ray	Slip
Gold	Letter	Offer	Reaction	Slope
Government	Level	Oil	Reading	Smash
Grain	Lift	Operation	Reason	Smell
Grass	Light	Opinion	Record	Smile
Grip	Limit	Order	Regret	Smoke
Group	Linen	Organization	Relation	Sneeze
Growth	Liquid	Ornament	Religion	Snow
Guide	List	Owner	Representative	Soap
Harbor	Look	Page	Request	Society
Harmony	Loss	Pain	Respect	Son
Hate	Love	Paint	Rest	Song
Hearing	Machine	Paper	Reward	Sort
Heat	Man	Part	Rhythm	Sound
Help	Manager	Paste	Rice	Soup

THINGS

400 General

Space	Sugar	Thing	Use	Weather
Stage	Suggestion	Thought	Value	Week
Start	Summer	Thunder	Verse	Weight
Statement	Support	Time	Vessel	Wind
Steam	Surprise	Tin	View	Wine
Steel	Swim	Top	Voice	Winter
Step	System	Touch	Walk	Woman
Stitch	Talk	Trade	War	Wood
Stone	Taste	Transport	Wash	Wool
Stop	Tax	Trick	Waste	Word
Story	Teaching	Trouble	Water	Work
Stretch	Tendency	Turn	Wave	Wound
Structure	Test	Twist	Wax	Writing
Substance	Theory	Unit	Way	Year

200 Picturable

Angle	Branch	Dog	Hand	Neck
Ant	Brick	Door	Hat	Needle
Apple	Bridge	Drain	Head	Nerve
Arch	Brush	Drawer	Heart	Net
Arm	Bucket	Dress	Hook	Nose
Army	Bulb	Drop	Horn	Nut
Baby	Button	Ear	Horse	Office
Bag	Cake	Egg	Hospital	Orange
Ball	Camera	Engine	House	Oven
Band	Card	Eye	Island	Parcel
Basin	Cart	Face	Jewel	Pen
Basket	Carriage	Farm	Kettle	Pencil
Bath	Cat	Feather	Key	Picture
Bed	Chain	Finger	Knee	Pig
Bee	Cheese	Fish	Knife	Pin
Bell	Chest	Flag	Knot	Pipe
Berry	Chin	Floor	Leaf	Plane
Bird	Church	Fly	Leg	Plate
Blade	Circle	Foot	Library	Plough
Board	Clock	Fork	Line	Pocket
Boat	Cloud	Fowl	Lip	Pot
Bone	Coat	Frame	Lock	Potato
Book	Collar	Garden	Map	Prison
Boot	Comb	Girl	Match	Pump
Bottle	Cord	Glove	Monkey	Rail
Box	Cow	Goat	Moon	Rat
Boy	Cup	Gun	Mouth	Receipt
Brain	Curtain	Hair	Muscle	Ring
Brake	Cushion	Hammer	Nail	Rod

THINGS
200 Picturable

Roof	Shoe	Star	Thread	Trousers
Root	Skin	Station	Throat	Umbrella
Sail	Skirt	Stem	Thumb	Wall
School	Snake	Stick	Ticket	Watch
Scissors	Sock	Stocking	Toe	Wheel
Screw	Spade	Stomach	Tongue	Whip
Seed	Sponge	Store	Tooth	Whistle
Sheep	Spoon	Street	Town	Window
Shelf	Spring	Sun	Train	Wing
Ship	Square	Table	Tray	Wire
Shirt	Stamp	Tail	Tree	Worm

QUALITIES
100 General

Able	Dependent	Healthy	Physical	Smooth
Acid	Early	High	Political	Sticky
Angry	Elastic	Hollow	Poor	Stiff
Automatic	Electric	Important	Possible	Straight
Beautiful	Equal	Kind	Present	Strong
Black	Fat	Like	Private	Sudden
Boiling	Fertile	Living	Probable	Sweet
Bright	First	Long	Quick	Tall
Broken	Fixed	Male	Quiet	Thick
Brown	Flat	Married	Ready	Tight
Cheap	Free	Material	Red	Tired
Chemical	Frequent	Medical	Regular	True
Chief	Full	Military	Responsible	Violent
Clean	General	Natural	Right	Waiting
Clear	Good	Necessary	Round	Warm
Common	Great	New	Same	Wet
Complex	Grey	Normal	Second	Wide
Conscious	Hanging	Open	Separate	Wise
Cut	Happy	Parallel	Serious	Yellow
Deep	Hard	Past	Sharp	Young

50 Opposites

Awake	Dead	Future	Narrow	Simple
Bad	Dear	Green	Old	Slow
Bent	Delicate	Ill	Opposite	Small
Bitter	Different	Last	Public	Soft
Blue	Dirty	Late	Rough	Solid
Certain	Dry	Left	Sad	Special
Cold	False	Loose	Safe	Strange
Complete	Feeble	Loud	Secret	Thin
Cruel	Female	Low	Short	
Dark	Foolish	Mixed	Shut	

[6]

How to Become
an Interesting Conversationalist

Most "CONVERSATION" between strangers is confined to the weather. Most "conversation" between friends is confined to gossip. And you can hardly call these subjects real conversation.

Conversation means: *having words with*. Since words are supposed to represent thoughts, true conversation is *having thoughts with another*.

In your attempts at striking up conversation with strangers you have come to the disarming truth: people don't care about you. And the concomitant fact, if you will be honest with yourself, is: you don't care about other people.

There is a simple device for hurdling these two stumbling blocks: It's all right to say you should care, but it's not easy to reform yourself quickly. If you can prove you care about others, they will come out of their shell and begin caring about you. But this self-education process may take too long and you will be tempted to quit the crusade before you can re-make yourself.

The device I offer here is really a little game, diverting and intriguing. What you know about the other fellow is this: he is locked up, he will not open up and give you a good look at his real self. (You strike him the same way.) Since he is under lock and key, the device or game is this: *Find the key that will unlock him.*

He may be under a special, complicated lock that defies you to find the key. But go after it. It is a wonderful game.

First, look him over and come to some theory about his inner personality. Study him. Speculate silently on the real man, what he feels, what he thinks, what he *loves*.

Study him on the surface and there doesn't seem to be very much there. Scratch the hard surface once or twice, and real *gold* may suddenly appear.

No one likes to be examined or interrogated, but deep down everyone is crying for sympathy and understanding. That man will reveal his true self to you if you work long enough and smoothly enough at unlocking him. Do not write anybody off as shallow or uninteresting until you have unlocked him; with the lock removed and the door to his heart wide open, you will find him an eager conversationalist and perhaps a real friend!

If you thirst for conversation and decry the small number of people with whom you can make fine conversation, tell yourself it is your own fault. You have not developed sufficient skill in opening locks. Practice. Stab around for subjects. Avoid the banal things, such as sports or politics. Move into the realm of philosophy, self-knowledge. Try a few abstract subjects; for the richest conversation is generally centered around the abstract.

Don't be so infernally *concrete* and matter-of-fact! The other man is really not matter-of-fact underneath and neither are you, though he thinks you are because your remarks seem to say so. Reveal as much of yourself as you dare to without seeming egocentric or autobiographical. Eventually a spark will come, the rusty lock will creak a little and slowly open.

What a game! Try to find the key to the other person. Even though you fail and no conversation in the real sense follows, still you have enjoyed yourself immensely. You have gotten in some mighty fine practice. You have improved yourself, increased your skill. Other locks will be easier to open.

Once you have unlocked anybody, conversation with him becomes rich and natural and high class.

I once boarded an airplane in Los Angeles, nonstop to Chicago, and an engineer from Buffalo sat down beside me. In two seconds we had each unlocked the other. For six and a half hours we talked continuously, philosophized, speculated, traded personalities prodigally. Few facts were brought up, all discussion was a lavish interchange of mind and feelings. The six and a half hours of the flight seemed to pass in ten minutes! It was a GREAT CONVERSATION, and like all forms of greatness it made time stand still!

Conversation is a great and noble thing. It is man at his best. It is self-rewarding because it so cleanly justifies your status as a human being.

People should care about you, and they will, if you can get them into real conversation. And you should care enough about every man you meet to try to unlock him. That you sell yourself to him, that you gain his everlasting respect, can be viewed as incidental. The real advantage, immensely practical and valuable, is: *Get to know a few people through excellent conversation, and you have gained a golden knowledge of all mankind!*

Some Tips

1. Recognize the high value of conversation.

Put a small price on conversation, view it merely as a time-killer and otherwise worthless, and you won't find good conversation. But regard it as one of the most precious activities of mankind, concede *it is an art,* give your complete respect to your converser or conversers. Acknowledge that the very *attempt* to make good conversation calls from you an important expenditure of your best faculties of speech, memory, and intellect. Put the value in and the value comes out, and instantly your conversational prospect begins to care about you!

Stanley Link, the cartoonist, had this faculty, and he was as good a conversationalist as a cartoonist. One day I was being funny with him on the subject of bald-headed men. "Why not," I proposed, "a fancy hair ribbon, or rosette or silk ornament that baldies could paste on their domes?" Stanley thought it was funny, but important to remember, he thought it was a *valuable idea*. So he used it for two months in his *Dan Daily* comic strip!

2. *Submerge yourself.*

Quit using such words as "I" and "Me" and "Mine." These are automatic conversational shutoffs, because people are not interested in you—they care mainly about themselves. Frame your conversation around them. Think from their point of view. Forsake the long-standing practice you have in seeing things from your point of view, and try to imagine yourself as the man who actually bears the other fellow's name, wears his clothes, and has the exact duplicate of the other man's knowledge, experience, and quirks of personality.

Try it for a day. For twenty-four hours, decide to be the other fellow, and let your emotions, your words, your instincts express themselves openly as if you had veritably transposed your very soul into his body. It's not a big sacrifice—it's fun.

3. *Honor their opinions.*

How can anyone engage in conversation unless he is allowed to express his personal opinions? How can he be drawn to you if you indicate you don't think much of his opinions?

No matter how commonplace the opinion be, no matter how often you have heard it expressed by others, STOP and hear it! Give outward sign that you are considering it. Be it stale, empty, or totally irrelevant—think about it! Take time and go over it mentally. Repeat it, perhaps. Let your mediation of the opinion be visible, audible.

Such honor to another's opinion is so unusual that he *must* like you, be drawn to your irresistibly. You become one out of a thousand to him. He wants to talk with you more, confide in you, know you better.

Strangely, in putting on the "act" of honoring his opinion by giving it your concentrated attention, you *do* get something new and fresh out of the opinion. As you force yourself to take the frayed old opinion, you believe you are in for a bad time.

But *honor it,* and you suddenly find you are enjoying yourself. You are giving *care* and thereby winning *care.* You are thrilled because he is thrilled. Nothing is wasted, much is gained.

4. Don't be "nosey."

Be personal, by all means, in your conversational contacts with others, but never get "nosey." Don't try to find out the persons age, what his suit cost, what he paid out in taxes, or the answer to the intimate, private things of his life that he has the right to guard. The rule here is simple: Never ask from another information which you yourself would refuse, if you were asked the same questions.

Even if you know you are not nosey by nature, be careful not to get involved in any kind of questioning which may seem nosey to the other. You want him to like you. Before he will engage in anything like good conversation, he must like you. Good conversation is not easy to find, nor easy to make. Don't kill off your prospects with frightening questions.

How to Start a Conversation

I have a friend who retired from business in Chicago and moved to a middle-sized city in California. My friend loves conversation. He loves his adopted city, too, but has one great fault to find with it. Already there for two full years, he finds it almost impossible to strike up a real conversation with anybody!

My friend is loquacious and articulate, and a very well-educated man with several university degrees. He cannot understand his fix. He concludes the people of his adopted city are cold, unfriendly because the conversational devices that worked in Chicago do not seem to work in this California town. I'm afraid he has missed the point (and, incidentally, missed a lot of good conversation that could make his retirement much happier.)

My friend is too eager to make friends. He shows his conversational hunger too openly. He rushes into each meeting with a stranger as if he were digging a ditch in a big hurry, running to catch a departing train, swimming for his dear life in stormy waters.

When you meet a person with whom you desire conversation, or walk into a group that is supposed to be ready for conversation, don't speed up, *slow down*. Too much revealed zest marks you immediately as a bore or a windbag. Conversation is often exciting, but conversers usually fear excitement.

My friend, when in Chicago, knew many people, and they knew him and understood him. But now he's meeting *strangers who do not know him* and cannot yet regard him as his former friends did. His initial torrent of words and ideas is so baffling, they have to seem cold or unfriendly to maintain their own poise and self-esteem. Their seeming aloofness is nothing but a natural attempt to *slow him down*.

Conversation is one of the great arts, but it is not the only thing in life worthwhile. In your attempts to find good conversers, please remember *you cannot succeed every time*. Try too hard to prove your ability to make everyone like your talk, and you'll find that nobody likes your talk.

Learn to live with yourself; learn to converse with yourself. If your own thoughts and deliberations—your inward personal conversations—can satisfy you, you will not be too expectant when you meet strangers nor too anxious to win them over into talking companions. Try talking silently to yourself at the time of meeting these strangers. Somebody has to say *something*, but it is not up to you immediately to show how smart you are by commenting on that something. Listen. Think it over. Your eyes will show that your ears are working.

You can't hit a home run every time you come up to bat in conversation. Be philosophical. Just aim to hit 300, which should satisfy any conversational big leaguer.

After the weather, what are you going to talk about? If you are going to make a study of high conversation—which is the only conversation—you should compile a list of surefire topics. All of them need not always work on everybody, but some of them will, and most of the following have a good chance of succeeding under most circumstances:

1. *Find the man's work.*

The next man you meet is a carpenter, an artist, a janitor, a something. It shouldn't be too hard to find out his work. Now talk about it. But don't start to tell him what you know about his work. Ask him to tell you. Every adult person by instinct is a teacher. Ask the carpenter about his work, how to saw a board properly, how to hit a nail, anything simple which you, as a humble listener, would like to know.

Any craftsman, once he sees you as a sincere inquirer, will begin to tell you about his work; sometimes he will tell you only the superficial side. At other times, if he sees you as having a deeper mind than usual, he will begin to discourse on the rich side of his work, his life, his ideals. He wants to pass on to another worthy soul some of the fine things he knows. This is true conversation.

Never advise others in conversation till they demand advice; advice is ordinarily resented, though it is temptation that eternally hovers over every conversation.

But if another is advising you, listen intently: don't argue. Sometimes you can go so far as to take notes on what the other is saying to you. This act, if smoothly handled, is a superior compliment, indeed.

2. *Inquire about their children.*

Ask a father or mother about his or her children, and you may be in for a cascade of words, a torrential monologue which might be called a conversation.

Do not open up by *talking* about their children; simply *ask*. The most reserved stranger in the world, given a chance, will try to say something about his children. And what he says may furnish you with the key to unlock him.

BUT NEVER TALK ABOUT YOUR OWN CHILDREN! And if you are asked about them, be brief and unexpansive in your answers. This will mark you as a person whose friendship should be further cultivated.

3. *Talk about the other person.*

If you see the man is wearing an expensive necktie, or one in very good taste, praise his necktie. Oh, it is such a little thing, but what a conversation-opener!

Talk about his dog, his lawn, his town, his school, his house; if a woman, her hat, her dress, her voice, her club.

Never talk about yourself till it is clear you are being forced into it.

4. *In meeting an absolute stranger, say something either very friendly or very unusual.*

I moved into a small town in Illinois eight years ago. The only welcome I got was from a young boy who stutters miserably. Would you believe it? For eight years, I have constantly enjoyed a hundred conversations with him and he with me. By showing a degree of friendship which others dared not show, he won my respect and affection.

But strangers ordinarily are suspicious of too much sudden friendship. The best way to open up a conversation with a stranger is to *say something strange.* "A 34-inch rainfall in Japan—" "A recent feat in baseball by a player in Vancouver, B.C.—" "The wind seems to be coming straight down." "Can you hear that blasting in South Chicago?"

Such a strange approach, if not offered in a light way, gets instant attention. The stranger looks up to you as a man of discernment. He may want to change the subject, but at least he will begin to *talk.*

5. *Their accomplishments.*

The first time I met Gene Tunney was on a sidewalk in Hot Springs, Arkansas. Others were talking to him about prize-fighting. I butted in with: "Gene, let's hear you recite four lines from Shelley." He immediately accommodated with eight. Then with a passage from Shakespeare, one from Swinburne, and one from Keats.

A few years later I saw him surrounded by a group of ad-

mirers in a Chicago hotel. Since he retired undefeated as heavy-
weight champion of the world, everyone wanted to talk prize-
fighting with him, and on this occasion it was no different. He
looked bored, till he caught my eye and he stepped forward
eagerly to shake my hand, though I had met him just once two
years before on that Hot Springs street.

Without any ado, and ignoring the rest of the crowd, I said:
"Gene, your association with George Bernard Shaw added immensely to your public stature." Tunney replied: "Rather to
my private stature." And then the two of us engaged in a single
two-way conversation for one hour, the subject: George Bernard Shaw. Anyone else in the crowd would have been delighted
to hold Tunney's attention for two minutes! But they never
suspected that Tunney was more interested in his other accomplishments than in prizefighting.

6. Nostalgia.

If the person is from the old neighborhood, the old school,
the old game or activity, you certainly can get the conversation
started by referring to things past that you both lived and
loved.

7. His accent.

He does say something, though it be but a couple of words.
His accent? What is it? Scotch? French? Italian? Austrian? Comment on it, ask him about his origins, and you are unlocking a
world of rich possibility. Though he be an American, his accent
suggests he is from state or section, about which you would like
to know more. He will quickly accommodate.

8. Medicine.

Not a good working topic of conversation, but a surefire device for getting a conversation started. Sickness and possible
cures as a topic is almost as universal as the weather, but much
more varied and fruitful of many more words.

Mention *doctors* in a roomful of people, and *doctors* will probably stay the subject of conversation for half an hour. For misery does love company, especially conversational company. However, you can't get too much good for yourself out of discussing sickness, operations, or miracle medicines; but here we are only talking about getting the conversation *started*.

9. News.

I mean real news, not gossip. I know a young salesman who as he travelled in his car kept his ear glued to a radio program by a down-to-earth announcer named Vince Garrity. Vince talked about a fire three blocks away, a woman who had just broken her leg, a celebrity's dog that was lost, and a host of other human things. The salesman stored these news bits in his brain, and on each succeeding call passed them on to his prospects, who did not even know there was such a program on the air. He was welcome *everywhere* as a man who had a lot of fresh news to pass out.

HOW TO KEEP CONVERSATION GOING AND MAKE THEM COME BACK FOR MORE

Good conversation helps you sell yourself to others. Good conversational power makes you a wanted man. You get invited into homes and to parties you would otherwise never see or know. You make acquaintances in all walks of life, and inevitably you come to meet influential people who admire and respect you for your smart conversation and who want to help you both socially and in business.

No intelligent host or hostess will invite a mummy or a silent person to the party, unless it is absolutely necessary. All entertainers are on the lookout for personalities who keep the conversational ball rolling and prevent the party from dying on its feet.

If you know how to start a conversation, you should know how to finish it. A reputation as a continuously good conversationalist is priceless. It opens business doors as fast as social doors and brings you many rich opportunities for profit or advancement.

The very best conversationalists are always trying to improve. They:

1. Deal in variety.

Don't stick with the same subjects forever. You will be labelled quickly if you do. Be unpredictable in your conversations —and enjoy it. Don't be always "against." Don't be always "for." Let them catch you now and then in an inconsistency, especially an ephemeral or unimportant one.

2. Employ the Montaigne "method" judiciously.

Re-noting, the great French essayist made this point: *the quickest way to create good conversation is to contradict!* This is an effective device, but dangerous. It is safe to contradict, if you know your adversary is broadminded, argumentatively inclined, and if he is a contradicter himself. Friendly argument speeds up the talk, lends excitement, and develops many new points of view.

But when you contradict, SMILE. Smile with your face, your eyes, and your voice. Do not contradict if you have nothing to back up your stand. Do not contradict a timid person, or one of shallow brains; they will take affront.

Some people can hold their own at proving black is white and vice versa; it's a great asset in conversation, but be sure you are in the right company for this very clever technique.

Be able to take contradiction. Prove you're big enough and accomplished enough to enjoy being crossed or challenged. This ability impresses everybody; you quickly become known as a man who can't be licked in verbal combat.

3. Recognize and acclaim every point scored by others.

All conversation should have a practical end, beyond being a pleasant use of time. If the people in the conversation are all trying to make a good point, eventually a point is sure to be made.

Don't let it pass without acclaiming it. If the others wish to hurry on with the conversation though a good point has just been scored, step in and hold them off. Expand on the point, refuse to shorten it. It belongs to another, but it is your duty to acclaim it and do justice by talking it up at greater length.

Act to prevent the weak defender of a good point from being defeated, and you will be loved by all and long remembered.

4. Finish all sentences.

Few people, though intelligent and well-educated, are in the habit of finishing their conversational sentences. There is too much hurry; thoughts and interjections seem to come too fast; interruptions are many, and the average educated man would never dare to write down on paper the words he utters in informal conversation.

Have you ever read the literal transcript of a recorded telephone conversation? It's full of grunts, hesitations, oh yeah's, broken English, and very, very few completed sentences.

Social and business conversations are much the same. But the man who insists on his native right to speak a formal sentence, with subject, predicate, object and modifying phrases and clauses in perfect grammatical form, is a standout in any company.

This is your right. It is not as difficult as you think. The rule here is simple: *Frame the complete sentence mentally before you utter it orally.* Be different from the common run of conversationalists; complete your thought before you give it utterance. Don't start with a half thought believing you can make up the rest as you go along. You can make up something, but the chances are it will not be rhetorical.

Right now think of someone you consider a good conversationalist. Isn't he or she a person who finishes his sentences and speaks in perfect form? If you can think, you can write. If you can write, you can speak what you would write just as perfectly as if you had written it!

5. *Take the ball and run with it.*

Don't leave it to everyone else to introduce all the subjects and hold the floor forever. Each member of a conversational party must take the ball every so often and hold the floor, discoursing, defending, extending the subject under review.

You are not there as a mere spectator—you are an appointed member of the team. Take the ball and run with it—it's good for the soul and good for the party.

6. *Don't talk over their heads.*

You seldom find yourself in brilliant company. The average affair that asks for your conversation is attended by ordinary people, some uneducated and most of them uninformed on the subject you may wish to expatiate upon.

Though you can boast of no great educational or reading background you can easily fall into the error of talking over their heads by picking a subject at which you are an expert and about which the others know nothing. A conversational bore who is a retired sign painter insists on endlessly recounting all the ins and outs of the sign painting industry to the eternal consternation of whatever listeners may temporarily be his captives.

Talk *down* to them, not in the sense of a superior talking down to an inferior, but *talk down* by using *their* kind of language, *their* channels of thoughts. Under no circumstances throw a powerful vocabulary at them; for big words, strange words, may lose an audience.

If it is too difficult for you to commit this kind of vocabulary-suicide, then use as your link references to their kind of people, people whom they know are ordinary "Joe Blows" and communication will be saved.

7. *Welcome humor.*

Don't be so serious that you show distaste for humor and fun creeping into the conversation. Humor is the oil that keeps the machinery of conversation working perfectly. It allows all present to feel they are in safe company, and to relax frequently from the strenuous nature of talk that is too deep and complicated.

You do not have to be brilliantly witty and clever. A sense of humor can be rightly shown in your *appreciation* of someone else's humor. Your laughter all by itself can be enough to hold up your end of the conversation in the company of very witty people. Just laugh, chuckle or giggle in the right places. Be natural.

Do not force your laughter; follow the wit of others and show you enjoy it by your smiling good nature or your laughing good nature. Never laugh deliberately; this is a giveaway and unpleasant to all who hear it.

If you truly enjoy witty remarks and clever "wisecracking" and at the same time know you are incapable of this kind of wit in conversation, do not despair. Don't try to be witty, when you know you're not; you can still be a generous wit-producer by assuming the role of "straight man."

A straight man in comedy is the one who furnishes the sober material which brings a witty riposte. This is an easy role. Keep feeding sober, matter-of-fact lines to the clever one who is displaying his wit, and he will quickly begin to lean on you to keep the grand game going.

Others, enjoying the fun of the conversation, will quickly forget that you are nothing but a straight man and will rank you as an equally clever and witty person.

On the stage, in professional comedy, the straight man feeds material to the comedian for a clever comeback and generally receives the brunt of the joke. But in conversational repartee, the straight man always has the privilege of outwitting the riposter. Thus he can take his share of the tricks by being too sharp in his straight observations for his witty comrade to answer him. Or he may feed a line to draw a corny comeback and have ready a still more clever comeback to the comeback.

8. The best place to practice conversation is at home.

If you think you are conversationally inept, and hate to enter into a talkfest with people you consider better conversers than you, then do what any sane person must do to acquire any necessary skill—PRACTICE.

Practice in the best place of all—*at the family dinner table*. The family meal is at its best when the food is mixed with gay words, fast words, slow words, every kind of words except negative words, grumbling words, sorrowing words or, worst of all, *absolute silence*.

Don't let on to your wife or children that you are using them as conversational sparring partners but go ahead and try to produce the best conversation in the world at your own dinner table. Try to draw them into substantial conversation with yourself. On one occasion, you may try being as formal and correct as you would be in high society. Another time, try to copy a business conference.

Or look over your family and try to find out which is the funniest, cleverest, wittiest one of all. Then try acting as a straight man for his or her wit. Keep imagining that every person at this table, young or old, is someone else, a matron of society, a millionaire businessman, a magazine editor, or a child prodigy. Speak to them in their imagined status, while still acknowledging their real being. Keep practicing.

Follow and experiment with all the suggestions offered in this chapter and other devices for conversation which you have already mastered.

A miracle will happen! Not only will your conversational powers grow with mercurial speed, and each family member develop new speaking gifts, but the dinner table, *your own family dinner table* will change into a magic, thrilling play, your biggest event of every day, and your own wife's cooking will be the most delicious in the world!

Good conversation involves a great deal more than merely talking about the weather.

A man whom I regard as one of the great conversationalists of our time discloses a very effective trick of the trade:

"Many years ago," he relates, "I deliberately began to cultivate the acquaintance of city policemen. In private, policemen love to talk and their experience has given them a marvelous stock of worldly wisdom. Their ideas are fresh and to the point.

Their thinking makes no attempt to avoid the heart of the matter. Their worldly knowledge inspires one to be worldly wise also, in his own conversation and on subjects in no way related to police work.

"So today, when I converse with anyone I try to talk like one policeman would talk to another, without of course, seeming to be a policeman. The subject matter may be philosophy, economics, politics, religion, any subject plain or abstruse. I try to get at the heart of the matter. I never attempt to push in any fancy language. I treat the subject as if it were a CRIME and then go out to solve the crime!"

I saw him engaged in a long conversation with a typewriter salesman. Later, the salesman came to me and reported. "Never in my life have I had a conversation like this. That man put more into an hour than all my college professors did in four years," said the thrilled salesman.

Standing at a bar one day he began to talk to a stranger, pouring out words of wisdom in his free, reckless way. A friend pulled his sleeve, and whispered: "That guy you're talking to is an ex-convict—look out." Our conversationalist, undismayed, asked the man if he were annoying him: "Cripes, no," replied the tough hoodlum, "I never heard anyone talk like you talk in my whole life. Keep goin' till you get tired!"

Good conversation does not necessarily please all people. Many people can cope only with prosaic subjects like the weather or sports or politics. Good conversationists, too, are apt to be loquacious and want to do a good share of the talking. If the listener does not appreciate real conversation when he hears it, all the golden words are wasted.

But the ability to converse with readiness, even brilliance, is a marvelous asset when you are thrown in with "higher-ups", with high society, or important people who can help you attain your career objectives. To the right person at the right time nothing sells you as fast as your conversation.

[7]

How to Speak
in Front of Others

*(Small Business Meetings and Conferences, Large
Groups and Civic Gatherings; Quick, Easy Steps
to Personal Prominence)*

You're at a conference inside your own concern. The boss is
there. The other top executives, also.

Ever notice how often some individual of much lower rank
grabs the floor—holds it for a long time—gets the ear of his
superiors while they silently mark him down as a very good
prospect for promotion?

His ideas and opinions, to you, may seem ordinary and uninspired. Yours are much better. *But he speaks while you remain silent.* You, with the better ideas, are not heard from!

Step up and take the ball. Take the floor! The floor belongs
to anyone with enough guts to grab it. Your ideas are no good
if kept to yourself. Speak them out and they're twenty times as
good as you suspect they are.

Take a chance—show the big shots in your company that you
are aggressive, expressive, confident and reliable. It's your duty
—to *them* and to *yourself*.

Then go out and get some preliminary training as a public
speaker. Certainly if the company officers have heard that you

have been giving speeches elsewhere, they will *expect* to hear from you at company conferences. They will insist on it. The public-speaker reputation you have made in other places lends your words and your ideas extra importance and force.

No matter how bashful, timid, and weak you feel about becoming a public speaker, decide right now to give it a fling.

You'll concede it's necessary in getting ahead.

You'll also concede that sooner or later, if you're going to make a success of *yourself,* you'll have to do it.

Chairman a few meetings in your own social, community or church world.

Emcee a few shows or special events.

Get your practice on any kind of an audience, large or small.

Once you find you make a satisfactory chairman or M.C. in outside meetings, you'll realize that you are the logical candidate to run:

Company sales meetings

Company drives of all kinds

and you will indeed enjoy the prestige and power such a post delivers to you.

NOW—you are well on your way to becoming a public spokesman for your company or your industry, a man who can stand on his feet, make a formal speech, hold the attention of any audience and force it to think, applaud and approve.

Make this success-resolution: "I AM GOING TO BE A BETTER-THAN-AVERAGE PUBLIC SPEAKER."

How To Be a Better-Than-Average Public Speaker

Everyone who intends to sell himself must learn to speak in public. A tall order for you? You're super-sensitive? Hate the spotlight? Have nothing of importance to say? Would gladly die before you tried it? That kind of alibi is for the birds.

You have to get up on your feet and say something sometime. Might as well rush this appointment with frightening destiny and *of your own free will* arrange to make a public talk before you're forced to by emergency or necessity.

I am not going to waste any time telling you why you should do it. You already know you should be able to talk on your feet. You see so many others with so little to say spouting in public, sometimes making asses of themselves with their empty mouthings. Again, you see and hear men of importance making solid and impressive speeches that increase their importance.

If you have set your sights on a job in higher echelon in your firm, no doubt that job will call for some public speaking ability. You simply can't be eager for promotion and dead set against public speaking at one and the same time.

So let's skip the rest of the reasons *why* you should be a public speaker in line with your personal crusade for selling yourself. I want you to be more than *able* to talk in public, I want to see you become a crackerjack speaker!

Take all the public speakers in the world and average up their quality. The quality is pretty low; public speakers are generally bores, who have a stale message or none at all, but say what they say with dullness, pointlessness. As long as you *have* to be a public speaker eventually, and might as well be one *immediately*, decide that you will be better-than-average.

What incentive is there to becoming a public bore? But there's much to be desired in turning yourself into a stellar performer, a salesman-in-public, a colorful showman, or that greatest star of all—a great orator! A series of drastic moves are suggested:

1. *Take the plunge suddenly.*

Without thinking about it for even a moment, stand up in a public meeting and say a few words on the spur of the moment. Don't plan it or think about it for, if you do so, you will probably chicken out. Just be there and suddenly get up for no good reason. The very act of getting your body into an upright position, the suddenness with which you have ambushed yourself will surprise some words out of you. I'll make a bet that if you take the plunge this way, you'll probably get up *twice more* at the very same meeting. For just demonstrate once that you can talk on your feet and you'll like the action for ever after.

2. *Quit that public speaking class or abandon the idea of joining one.*

Don't get me wrong. I am not against courses in public speaking; they do a world of good in bringing thousands of timid souls out of their shells.

But to some the idea of joining a public-speaking class is almost as frightening as making a speech in public.

And to many members of public speaking classes, to step out of the class and actually make a speech in public is a move too drastic to imagine.

I don't object to "sneaking" your way into public speaking, such as serving on small committees, getting yourself appointed an officer of a small club, (finally being president and thus proving you can chairman a meeting). But don't dabble around with one speaking course after another in the hope of *graduating* as a public speaker!

I know dozens of individuals who have been attending public speaking classes for 25 years! They are still studying! I have spoken before several of these classes and observed these "ambitious" speakers. They get up, they giggle and titter like school girls, and confidently smile at their audience (their own kin) as much as to say: "I'm doing pretty good tonight, huh?"

Years ago my friend Les Lear was directing one of these classes and asked me over to comment on the performances of his pupils.

After hearing the customary round of tittering and pseudo-confident speaking, I said to Les: "Can any of these people SHOUT?" He had a few try shouting, but they couldn't deliver much power. "Perhaps you will demonstrate what you mean, Jim?" said Les. With that, I let out a shout that almost brought the walls down and scared the class right out of its jeans! It was my atomic protest to this namby-pamby approach to public speaking.

3. *Try a real SHOUT.*

Next time you're on your feet, and without any warning to your audience, try a sudden *shout or scream.* Give it everything you have. Give it more than you ever suspected you had. As one man, put more wild spirit into your shout or scream than the entire audience *combined* might be able to do.

You may frighten yourself a little but that will be good; for a good shout frightens your own fear out of you. And the shout can be easily related to what you are extolling, reviling, or selling in your speech.

4. *Make an honest-to-goodness speech.*

A lot of men claim they are bona fide public speakers and *they have never made a speech in their whole lives!*

What folly! Whom are they kidding? Talking for five minutes in a small conference isn't a speech. Taking your turn in a sales meeting isn't a speech. Filling an assignment in a public speaking class isn't a speech.

Your speech is a *solo* performance in which you talk on your feet for a minimum of *forty minutes.*

Your speech is a speech before a *meeting* and the only reason people came to that meeting was to hear your speech!

Printed notice is issued in advance of the meeting telling the people what you intend to talk about.

That's a speech. It's that simple, and that terrible! It's the lowest step on the ladder and it's the top of the ladder at the same time. Why not save a lot of fretting and temporizing, why not take the richest short-cut to public speaking and make *a real speech?*

One dose of medicine, potent and health-bringing, is a thousand times more desirable than a thousand little doses, puny and bitter, that don't effect a real cure.

Arrange to make a speech that fulfills the three stated essentials of a speech. Get on a program. Program makers are always looking for speakers. Tell the right man you're ready for a speech. Don't tell him this is your first speech; he doesn't care if it's your first or your fortieth, he's looking for a victim and you are IT. Take the rap. Take the speech!

How to Fortify Yourself for the Crisis with a Bag of Tricks

I am not urging you to commit suicide. I am not trying to turn you into the laughing stock of the world. No sane person allows himself to get suckered into making a formal speech unless he has insured himself against catastrophe. Take out some insurance policies that will guarantee your survival of the ordeal. Here are a few:

First, seek and expect a mediocre performance.

Don't try to kid yourself into thinking your maiden effort will be another "Cross of Gold" job. Don't try to be brilliant; *try to be mediocre.*

This doesn't sound like inspirational advice but it's supremely safe and practical! Great speeches are seldom made "on purpose" even when the speech-maker is a professional and a veteran. Now (mind you, I did not say to be *amateurish; I* said *mediocre,* meaning unsensational) by deliberately not seeking to set the world on fire, you will successfully cover up most of your amateurism and inexperience.

Second, prepare.

This is something you need not be told. Preparation time should be equal to ten times speaking time; in other words, if you are to speak for forty minutes, spend at least four hundred minutes in preparation.

Prepare *more* than enough. If the speech you prepare is twice as long as the time it will take to give it, that is fine.

You're going to forget parts of your speech in the act of giving it. Some point will slip your mind. When it does, let it go—be rich about the matter. Don't stop and try to recall it.

Extemporize with your omissions and elisions; it will make you feel free and liberal and somehow inform your audience that your preparation had been beautifully complete.

Third, just before zero hour exert yourself physically.

Take a fast hard walk outdoors. Exert yourself enough to work up a quick sweat. Move some chairs around. Don't try to be relaxed *before* the speech starts, don't try to remain cool and calm.

Best to feel a little sweaty, a little exercised. This is a good way to work off your *fear.* Don't try to tell yourself you have no fear; make no mistake, you are *afraid.* And the best way to get rid of fear before a speech is through sweat and exertion.

Fourth, take the first kick in the pants like a man.

Just as you start your speech, something adverse is bound to happen. The toastmaster will mispronounce your name or give you the wrong middle initial. People will be standing out in the corridors engaged in loud conversation, trying to drown you out. Or waiters will be collecting dishes, scurrying back and forth under your nose.

Don't expect help from the toastmaster—you won't get it. You have to make your own way. You have to fight. Fight these distractions with directness and gusto.

Talk a little louder. Dig in and start swinging. Don't, under any circumstances, brood over the frowsy treatment you are getting. Every speaker faces this competition, this conspiracy; but the audience knows nothing about your troubles and is concerned only with what you do and say.

Fifth, move your body.

Much stress is put on proper gesturing in public speaking but, to my mind, the greatest gesture of all comes when the speaker decides to move his body around, *to walk as he talks.*

The Spaniards are great at this, and the Spaniards are great public speakers because they *move all over the lot* as they speak. It's an incontestible proof of poise, of audacity, and the audience loves it.

Remember, every speech is a contest between you and the

audience. Shall you dominate them or will they dominate you? If you fail to dominate them, they begin to look for flaws in your speaking—mistakes, repetitions, sloppy rhethoric—and you're a goner.

Physical motion is a good device for getting domination. They are glued to their seats, can't move—but you can. Take advantage.

But what if you are stuck to a microphone and can't get away? What if you are *reading* your speech, or consulting notes, or behind a lectern? Or wedged in a small spot with an immovable gentleman on each side of you?

All I can say to that is don't allow yourself to be placed in such a spot. Don't read your speech. If you have prepared properly, you don't need to. Keep your notes in your pocket—just for comfort. Demand and get moving room before you start.

If you're using a mike, walk away from it once in a while and raise your voice accordingly; prove to your audience you have a voice that does not need electronic assistance.

Sixth, use your left hand, forget your right, in gesturing.

Right hand gestures are clumsy if the right is all you try to use. But get your left hand into the action; force it to gesture.

Sure it may be clumsy but that is what they expect it to be, and by being awkward it actually becomes natural. Then your right, unknown to you, picks up the play, synchronizes beautifully with the left, becomes doubly effective.

Seventh, change your pace during the speech. Speed up, slow down; move, stand still; freeze your hands, then gesture suddenly; get hot, cool off; mix up your pitches.

Eighth, never ask yourself "How am I doing?" while your speech is going on.

Do the best you can. Use your bag of tricks and they will work. You have promised yourself a mediocre job only; and anyone can be mediocre. You have done all you can, you cannot do any more.

Later on, perhaps, after you have got *several* speeches under your belt, you may want to study your execution, try to feel your audience in the middle of the speech, try to change their temper—but not now.

This, then, is your first speech. You have deliberately dived into water over your head knowing you shouldn't be able to swim in it. By all the rules, you should sink and drown; but you won't. I tell you, my friend and reader, you will float, you will come out alive, you will not be disgraced!

That audience is there to scare you but it is also there *to be used by you*. That audience represents just so many human animals, with a necessary measure of eyes, ears, and brains, who are in this place to afford you the opportunity of making your first speech. Without them, you could not make a speech. With them, if you stay up there forty minutes or longer, *it is a speech*, and better than you ever hoped it would be.

Make that first speech and you'll make many more. Get a taste of those floor boards and you'll find it hard ever to forsake them. Make that first speech and talking on your feet for a few minutes at a company meeting will be a snap by comparison. Make that first speech and overnight you have licked every problem of public speaking, probably the biggest hurdle you face in your campaign for selling yourself.

And you won't have to work very hard at your other problems of private speaking and conversation. You now have a tongue in your head. If you can use it in public, you can certainly use it in private. You will speak up at every chance you get. You will be heard from in every kind of a situation.

Demosthenes said the three essentials of oratory are first, acting; second, acting; third; acting. But unless you are a natural actor, ignore the old Greek on your first speech. Another group of speech experts insist: "It's not what you say, but how you say it!" This advice could mean acting, too, but it could also apply to a open show of the planning, organization, and preparation you have put into the speech.

Thorough and sincere preparation will always show in a speech and carry the speech through successfully when other qualities such as eloquence, acting, and salesmanship may be

missing. Preparation compliments the audience; lack of preparation is a slur and an insult. Many experts say, "Never de-
claim," meaning never recite your speech word for word from
memory. I do not agree. If you are able to remember everything you want to say word for word, the audience will never
protest at declaiming, for people know you are honoring them
by having gone to a terrific amount of preparation. However,
I do not advocate declamation in speeches by seasoned speakers,
unless they are great actors, and wish to extemporize in their
acting as they go along with the speech.

So the biggest trick in the speech bag inevitably is PREPA-
RATION. In this regard, please realize that it is better to be
able to give the same carefully planned speech over and over
than to be able to render forty rambling speeches on forty
different occasions. I have given the speech, "The Knack of
Selling Yourself," on a score of occasions with little variations.
Repetition to new audiences is not repetition at all, but superior
preparation.

As a public speaker, I am not trying to liken myself to Patrick Henry when I tell you that Patrick Henry, one of our
country's founding fathers, rendered his famous speech ("Give
me liberty or give me death!") *one hundred times* before the
great day on which the speech finally set off the spark of the
American Revolution.

Emceeing and Toastmastering

If invited to emcee or toastmaster an event, by all means
accept. Don't say: "I'm not witty enough, or clever enough, to
be a toastmaster."

The audience doesn't expect you to be witty; all it asks is
that you be a good *mechanic*. And under no circumstances attempt to be witty, if you know you're not. All you have to do
is introduce the speakers properly.

Pronounce their names *clearly* and *correctly*.

And make the introduction completely *plus*. Don't kid the
speakers or belittle them or joke about them. Praise each

speaker to the skies. Let the audience figure they are about to hear from another Demosthenes, a da Vinci of accomplishment, an Aristotle in wisdom.

Know this about your role as toastmaster: *The audience is more than ready to believe everything you say.* And the speaker, having been built up so well by your introduction, is bound to make a good speech!

M.C.'s can take the above advice with or without a grain of salt. I make the point here because many introductions are so dreary and so depressing both to the audience and the speaker. If the M.C.'s of the world will only start to upgrade their introductions, we will have a general improvement in the quality of all speeches.

If you are running a meeting as chairman, or master of ceremonies, or toastmaster, here's a surefire trick that never fails:

You can key your audience up well in advance of the actual speaking by standing up every few minutes and making an announcement!

The announcement need not be of epochal importance; trivial announcements will do as well. "Will Mr. Jones please come to the speaker's table?" "You have a choice of pie or ice cream for dessert." "Our next affair will be two weeks from Wednesday."

If you have a series of announcements which must be made, do not make them all at once. One at a time is much better. Jump up, say just one little thing, and sit down.

This is a splendid device for killing the time that must go by while people are eating, or if it is not a luncheon or dinner, while they are still coming into the room and the meeting is forming. Let the latecomers miss some of the announcements if they must; it doesn't matter. Scatter your announcements all over the place. By the time the speaking starts, everyone will be on edge.

I once emceed an affair where a lot of entertainment was promised but the talent was late in coming. The crowd was getting unruly. I hoped I could tame them with short, terse, intermittent announcements.

I gave them everything, told them what time it was, the count of the noses, the names of some in attendance (and introduced several unknowns); and finding the audience in the palm of my hand, put on an act that turned out to be much better than that of any of the professionals on the program. *I asked the janitor to sweep the floor.* For fifteen minutes the crowd gazed spellbound as the janitor swept up the place!

Don't ask me why announcements work—I don't know. They certainly key everybody up. They seem to presage a bang-up program. Most of all they inform the audience that the M.C. is an experienced hand.

Eliminate every trace of the negative. If a celebrity was promised, but failed to show, don't mention it. Don't apologize for his absence; *never apologize to your audience for anything.* To show the slightest sign of weakness is to lose their respect and attention. Be strong. Be positive.

Never tell them you have a cold or a sore throat. Cough all you want, blow your nose, sneeze. The cold may want to speak for itself but don't you ever condescend to speak for *it!*

My friend, Jim D., is a thirty year veteran pilot with one of the largest airlines. He had to make a speech to his fellow pilots, some of them almost as long in service as he. This darn speech, Jim confided to me, was an annual affair in which latest flying techniques, safety precautions, all the latest and most advanced developments in flying were discussed. Doing the speech in the same way for years, talking to the people who knew as much about the subject as he had become monotonous to Jim.

He came to me for a tip. How could he make a different speech? Something that fulfilled the assignment and yet was off the beaten track. Something with some life, excitement, and suspense in it.

There are so many different forms of writing and so few forms of speaking! A public speech is a "speech." How can it be anything else? But imagination frees a lot of hidebound concepts and in a matter of minutes I came up with the answer, which Jim enthusiastically endorsed.

Since his audience of veterans flyers would be seated in about

25 rows of ten seats each (250 in all), he would start his speech picking a man indiscriminately out of the last row, mention some outstanding characteristic of his flying that brought out or emphasized a special technique or salient point. Pick a man in a different seat in the next row (Jim knew all the men intimately, all their special gifts and abilities) and thus proceed forward to the front row. Each flyer in the audience was thus alerted that he might be a useful object lesson. Tenseness, complete attention and interest, ruled the session.

Maybe it should not have been called a "speech." It was really a public diagnosis of the flying skills of the airline company, a composite case study in live material all in a single hour. The officials present were indeed impressed. A week later Jim was made manager of his entire division. And months later, when the company was hit by a general strike of its pilots, Jim's division was the only one that did not go on strike.

Often the physical make-up of the building or hall may make it necessary for you to shout, in order to ask a question if the meeting speaker invites questions from the audience.

If you have a question, ask it. If you have to shout to ask it, SHOUT. Shout louder than the speaker has been speaking. The shout will surely loosen you up. It will be appreciated by the audience which always has difficulty in hearing questions asked from the "floor."

I once attended a conference in a big tent out in the open. The speakers invited questions, but they had microphones and could be heard. The questioners sitting far back could not be heard unless they really shouted.

So for the first day of the conferences I consistently shouted questions from afar. The questions were pertinent and appreciated. At the end of the first day, several men came to me and asked, "Why are you not on this program?" I replied, "Nobody put me on and now the program is set and cannot be changed." One man did something about it. He called a "rump meeting" for the following day for a sort of rebellious session aimed at throwing more light and more discussion on the topics involved in the formal program. I was asked to be chairman of this meeting. Nearly 300 conferees attended the rump session and it lasted for nearly four hours without anybody walking out. It was the high spot of the whole conference.

A stunt like this might be called "stealing the show." My answer is this: when you're out to sell yourself to others, and you are not afraid to speak in public, "stealing the show" is thoroughly delightful and completely legitimate.

[8]

How Writing Helps You
Sell Yourself to People

Good Lord, I believe I'll have to write it myself!" Sooner or later you'll face this formidable challenge. You discover you have to put your plan, your announcement, your thinking ON PAPER. You agree that, if you do not, it *can't begin to work for you.*

You now realize how indispensable writing ability is in your drive for success.

Your thoughts, to get distribution, to reach a large number of people, must first be written and then be printed and published. "Scripta manent" (writings remain) goes the old Latin quotation. Long after you have written your words and sent them to their proper destination, they will work and sell for you.

Some people are professional writers, others semi-pros. Many others would like to become writers and occasionally do something about it. You have heard countless people exclaim; "I could write a book on" one subject or another which might seem to indicate that everyone, whether near the writing stage or remotely wishful about it, subconsciously recognizes the utilitarian benefits that result from being able to write.

No one is ever going to coax or force you to write a book. But

111

sooner or later you will have to write something—a postcard, an invitation, a set of instructions, a letter, or another "insignificant" piece. But no writing is really insignificant. Your writing reveals you, and whether flimsy or trivial, people judge you by it. Yes, you can sell yourself with a simple postcard, and a short personal letter of yours can be almost as potent in its own way at winning or consolidating a friend as Lincoln's Gettysburg Address was in selling Lincoln to posterity.

Joe, the bus driver, may have a refund coming from his insurance company; or he may have to write a statement about an accident claim. Will this letter or statement be a moronic debacle of mixed-up thinking and slaughtered English which his superiors will laugh at, mentally pegging Joe as someone who must drive a bus for the rest of his life? It need not be so if Joe will wake up right now and do a little "dabbling" in the writing game.

Remember your English classes at high school or college? The teacher often gave you "themes" to write. You probably hated "themes" then. But, on your own now, make yourself do a few new ones. You're a lot wiser and more experienced now and just for the fun of it, drive yourself to write a theme or two on any subject at all. Be your own teacher. Be a martinet. Force yourself. You do not have to earn a passing mark, you need not seek to turn out a masterpiece. Just write something, anything, and do not use it for any purpose other than to look at it, as if in a mirror, to see exactly what YOU look like in your own writing!

Write a funny postcard to someone you want to joke with. Better still, buy a stock of three-cent postcards and use them up fast. It's fun. A lot of people will suddenly become aware of the fact that you are alive and breathing!

You can actually write your own boss a letter. Do not make it in the form of a letter if a letter seems uncalled for—but call it an idea or suggestion for a new improvement, an invention, a time- or money-saving thought that has been resting in your own mind for a long time, unused.

A man in Oakland, California, heard about a new product

that was being developed by a large company in Chicago. The Oakland man had had nothing to do with the development but the progressive nature of the product appealed to him. So he spent six weeks of his spare time writing a prospectus on how the new product should be marketed, covering every angle, every facet. He had never written a prospectus before, but this thinking and his enthusiasm fed his writing so richly that the prospectus turned out to be a most amazing and convincing piece of work to the Chiacgo people. They called him in for a conference, for strangely, no one in Chicago of all those participating in the development had ever bothered to write a comprehensive prospectus about the project. The Oakland man not only got a good job with the company, he ultimately was made vice-president. When the new product went to market, little of his original plan was used—but he, the writer of the plan, was made the principal marketing figure.

One of the principal, and year-round, items of daily mail arriving at your house is probably solicitations for your subscribing to certain magazines. Most of this direct mail fails to get any action out of you—and deep down in your own heart, you know why. It sells you partly but not all the way to the point of attracting your signature to the dotted line. Here's a good exercise. Try writing a human statement about "40 ways in which I have not been solicited for a magazine subscription." You may not be able to think of 40 new ways, but you should hit on eight or ten. And maybe your new ways will be good ones and saleable.

You've heard it said of many a successful man: "Every place I turn I bump into something by him or about him." By breaking into print, you have the chance of meeting a thousand unseen people for everyone you can meet with your spoken words. This unseen audience respects you, acknowledges your prominence, remembers your importance. Without putting the thought into words, the public says: "That man is working hard for success; he writes well and it's something he had to learn all by himself!"

Don't say, "I can't write." You can. YOU MUST.

There are hundreds of ways in which *business writing alone* can take form. For example:

Personal Letter	Set of Directions
Business Letter	Trade Paper Articles
Circular Letter	Recording of Ideas
Personal Acknowledgments	Invention Claims
Thank-you Note	Suggestions
Greetings	Maxims
Advertising	Epigrams
Individual Advertisements	Charts
Sales Promotion	Application for Employ-
Publicity Release	ment
Bulletin	Resumé of Experience
Memorandum	Testimonials
Announcement	Credits
Product Names	Petitions
Slogans	Dedications
Brief	Resolutions
Survey	Log of Events
Report	Business Diary
Synopsis	Minutes of Meeting
Critique	Programs
Speech	Terms of Proposition
Introductions	Contracts
Toasts	Booklets
	Brochures

—and as the highest goal of all—a BOOK!

SELL YOURSELF BY ACQUIRING SOUND WRITING ABILITY

You hear a so-called "big man" give a speech. He has to read it. As you listen to him read it and detect an occasional stumble or mis-pronunciation, you suddenly realize that this man did not write his own speech—someone did it for him. Your estimation goes down. He unsells himself.

Abraham Lincoln wrote his Gettysburg Address, we have his own handwriting to prove it. Supposing some researcher could prove that Lincoln never wrote the short speech, that some "ghost" did it for him. Wouldn't it rob "Honest Abe" of a little of his reputation?

Woodrow Wilson wrote all of his own speeches and public

announcements, composing them on his own typewriter. Many students of history are now of the belief that Woodrow Wilson will someday be definitely known as the greatest of U.S. Presidents. His writing ability alone keeps on "selling" him and his works to posterity.

Writing ability not only sells you but has a definite tie-in with success. Success is "getting ahead"—ahead of what or of whom? In most cases, of competitors or associates in business who lack this skill.

Think. How many people in your own business circle do you know who could honestly be called WRITERS? Probably very few. Competition at writing, especially business writing, is very mild. With competition weak in this activity, it is clear that the way to be a standout yourself is much easier. With writing you can engrave your thoughts and your ideals on the public mind for years to come. Your writing, read long after you have written it, re-creates a public image of you that is worthy, respect-getting and important.

I would say that it is much easier to be a superior businessman-writer than a public speaker. And the rewards can be much greater. So this chapter on selling yourself to success in your chosen field concentrates on the tricks, devices, and shortcuts for learning to write.

One or more of these writing opportunities is open to you every day of the year. Are your business letters routine, conventional? Spice them up with a new phrase, an unusual word or two, a fresh style. Every improvement in business writing is not just a personal improvement in your skill, but inevitably results in promotion, salary increase, a higher status for you in your organization.

And think of how well you have "sold yourself" if your written words become *quotable!* One solid business maxim, clever or sharply pointed, may put your name before millions.

"Few people do business well who do nothing else."
—Chesterfield

"The fundamental principles of business are so simple that a fool can't learn them, so hard that a lazy man won't."
—P. D. Armour

"It is a great art to know how to sell wind."
                                    —Gracian
"When I hear of artists or authors making fun of business men
I think of a regiment where the band makes fun of the
cooks."
                                    —Charles Schwab

A three- or four-page letter is impressive and goodwill-winning merely because it tells the reader that you spent a lot of time and thought on him. If it is handling a complaint, it dignifies the complaint of the customer, and automatically tends to soften it. Though you may be able to say just as much in a short letter as in a long one, remember this: Nearly every businessman writes short letters, giving the impression the reader is only worth a little time. The long letter builds up the receiver and thus helps the writer sell himself as a thinking and considerate man.

Skeleton of a Letter

A. OPENING. Open with a condition in which the reader—not you the writer—may be finding himself. Put the word "you" into opening sentence. Sample: "The paper said yesterday that the temperature in your town reached 85 degrees."

B. TIE-IN. Tie in the opening with a need of the receiver. It might be a lightweight suit, some fishing tackle, some printings, etc.

C. EXPLANATION. Explain what you are offering in terms of filling the possible need. Keep the explanation free from exaggeration or fulsome adjectives. Make it plain and simple.

D. REASON WHY. Give the reason for acting now.

E. CLOSE. A special offer with a time limit, a scarce or limited supply, and temporary low price may all indicate the reader will lose something of value by not acting at once. And give him the *materials for acting:* return, postage paid envelope, order card that preferably requires no signature; or if a free inquiry is wanted, the unmentioned inference that the inquiry will be honored with all the deference and attention of a $1,000 order.

See also "The ABC's of How to Write a Good Letter" a little further on in this same chapter.

In tackling every job or exercise in writing, you must forever keep on repeating to yourself: "I am not doing all this writing in order to become a literary giant or to make a fortune by selling the words I write to some editor or publisher."

Know this: You are writing for *nothing,* practicing it because writing skill is an immensely valuable asset in any business or profession.

The tips and "How-To's" that follow have been gleaned from the working habits of professional literary men and should help you acquire business writing skill much faster than if you were to go about it in haphazard fashion.

You should gain a better perspective on the matter if, in your private writing forays and secret practicing, you keep the subject matter on business topics only. This will help prepare you for more formal business writing when it is demanded. And there can often be this happy accident to your practicing: you may like a particular piece you have done "just for fun." It may fit a definite business need. The naturalness you put into the job, not ever thinking of it for publication, may have made it extremely worthy of publication.

Be a writer. Be known as a practical writer. He is accepted everywhere. He is always of possible use to the scores of people around him. He sells his way to his own success by achieving a worthwhile skill other men of his same ability do not possess.

SOME TIPS ON GETTING STARTED

1. Write RIGHT NOW!

Try writing a set of directions on how to use the product you are working on. Or take any other product, read the directions that pertain to its use, and try to improve them. Goodness knows, you are seldom satisfied with the directions on a new product you have just purchased; they seem so vague, so unintelligible, you are sure you could write them better.

Well, go ahead and improve on them. No style is required, just clarity, and a little consideration for the reader. In an exercise like this, you will instantly see the connection between *thinking* and *writing*.

Write an advertisement for your firm or its products. Though you are not in the advertising department and though no one has asked for your ideas, write an ad based on your own knowledge of the product, your intimacy with it. You are as well equipped to write such an ad as anyone. Send it to the advertising manager or the advertising agency as a suggestion.

If there's something to write, *write it at once*. In my own career in copywriting, I always got special satisfaction by writing an ad, an announcement, or any kind of composition while the client sat in my office and I pounded out the copy on the typewriter right in his presence! The spontaneity of the act made a big impression, and the O.K. was much easier to get that way.

2. Try a big volume writing task.

A middle-aged business man has just secured national distribution of a new product. This man is only a grammar school graduate and has never written 400 consecutive words in his life.

But because no previous copy exists on the new product he sits down and proceeds to write a *15,000-word* prospectus on the product! His brain, supported by his enthusiasm, did the job.

Once the boss and I were in consultation about a big beef by a valued customer. This man, who purchased a million dollars worth of goods a year, had just sent in a serious complaint and proclaimed: "I'll never buy another cent's worth from your firm."

My suggestion to the boss was: "Don't write him an ordinary letter; write him a really LONG one." Between the two of us, we composed a fifteen page single-spaced letter that amounted to 6,000 words. It wasn't at all hard to write!

The customer responded with: "Thanks. I understand. And to prove it, here's a nice order."

Try a very long letter of your own—a personal letter or a

business letter. The Frenchman who said: "Pardon this long letter, I didn't have time to write a short one," emphasized unconsciously that long letters are easiest of all to write.

3. Make notes.

In a conference, a discussion, or conversation make notes. Making notes is a form of writing. The ideas worth noting are often subtle, elusive, and unless you pin them down on paper, you will quickly forget them.

Get in the habit of making a lot of notes. You will soon be amazed at the number of rich, meaningful words you have written.

When you make notes, you honor the speaker. He thinks, as he sees you writing, "There is one man who appreciates what I am saying!" Regardless of all the other benefits in the making of notes, this is the greatest benefit of all in selling yourself to others.

4. Ask questions.

Suppose you are planning an article for a business journal. Get down as many of your own ideas as you can, and you may have to stop because you think you haven't enough material.

But start discussing your subject with everyone you meet (without informing him you are preparing an article) and you will soon come up with more material than you can use in just one article!

Ask questions. Make provoking remarks. But don't let the other know he is collaborating, for then he will want to give you stilted, conventional material.

5. Offer to write.

A conference ends, and the question is asked: "Who'll write this up?" Commit yourself. Say: "I will!" You have been taking notes while the others present have been relying on memory.

You have been seen taking notes, so you are the natural man to do the writing. Volunteering for the task wins everyone's good will because they all probably hate to write. Committing yourself publicly, will force you to complete the task. When *forced* to write, everyone can write!

6. *Experiment with brevity.*

"Long-winded" writing is as bad as "long-winded" talking. Though volume on occasion is impressive, and though volume gives you much needed practice, the ordinary "reader" much prefers something short.

In mastering brevity, a very good device is to read articles written by others and then attempt to put what they have tried to say in a sentence or short paragraph. Write your abbreviated synopsis. Yours is probably better writing than theirs!

Richard Crashaw, the great English poet, was once a student at Oxford. One day his class was given the assignment of putting the Biblical story of the Marriage Feast at Cana into a Latin poem, of any length desired. Crashaw wrote it in a single line: "Lympha pudica Deum Videt et Erebuit." (The modest water saw its God and blushed.)

7. *Try verse.*

Seems silly, but versifying makes you nimble with your words. Make up rhymes in your head; make up others on paper. Don't try to make them into full-fledged poetry, keep them light and reckless. Now suddenly turn to serious prose. Your prose will have that easiness to it that invites reading.

The famous copywriter, Gordon Seagrove, and I worked in the same bull pen for many years. One day Gordon received the assignment of writing a sober article for a farm paper. Immediately he put his thoughts into verse. The chief copywriter rejected the composition and delivered a lecture on what farm paper editors want in their journals.

That same day Gordon, unsatisfied, privately sent his poem to the editor. Almost immediately the editor wrote him: "Just what I want. Enclosed find check for $50!"

Maybe your verse won't bring you money, but it will bring fun, looseness; and greatly decrease your fear of writing.

However, unless you are completely satisfied that your verse is extremely clever, do not expose it to the public eye. Sophisticated people will only laugh at you if it is clumsy and inept.

In everything you do in the process of selling yourself, you must always hold to the belief that in your audience there may be several educated, critical people who can detect the difference between good work and poor. Though you know not who they are or may be, aim at selling them if what you are doing seeks to be professional. The professional thing will impress the *hoi polloi* just as surely as it impresses the *cognoscenti*.

8. Inject the classic touch.

Perhaps you seek a touch of statesmanship, grandeur in your writing. If so, here's a simple trick:

Write parts of your article *as if you were writing poetry*. In the first draft, put your thoughts into separate poetic lines. Do not rhyme anything, but proceed as if it is to be "free verse."

Then on the second draft join the short lines together into paragraphs. Your words are now in prose form but they have real poetic content.

9. Write about yourself.

You have nothing to write about? How about yourself, your own life, the infinite experience you have had over the years?

You like to talk about yourself, don't you? Then do a little writing about yourself. (There's nothing inordinate about it, either, for most judges of good writing maintain that at least 50 per cent of all published writing is autobiographical.)

This gift comes in handy when writing a resume of your experience in seeking a new job. Most resumes are immensely dreary and difficult to read. Stick to the facts, of course, but try to inject here and there odds facts, strange facts, human facts that reflect on your special abilities.

The fullest immediate meaning to the phrase "selling yourself to others" comes into play when you are trying to get a new job. The whole art of selling yourself must often be rolled into your skill in personal speaking and selling and in putting down on paper the facts about yourself that most appeal to the prospective employer.

Suggestions for Three Different Kinds of a Job Resume

First Kind. Very short and condensed. Contains only the bare facts of your personal history, education and experience since you have left school. But do not neglect mentioning names of former employers.

A short, telegraphic resume often fills the bill where the employing company has no formal employment or personnel manager, and you are dealing direct with a foreman or executive. Many "old fashioned" business people still have a sharp distaste for resumes of all kinds. Where they expect none, but get one that is pleasantly abbreviated, they are often intrigued and gladly give the time to get the rest of the information in a personal interview.

Second Kind. This is the complete, comprehensive record of every detail of your personal and business history, with appropriate sub-heads, covering every item down to your special hobbies. This is something for the professional personnel man to feast on. Nothing is left to the imagination, nothing concealed or hidden.

Later in this book (see chapter on Publicity) I suggest that you have a stock of glossy print photos of yourself, size eight by ten inches. Enclose one of these large prints with this type of resume. Ship resume in same large envelope with photograph; the typewritten resume should be unfolded.

Third Kind. Expansive and replete with salesmanship. Besides giving all necessary facts of your history, quote what some other people have said of you, mention special problems you have solved, accomplishments at overcoming obstacles, and any other spectacular or noteworthy things you have done.

This type of resume makes it clear to the prospective employer that you *want the job*. When two applicants by their records are qualified for one job, the job generally goes to the man who has proven he *wants* it.

10. Make writing a "must."

Most successful men are good talkers.

Most successful men are good writers.

Writing takes energy—so when your writing is seen, you are instantly known as a man of energy.

Writing takes intelligence—if you believe you're intelligent, *prove it by writing.*

Writing identifies you as "a man on his way," and once the world sees you have a goal, sees you want to sell yourself, it accepts and applauds you.

Writing is one of the fastest ways to sell yourself because competition is light. Others feel as you do now about writing. They claim they can't write, they don't want to write, they hate it.

This leaves the field wide open to the man who writes.

Make writing one of your biggest "musts" on your self-advancement program. Not just one composition, one business article, one creative letter—but a hundred!

Follow up! Follow up your audience, your editors, your public, your prospects relentlessly—by writing.

For instance, to write just one letter asking for a difficult concession or improvement is ridiculous.

As you begin your project, tell yourself you are going to write 20 letters if need be; follow up on this one matter 20 times! Agree to the 20-shot campaign, knowing that one shot only will not work. And long before you have reached your twentieth follow-up, *your request will be granted.*

How To Learn To Write

Someone says: "Write simply!" That's the most complicated advice of all.

What does he want? Short sentences? No adjectives? Perfect communication with complete economy of words? If that is "simple writing" it's wonderful.

You're supposed to get it without even trying; if the subject you're to write about has a subtle color or condition or some special distinction, forget it.

Such advice is a joke. Simple writing is not a way or a means. It is a *result* and amateur writers just haven't the ability or cleverness to produce simple writing at the outset.

Be carefree. But I can say to any amateur: "Write loosely!" Meaning: "Loosen up!, be free!, break loose from all the old patterns" and it will be good advice; at least, advice that can be followed.

When you tackle your first job of writing, you are as stiff as a board, and as shaky as a high stilt. You feel that what you produce must be perfect. Well, you know it won't be, it cannot be, yet you insist that this first paragraph is going to be PERFECT.

Make your first paragraph wild and woolly. Turn yourself around, say, "This first paragraph is going to be wild and woolly." Get as loose as a goose and let the words come forth like alphabet soup.

Well, well, well! This first paragraph done by a first-class slob turns out to be a first-class job. You put all of yourself into it— your idiotic notions, your moronic emotions, your giggles and snickers—and you kept out of it *all that was not yourself*—the fine style of Washington Irving, the epochal utterances of William Jennings Bryan, the clever epigrams and philosophy of Will Shakespeare.

You broke all the rules of grammar and of form; but by deliberately seeking to make it imperfect, you came much closer to a good and unusual result than by proceeding as if you desired to be perfect.

Write loosely. What does it mean? Forget about form. Be unashamed, and proudly so, of your awkwardness, your meagre thoughts, and your terrible private and unconventional feelings. It is not easy to throw away your school teachers, your parents, and the hard, tight books you've read or heard of as great.

Insist: "The right way to write is not the way for me. I suppose I may have admired that stuff in the past, but actually I never believed in it and my true feelings do not concur with it."

You must be free in your heart, in your blood cells, *in your toenails,* before you can be free in your mind. Follow these steps:

1. Say what you feel, shamelessly, no matter how awful it is, how disparaging or incriminating to yourself.

2. Practice at "reading yourself outloud." An easy experiment is this: ask yourself a conventional question such as, "How do I feel?" Then answer it in a conventional way, such as, "Pretty good!" Now take the opposite of your conventional answer, *"Terrible."* Now describe this terrible feeling in words, though the conventional side of you still insists you feel pretty good.

3. Make up a few similes, fresh and shocking. "He looked as big as an observation car with vistadome." See how much shame you can shed in your next simile.

4. Coin some new words or phrases which of themselves immediately tell what you intend them to mean. Change a line like "A situation in which you would not want to be found" into "A situation which you would not want to be infound."

Again: "A preposition is a bad word to withend a sentence."

You can work wonders with the most trite and commonplace phrases by just changing them a little bit. No law on earth or in heaven forbids you from making as many of these changes as you wish.

5. Don't fear mistakes—invite 'em; they make the most human kind of writing. Mistakes in reading, spelling, pronunciation, phrasing; in seeing, hearing, smelling, surmising; in mechanics, such as tripping, slipping, dropping, falling; in speaking, a frog in the throat; accidental mistakes like spitting in another's eye, tickling accidentally, stepping on another's foot, scaring someone accidentally. Record them all. They are human. They are you. Anything else coming from you might not be you.

6. Keep your nose to the grindstone. Write a little every day, or make a definite day, like Sunday, your writing day. Don't merely take a fling at it, say, "Oh bosh, I can't write," and give up. Stick.

But do not get too serious. Always stay loose. Tom Wolfe, a tall man, wrote longhand standing up with an empty Frigidaire as his desk, often staying at his writing for two or three days and nights without stopping. But he stayed "loose" by not counting the words or the written sheets; he threw the sheets on the floor as he filled them, and then proceeded to fill the whole room with his product.

Face the duty of writing, the hateful task of writing as a foolhardy lunatic game that has no rules, no innings, no runs, no victory, no defeat. Only two requirements, (a) to start, and (b) to keep going.

7. If you can, as you write, *giggle*. Most of us are gigglers who would like to keep on giggling forever. If your writing is loose, it should make you giggle; giggle to your heart's delight and the giggling will make your writing even looser.

8. Try describing your miseries. Misery loves enunciation and challenges description. If your writing can do justice to your misery, the misery will evaporate. Write about your vegetable nature. How much does your head weigh? Your mysteries. Where were you before you came to earth? Your dreams. Try to describe the hundred thousand strange people in your bureau drawers. Your fears. Delineate them in writing (honestly and completely) and they will also vanish.

Your problems. Goodness knows you have plenty of problems. Take your biggest problem and "write it out" at length. When you finish, you will find you have the problem's solution!

How to Get in the Mood For Writing

Even the most capable professionals seldom *like* to write. Thomas Carlyle, complimented on his "smooth" and "easy" style, commented: "When I turn it out, every line is as painful as childbirth!"

So don't get the idea that writing is not for you because you hate it. You have to force yourself to write or, better still, "seduce" yourself into it. Here are a few tricks for getting yourself into the mood for writing:

1. Stock up on the kind of writing paper that fascinates you; the weight, the color, the texture of the paper may intrigue you into putting words on it.

2. If you compose on the typewriter, always have the machine in tip-top condition, responsive and obedient to your every touch.

3. If you have received any fan mail in the past, letters praising you for your accomplishments, re-read and re-smell the bouquets as you sit down at the typewriter. This sounds childish but if it dissolves writing-hate, it is admirable.

4. Keep a book of inspiration handy and read a few paragraphs that tell you you can be better than you are. Believe the inspiration. The typewriter is there to certify this belief.

5. Read some of your former writing. Something which was printed.

6. Find an old manuscript of yours which was never printed. Perhaps you wrote it years ago and tossed it aside in disgust. Read it now. Pretty good, isn't it? You're not as bad a writer as you thought you were.

7. Memorize and repeat these statements constantly:

"Anyone who can think can write."—WM. RANDOLPH HEARST
"Anyone may write if he will set himself doggedly to it."—SAMUEL JOHNSON

8. Find a nice quiet spot, make yourself as comfortable as you can. There's no law that says you must sit up straight in a hard typewriter chair. I prefer to write sitting in a big, low-slung upholstered chair.

9. If there's noise around you, as you begin, face it like a soldier. The dog howling next door, the neighbor indulging in loud piano practice may not be conducive to the creative effort but can help you resign yourself to the ultimate writing philosophy: *when you gotta write, you gotta write!*

10. Work late into the night. While the city sleeps, you can get more done. Some night, just for kicks, *stay up all night writing*. Call it a "writing bender."

11. Make a mechanical outline of your story or article. Try to put literary quality, art and invention into the heading and phrases. If you know what you want to say, the outline will not be difficult, and the eloquent literary interjections may oil up your writing apparatus for the production ahead.

12. Relax your face as you face the job. Smile, giggle, laugh with your eyes. At taut expression on the face closes many doors to thinking. An amused expression, though deliberately forced, ventilates the mind and invites a swarm of new thoughts and ideas.

Our most practical outlet for our writing ability comes in the writing of letters. Personal letters, business letters, legal letters, letters of every variety.

None of us write as many letters as we should. We are constantly conscious of owing many friends letters. We feel guilty of not following up the good business prospect where we made only a half-sale. A mountain of unwritten letters faces us all.

Yet we realize the power of a letter as revealed in my essay, "Write a Letter!" (This essay was used by the United States government to promote the use of the mails, and is considered one of the best advertisements ever written.—Ed.)

Write a Letter

It's only a few steps to the nearest mail box—write a letter! Take a little chunk of your heart and spread it over some paper: it goes, oh, such a long way!

Write a letter to your mother or father, to your sister, brother, sweetheart, loved ones. Are they dear to you? Prove it with a letter! Are they far from you? Bring them near to you with a letter! Write a letter and give them the same thrill you had when you last received that same kind of a letter. Think of the joy of opening the mail-box and drawing out a warm envelope enriched with old familiar handwriting! A personal letter—it's good to *get one*. So *send* one—write a letter!

Write a letter to the aged relative who hasn't many days to live, the friend of your father, the friend of your family, the one surviving link between your own present and past. Don't wait for that dear soul to die till you act. Act now with a message of love to cheer those last few days on earth. Sit down and *start writing!*

Write a letter to the author whose story gave you that delightful half hour last night. Write a letter to the cartoonist whose serial strip you avidly devoured this morning; to the teacher who inspired you twenty years ago; to the doctor who saved your baby's life; to your old employer to show him there was something more between you than a pay check. Be a human being—write a letter.

There's a man in public life you admire, believe in, rave about. Write him a letter of praise, of encouragement. To be "with him in spirit" is not enough—show your spirit with a letter. We can't all be pioneers, crusaders, presidents—BUT we can help those brave men stay on the track and push through to a grand and glorious success if all we ever say is "Attaboy!" Write an "Attaboy" letter!

Write a letter and—give. Give praise, encouragement, interest, consideration, gratitude. You don't HAVE to give these things; but the real letter is THE ONE YOU DON'T HAVE TO WRITE!

The sweetest, gentlest, and most useful of all the arts—letter writing. Great, grand characters like Washington, Franklin, Lincoln and the greatest men of all nations, have been regular letter writers. Write a letter! Write it with pen, pencil, or typewriter. Use any kind of paper, any kind of spelling or grammar. It doesn't matter how you say it, and it doesn't even matter what you say; its beauty, its *gold* lie in the pure fact that it's a *letter!* Each mistake is another hand-clasp; every blot is a tear of joy.

Do you see a job? Do you smell an order? Is your mind on business? Write a letter. Then write another letter. No business, no individual, built on the "write-a-letter" rule ever failed. Because you simply can't fail, if you write a letter. Try it, you'll like it. Great joy and many surprises are in store for you. You'll get letters back. You'll get help from unexpected sources. All that you gave in your letters will be returned to you a thousand-fold. For a letter is a 4-cent investment in bountiful good fortune.

Write a letter! Whether you say: "Attaboy!", "Thanks!", or "I love you!", always remember: A LETTER NEEDS NO EXCUSE!

How to Write a GOOD Letter?

Though we admit we write too few of them, we all think we know how to write a letter. At least we are acquainted with letter-writing form. But nearly all letters are too formal, too stiff; they *suffer* from form.

Some years ago, my friend, E. Willis Jones, started a campaign to drop the "Dear Sir" salutation out of a letter. Because there seemed no good reasons for calling males, especially strange males, "Dear." He urged substitutes like "Good Morning, Mr. Smith," "How Do, Mr. Johnson," and the like. It was a good idea. But to my mind, the reform should have been carried all the way through the body of the letter, through each separate paragraph and stilted phrase from beginning to end. For most letters look alike, read alike, and are alike.

The way to write a good letter is to kick tradition in the pants, throw convention up for grabs. A line or two may illustrate the point.

> Smith:
> Excuse me for not calling you "Dear."

> Johnson, Dear:
> One little change may cause a revolution.

Take any letter you have already written and start chopping it up. See in how many ways you can change the salutation. Now, maintaining the same changing attitude, see how many times you can change the paragraphs in the body to make them just as informal.

Whether it is a personal letter or a business letter, if it is radically informal, it will be unusual. It need not be over-clever, or full of artificial gimmicks. Just informal. That makes it *personal*. And any business letter can be as personal as the most personal of personal letters. The personal touch helps sell the person.

"THE ABC's OF HOW TO WRITE A GOOD LETTER"

(a) Don't dictate it, if you consider it important. If you can run a typewriter, compose it first on the typewriter. This first draft will then show balance, length, and be a good facsimile of the final letter.

(b) Play down the word "I," play up "you," whether letter is personal or business.

(c) If letter is an answer to an inquiry, answer all questions clearly. Answer them ALL—not just 75 per cent of them.

(d) Once more re-read sender's letter to see if all points are honored in your reply.

(e) Avoid technical terms and phrases which reader may not be hep to. Did you ever inquire to the home office of an insurance company and get an answer back in PURE GREEK?

(f) Before you start, make a short synopsis of what you are going to say.

(g) After letter is drafted, now synopsize it without consulting
original synopsis. Then compare the two synopses to see if
they match.

(h) Think of receiver in terms of his first name. Think of him
as a person with all your own fears, shames, weaknesses,
humor.

(i) Make your letter plus. Eliminate every negative, defeatist,
pessimistic, mournful note.

(j) Insert some good news. Praise the receiver if you have no
news.

(k) Think of a good warm letter you have recently received. I
recently reviewed two letters, one from a woman who had
never graduated from grammar school, the other from a retired school teacher with a master's degree. The first was
warm, human, every word reeking with human interest and
human flavor. The school teacher's letter concerned her recent journey to Hawaii and was dreary to the point of being
exhausting. I would love to be able to write as good a letter as
that from the woman who had little education.

(l) If you are supposed to know grammar, be sure to spell right,
follow the rules.

(m) But if you have no claim to a mastery of English, go ahead,
misspell, bust all the rules. In your own way the chances are
better than even that you will be able to say more and more
aptly than the good grammarian.

(n) Try writing a letter in ALL CAPS with telegram brevity.
John Patterson of National Cash Register Co. once said: "If
the toll were heavy enough, any message could be condensed
into ten words."

(o) If you write longhand, and your writing is normally very
bad, print or write very slowly and carefully. At least give the
receiver a chance to spell your words to himself. You are
honoring him in this letter, do not spoil this honor with
atrocious handwriting.

(p) Never write the answer to a letter on the back or bottom of
the first letter. Sending back the original letter is an insult of

the first rank. Yet this rule is broken ten thousand times a day by thoughtless letter writers.

(q) Never apologize for your delay in answering. The receiver knows you are late and nothing much can be done about it. An apology is simply salt in the wound.

(r) If you hate or fear to write this letter, hate or fear will show through and spoil it. Write loosely with a smile on your face as you write.

(s) If you simply are unable to compose a letter, due to sickness or dumbness, have someone write it for you and sign it yourself, even if you have to use an "X."

(t) If a business letter, either get it all on one page, or if you see it will run over, run it far enough to take up at least a page and a half.

(u) Have a purpose in your letter. Aim to sell, to take something back from the receiver, to get money, to get an order, to get an early reply, or tantalize him to produce a more urgent type of inquiry from him. Play checkers, especially in your business letters.

(v) Make the receiver the most important man in the world. Think of him this way as you write.

(w) Try a "passion" type of letter. Pour all your heart, your want, your sincerity into it in a most exaggerated degree.

(x) If you want an answer, make an answer possible by enclosing stamps, an envelope, perhaps a couple of blank sheets of paper. These accessories will speak louder than words.

(y) Have enough paper handy. Write big. Paper is cheap. Do not be afraid to waste it.

(z) Remember, this letter is a transport of you and your personality across miles of space. If the letter is not you, it is not a real letter.

If hard up for material to write about, and if a search of your own experience cannot, when desired, deliver the idea for a story or article, try listening, with full heart, to the stories and experiences of others.

Jack Norworth, famous songwriter, wrote the hit song, "Take Me Out to the Ball Game," in 1908. But Jack actually saw his first baseball game in 1942, thirty-four years later. All he needed for material was the wild baseball spirit all aound him. He realized he did not have to be an eye witness or a fan himself.

Sheridan Gallager, operator of the Board of Trade Observatory in Chicago, once went ten years without even glancing at a newspaper or magazine. Merely by overhearing the conversations of fellow humans in elevators, offices, on the street and in his own tower, he was one of the best posted men on "current events" in the whole city.

Listen to enough people, and though as individuals they may seem inaccurate and poorly posted, roll all remarks and conversations into one, and you come up with the basic information that is accurate, and amazingly fresh.

Buy $4.00 worth of stamps. And don't rest easy till you have used them up! The letter "you do not HAVE to write" is probably the one that sells you best of all.

By accidental turns of our work there was a certain politician I used to meet several times a week. We were polite to each other but a definite undercurrent of feeling always seemed to report that he did not like me nor I him.

Then one day I heard he was in the hospital with a serious operation. The inspiration came to write him a letter. I knew he had a legion of friends who would visit him there, but how many would write him a letter, how many ACTUALLY HAD THE ABILITY TO WRITE A PERSONAL LETTER?

So I sat down at my typewriter and wrote him a long letter, crowded with personal items, replete with friendly gossip about people he knew. It turned out that this letter was the biggest feature of his stay in the hospital! He showed it to visitors, many of whom had always been unfriendly to me. I myself felt a new and warming friendship for both the politician and all his cronies. I not only sold myself to him and all his following with just one letter but I automatically convinced myself that I was wholly unjustified in my previous feelings toward the whole group!

If you think you should write someone a letter, and do not know what to write about, put some gossip into it!

All authors like to get mail, like to see the written proof that their words have affected others, perhaps changed their lives for the better. Address your letter care of the publisher, and it will reach the author.

Professional writers have a very simple rule for writing. They gather all the material they can on the subject—publications, written notes, factual data of all kinds. Then they push all this material aside and write from memory, later checking the accuracy of factual items against the material.

This trick—writing from memory only—keeps the writing crisp, personal, and gives immense freedom in the execution. Sometimes too many facts can drain all heart out of a written piece.

Some seasoned and much-experienced businessmen sometimes make important "surveys" and business reports by a strict and piercing examination of their own experience, past and present. This technique can only be used by a few.

But a technique which any researcher, especially one seeking to make an accurate national survey, can employ is known as the "long distance survey" technique. Under this method, one simply gets on the long distance telephone and talks to key customers, distributors, and managers with a brief, incisive series of questions about the business being surveyed. Under no circumstances is the man interviewed told he is taking part in a survey. By the nature of the long distance phone, and the premium being paid for the time, he usually gives his answers fast and very much to the point. He hasn't the time to try to find out the ideal answers which are often sought in a typical personal survey, so his off-guard opinions come very close to the real truth. Such a survey can be made in a couple of hours at insignificant cost.

This same telephone technique can also be employed in your own city. But never tell the person you are calling that you are making a survey. You will be amazed at how just a few phone calls will reveal a pattern of truth that runs through all the answers and gives you the real answer you are seeking.

USING
SELF-TRANSFERENCE
(Part Two)

Words are not the only tools of self-transference.

You have many other assets the world is waiting to cheer; natural gifts you came by unknowingly; skills acquired by experience; instincts and inclinations begging to express themselves.

Everything that is PLUS inside you can be exploited and SHOULD BE EXPLOITED.

This exploitation calls for self-transference by means of:

> *Audacity*
> *Kinship*
> *"Connections"*
> *Finesse*
> *Showmanship*
> *Dependability*
> *Future Promise*

To transfer the good inside you is to *sell yourself* and to win, thereby, the *success* that is your proper due.

Let us examine these extra tools of self-transference. Let's see how to get them into perfect shape; sharpen them, align them, and then put them to work.

[9]

The Eight Avenues to Audacity

THE FRENCH have a beloved shibboleth: *"L'Audace! L'Audace! Toujours L'Audace!"*

Which means, literally: "The audacity! The audacity! Always the audacity!"

Which means in a free translation: "Guts, nerve, backbone, intestinal fortitude, always on hand, always in use, win the greatest prizes of all!" The French honor and cherish audacity in war and in peace, in private life and in business; in the person, in the race, in the nation. So do all people.

For without boldness you can never completely sell yourself to yourself. Act shy, follow the beaten path, avoid the new and the spectacular and, though you may lead a well-ordered life, you'll find success a long way off.

Many a multi-millionaire got his fortune through his boldness in investing for, without boldness in the heart of its possessor, money itself loses a great deal of its power.

Many a successful person reached his eminence by stepping into an opening others were better equipped to fill but lacked the courage to try.

What's the cost of audacity? Nothing! They cheer you almost as loudly if you fail as if you succeed. It's not the final outcome they cheer, but the sheer guts you show by walking into fire, risking your all, laying your very life on the line.

You think of the big move; you peer into the disgrace and ridicule and total loss ahead. You hear the whispered threat: "If he tries that, he'll be run out of town!" Yet in spite of everything, you make your move and ACT.

In the very act of stark courage, YOU SELL YOURSELF. No one, positively no one, can dislike conscious, real AUDACITY.

A girl of twenty-one, after graduating from college, decided to equip herself for a business career. She enrolled in a secretarial course at a business school. Before the course was over, she had made such a good impression on the owners of the school, that they offered her a good job at a fine salary.

Was the job a plush office job where this girl's charm and good looks might prove an adornment to the school? Not at all. She was told she would have to go around the country *making speeches* to university and high school groups.

And our young friend had never made a speech in her life, nor had she studied speech in school. BUT SHE HAD PLAIN UNADULTERATED AUDACITY. "No trouble at all," she told her employers, "I like to travel, I like to talk!"

I am asking you, how many people do you know who, having no experience in public speaking, would take such a job at ANY salary? How many bold, red-blooded MEN would do it? You'll admit it takes courage in a superlative degree.

Yet the courage that takes one into the unknown usually supplies the skill and ability to sail successfully through strange seas. Our young lady friend is now head of all promotional activities for the afore-mentioned school, but still keeps her hand in at public speaking by making all out-of-town speeches in recruiting new students.

She says: "Aggressiveness, nerve, audacity, or whatever you want to call it is a simple act of the will. Never ask yourself: 'CAN I?' because you may not be able to show all the experience to prove that you can. But make the question: 'Will I?', say 'Yes' to it, and things you never knew you could do become easy with the application of a little study and intelligence."

How to Build Invincible Courage

1. Initiative.

The poet Goethe said it this way:

> "What you can do, or think you can, *begin* it!
> Courage has beauty, power and magic in it.
> Only commence and then the brain gets heated;
> *Begin it* and your task will be completed!

That poem can be a shot in the arm. Memorize it. Repeat it over and over. Apply it to the subject at hand: *the project of your becoming successful by means of selling yourself to others.*

If you've read this far in this book, you should already be doing something about the ways and means. You should have started your personal success campaign. HAVE YOU?

Initiative is the quality that causes you to be referred to, in admiring tones, as a "self-starter" or a "stem-winder." The start must come from you. It's possible to lead a life of automatic routine where others, or the inanimate demand of the work itself, *make* you move into action.

There's no glory in this kind of a life. It's abject slavery. Initiative turns you into a free man, a man of pride and honor.

Thousands of things are waiting for you to do; thousands of new ideas waiting for you to try; thousands of good chances waiting for you to take them. ACT. BEGIN! The highest wall starts with the first brick. The longest journey starts with the first step. Goethe urges you to take that single, simple, easy move that *begins* the job, and then the same hidden magic, applauding your audacity in starting, will help supply the power to bring it to a successful end. Yes, initiative and "finish-iative" are practically the same thing!

If you are in a big waiting line coming out of a hall and only one side of the double exit door is open, step out of line and walk up and open up the other side of the door, without asking permission of anyone, without being sure you will be able to operate the closed part of the door.

If you are a lawyer or a copywriter and a client wants a contract or an ad in a hurry, pull the office typewriter over to your desk and right then and there—in full view of the client—start writing the contract or the ad. Such a display of time-saving initiative will surely help sell yourself to him instantly!

If you are thinking of a party, set the date, extend the first invitation.

If the event calls for the sale of tickets, accept the very first ticket money even before you have the tickets printed.

If you want a friend or acquaintance to visit you at your home or office, name the day and the time of day. Don't make the self-frustrated offer of "Drop in sometime," which is meaningless and impresses no one.

If you are backing a project that calls for small donations, make the very first donation. Do not wait to see what "George" does.

If you are thinking of entering the selling profession, make your FIRST COLD CALL, not merely to find out what will happen but especially to demonstrate your initiative to yourself.

Since you secured this book with the thought of attempting to sell yourself to others, make a specific attempt to sell yourself to somebody by some means *within the next hour.*

2. Get hurt!

Take your foot out of the bucket and stand up to bat with no fear of getting killed. *Want* to get hurt, *invite* it deliberately.

Before the football game, all 22 players are afraid of suffering the first bump from their opponents. The whistle blows, the game starts, and on the first play everyone gets hurt slightly. Then fear instantly leaves. The first hurt does it.

In winter you are often annoyed when you walk over a thick carpet and suffer a certain spark of electricity in touching something metallic. Instead of being annoyed, slam your hand hard against the metal, and in the slightly increased pain of the slam, you do not see or feel the electric spark.

Get hurt physically and get hurt socially and you come up fighting mad. Get hurt in business and you not only learn a lot, but pick up plenty of new audacity for a further try at success.

If you are a salesman, call today on your toughest buyer, the one who told you positively not to come back for six months.

Take the insult, hold your temper, be pleasant and persist.

Risk ridicule at a business meeting by proposing a move which is a radical move but which you believe is right. Such as: "We ought to sell mail order! Or we ought to open retail stores!" Somebody in old Sears, Roebuck must have made a similarly shocking statement one day which must have brought down tons of ridicule on his head.

In a labor organization, or a fraternal organization, you may "get hurt" by standing up in open meeting and defying the entrenched officers. But it is good for your soul and for your prestige, too.

3. Always be aggressive.

Why does Hollywood score *aggressiveness* higher than *beauty* in its actresses? Because Hollywood knows that the public, which is supposed to be eternally smitten by female beauty, likes aggressiveness *more* and will pay *more money* to see it.

If you are aggressive, they will gladly pay you with their applause and acclaim.

To generate aggressiveness:

(a) *Force yourself to be aggressive,* especially if now you feel yourself too indecisive and passive.

(b) *Act quickly!* Waste no time in contemplating the danger, weighing the cost. Don't let the things that can slow you down enter your mind.

(c) *Do what you think you cannot do.* All that's required here is the decision to tackle it. Your surprise and satisfaction, when you find you CAN do it, deliver a great volume of additional aggressivness.

(d) *Repeat the "obnoxious performance" several times over.* Repetition gives added strength.

Speak up at your next club meeting and contradict the chair. Come early to an event. Or come late. Go to an event where you have not been invited, are not expected, but where you have every right to be. If you have never worn a tuxedo in your whole life, go to a tux affair and wear your first tux. Or wear a sport coat at any event where you expect most of the men will be in business clothes.

Break any rule, or personal habit based on fear, and you will develop new nerve quickly. A simple example is offered in the breakfast served on Pullman diners or in hotel restaurants. Here they invariably serve you your cereal *before* your bacon and eggs. I could never understand why. I have always regarded the sugary, creamy cereal dish as a sort of breakfast dessert. It ought to wind up the meal, and not begin it. So I insist on having it served last. (Does take a little nerve, too!) The thought of breaking any old rule, no matter how sensible you know the fracture to be, may seem terribly obnoxious in its contemplation. But wade right into the distasteful thing and you are elated—and what is more—noticed and favorably respected for your audacity.

(e) *Convert the negative into positive.* If you feel weak, suddenly act strong. If you know you are not strong, put it on anyhow just as an "act." If you feel tired, act energetic. If you don't feel like mixing, dive in and be the best mixer in the crowd. By acting contrary to your feelings, you become a new figure, and people turn their heads to look at you with respect.

Gerry H., office clerk, was a mild-mannered quiet young man. We all liked him because he always did what he was told to do, and did it well. And isn't that the standard idea of a good office assistant—do what you're told to do, don't question your superiors, don't invade the work of others around you, "stick to your last?"

But the offices of America are filled with a million such workers, all reliable, all knowing their places—and staying there.

The very nature of aggressiveness suggests selling yourself to others: reaching out to meet them and mix with them, reaching beyond the hard, tight restrictions of your own job, and acting in bigger terms and at higher altitudes.

Someone must have insinuated some of this aggressiveness into young Gerry; anyhow we have been separated for fifteen years and just yesterday I heard of his progress. He has moved from credit work into insurance, now is general agent for several companies, can talk and write FOUR DIFFERENT LANGUAGES, has three secretaries and makes a net income well over $50,000 a year. Through a third party he sent me greetings and this message: "I still take orders—it is good company policy. I also GIVE orders—because I have to. But at least once a day I force myself to DO A THING I DO NOT HAVE TO DO, just to keep my aggressiveness in good trim."

Gerry adds this advice: "All my mature life I have kept a model man in my mind, a man who inspired me in my youth. Once at a Christmas party—the man was head of the company— he said: 'Any person in this hall who wants to can make $50,000 a year.' He was a person of great force and aggressiveness, and I went out to prove he was right.

"He never let any grass grow under his feet. He always moved fast, worked fast, and avoided routine and repetition. From him I learned the importance of always ridding myself of deadwood, whether it was assistants too lazy to work, or a bunch of useless old files and records which could not be consulted in a hundred years."

People who are aggressive naturally, if not dumb and impolitic, generally get ahead fast. They do not need to force themselves. But those who are born shy and timid and over-sensitive are gifted with feelings and extra knowledge of people and things that the naturally bold person lacks. All the more reason for the unaggressive man to force his way into aggressiveness. His highly sensitized system will give much better balance to his new boldness. Force yourself! Force yourself! And then force yourself some more!

4. Bluff.

Bluff your fears, bluff your difficulties, bluff your worries, BLUFF THE NEGATIVE SIDE OF YOUR MIND.

The easy device here is: as each individual trouble or worry or fear arises, say silently: "Bluff!" "Bluff!" Your inner ear will hear the magic word and your whole being will respond with a new spurt of aggressiveness.

Good bluffers are not afraid to put their bodies in the foreground, to be seen and heard. They take a chance on getting "knocked down" but life is full of such chances whether you bluff or not.

When some one decides to call your bluff, accept the call and bend every effort to deliver. A woman employer heard a bashful young assistant inadvertently say he knew something about bonds. She called him. "I have had a bond in my desk for some time. See if you can get it cashed for me." It was a trick challenge because the woman considered the old bond worthless and dead, the original firm whose name was on it having gone bankrupt years before. But the bashful young man took off with the bond, went to one bank after another, followed a few wild goose chases, finally got steered to a successor company, and stayed there till they cashed the bond for one thousand dollars with interest added. He took the check back to the woman who was his boss and told her nothing of the work involved. "I was delayed because I had to go to several places." The female employer never challenged that young man again.

I do not know who wrote the following poem. It was clipped from a trade magazine and signed "Anonymous," but whoever wrote it should receive full credit for its golden inspiration:

THE GREAT GOD FEAR

The great god FEAR grinned back at me:
"I am the god men never see,
The hurt they never feel," said he.

"I am the wrong they never bear,
The poison they themselves prepare;
I am the shadow on the stair.

"I have no voice and yet I speak;
No strength and yet I blanch the cheek
And leave the strongest mortal weak.

"I am the blackguard man befriends,
Heeds most, feeds, cherishes, attends,
And 'gainst all counsel wise defends.

"Mine is the humor, ghastly, grim;
The lamp of reason I can dim,
Though I am nothing but a whim.

"I am man's cruellest, bitterest foe.
Yet past his door I could not go
Had he the wit to tell me: 'NO.'"

5. Despise "they say."

Ever try to find the people represented by "they" in the expression "they say"?

"They" have no existence at all. People care very little about folks like you or me—they're too interested in their own lives and personal problems to devote an extra second of time to others.

They haven't time to condemn you.

They haven't time to watch you.

Only when you succeed in selling yourself to them do they wake up to your existence. In *your* compaign for success, however, you must always pay attention to *them*. "They" do not exist to work on you—but for *you to work on them*.

The person who, to you, looks most at ease in public is probably trembling inside with nervousness.

The hero you applaud on the athletic field or in the prize ring was probably tempted to quit a dozen times in the last hour but could not, because he did not want to show his cowardice in public.

Since you and everyone else likes heroes, why not decide to be a permanent hero yourself? All you need do is act heroic at all times. Refuse to tell the truth about yourself *to* yourself. Insist: "I am not a coward, I AM A HERO!"

Though you can always feel like a hero if you make up your mind to feel that way, you cannot expect to be a real hero—except on rare occasions. If you play a hero in one field at a game which is not his game and beat him, that makes you a conqueror of champions (in an inverted way, to be sure). But sometimes a bunch of experts, top men in their line, will say a thing cannot be done. Take a look at the thing the supposed "heroes" say is impossible, and give it a try. You may surprise them and do it because you do not know or understand why it should be "impossible."

A permanent attitude like this in facing all the things you must do or may do builds impregnable aggressivness, which in turn delivers a rich flood of self-confidence and new ability for making the heroic image real!

6. Endure.

Success is not an overnight proposition. Aggressiveness is not an admirable quality if it only lasts for a day.

On undertaking any project, make a manifesto to yourself, a firm resolve, that you will not quit this thing till you've accomplished what you started out to do.

Better still, make a *public* manifesto of your intention to put the hard job over. Though the public may forget your manifesto, you will think they will throw your words in your face if you do not continue, and this imaginative threat will keep you going,

Why quit—ever? You invest time, work, and often hard money in a project. The harder the job is, the longer it lasts without completion, the more expensive it is. To quit when it is half done is to sacrifice all you have put in it. If partially completed, dwell on its cost; decide you will never pour this value down the sewer without carrying on to a finish.

But straight endurance, all by itself, may not be enough to keep you going. Endurance like everything else in life needs a constant supply of fuel, of food. Perhaps, the best fuel of an endurance built on passion is a sense of humor.

Some readers of this book may have heard of the author's making a legal claim, officially recorded, to all celestial space on December 20, 1948. 100,000 news stories and 5,000 radio and TV broadcasts over the ensuing years have reiterated his claim. The project, if I may say so, has been backed up with a

monumental amount of work, thinking, and personal energy—
and yet to this date, the world at large prefers to treat the claim
as ridiculous.

From the beginning, I knew I was undertaking a BIG project and instinctively, while deciding to pursue it to the bitter
end, realized that I would have to have a lot of fun with it if I
were to keep enduring.

So I constantly turned my studies toward the "human side of
space" and away from the technical and legal. Newspapermen
interviewing me and trying to knock down my claims—and failing—invariably make this remark: "How can you be serious
about this matter—it is clear that you are enjoying yourself!"
My pat answer may contain a useful tip for anyone who wishes
to nourish his perseverance: "There's no law in heaven or on
earth that says a man can't be serious and have fun at one and
the same time."

For a dozen years I have pushed my claim relentlessly and
loudly, have drawn many thousands of followers to my cause,
converted fifty well-known lawyers, downed many scientists
and engineers, and succeeded in getting one title company to
announce that space was real estate. Which achievement in
Celestial Space I like best is hard to say but one of the most
intriguing was the minting of Celestis's own gold money, an
outer space coin of genuine mint gold .900 fine. The startled
numismatic world finally woke up and realized that I had a
real nation with the right to issue its own currency. This coin,
called the Gold Celeston, has been used to buy goods and pay
for services and has already filled every purpose for which
money is intended.

If your project is big and long-lasting, and your objective a
real tax on your perseverance, it may be well to make a *game*
out of the project for a game will often keep you going when
the ridicule and discouragement of the world tempt you to quit.

7. Carry $100 on your person.

If you do normally carry a $100 bankroll, you will not con-
sider this act as very audacious. If you don't, you may say·
"Where on earth do I get the $100?"

That's a specious answer. You have access to the hundred. You can get it out of the bank or out of your next pay check. You don't need to carry it with the intention of showing off, but merely for the purpose of making yourself feel audacious.

Carry the money when you work in the yard. Carry it when you visit friends in their homes. Money is power and carrying one hundred dollars around with you tells you you are always powerful.

At this point, I am asking you again to carry the $100 as proof that you really want to sell yourself.

8. Speak up!

Gadzooks! And by the lord Harry! SPEAK UP! You are not a dummy, you have a voice, you CAN talk.

Do you want that stranger to remain a stranger? Then keep your mouth firmly shut. But if you want to turn that stranger into a human being, speak up!

You are being interviewed for a job. For goodness sake, speak up. Pronounce your name so that it can be heard. Tell your qualifications outloud. Remember, it's *you* who are being interviewed. It's up to you to do the major share of the talking. If you remain on a talking strike, all the prospective employer can do is look at you. And though your looks are good, the longer you go without talking, the uglier you become!

It's your first day on the job? Speak up. Ultimately you will have to find out where the washroom is, you'll have to speak up then. Speak up and find out where everything else is, take a walk, say "hello" to people, stop and ask them what you'd like to know. No one resents a sensible, practical question; everyone likes to give out information.

Suppose you are a clerk in a store. When a customer asks for something you know nothing about, do you have to question other clerks for the information? Why not use the time when you have no customers to tour the store or your department and find out *what* everything is and *where* everything is. Speak up when it counts.

Speak up your gratitude! Art Blitstein, owner of a succesful bindery, gives me a lot of credit for my book *You Can Do*

Anything. He says the book reduced his golf scores from 120 to the middle 70's. Every time he has a good score, or breaks a previous record of his, he sends me a gift. Now, *there's* a truly grateful man. I don't know how I helped him, but if he thinks I did, I did help him. He speaks his gratitude OUTLOUD and I hear him well.

If you have a good impulse such as gratitude, or sympathy, or inspiration, SPEAK IT UP. Follow the good impulse with a real act or action that your friend can hear and understand. Nobody's a mind reader, mental telepathy is far from developed. Speak up and your audacity in speaking up will delight the hearer as much as it delights you.

The ability to say "No" is tied in with many other abilities needed in selling yourself, but I firmly believe it properly falls in this chapter because there are times when it takes a lot of guts to say "No."

When you learn how to say "No" with finesse, it need not require too much bravery on your part. Some tips: You may not need to shout the "No" or even say it outloud. Simply mean it and put the meaning into your answer. Another way to say "No" is to thank the supplicant effusively for giving you the privilege of refusing his appeal. Or get confidential with him. One man, supposed to be very rich, had "the arm" put on him for a preposterous donation to a cause. "Let me tell you something in confidence," he said to the man who demanded he "hold his end up," "I am not a millionaire at all. I live on a very small pension and on my life savings. Please tell nobody but this is the reason that prevents me from making a donation of any kind."

Learn how to say "No!" Anyone can say "Yes." It's easy. But too many of us have never learned the art of saying "No" because it often takes a good measure of decisiveness. I am thinking now of Herbert M. who with his brothers owned and ran a big, rich company of several thousand employees most of whom quickly learned that Herbert did not know how to say "No." So there was always a steady stream of employees heading for Herbert's office looking for an O.K. on their plans, their changes in procedure, their side in their quarrels with fellow workers.

The saying went around, "Herbie has okayed it, but wait till the next man sees him." For any plan Herb okayed could easily be changed by the next man who got Herbie's ear. So all was confusion and disorder till a brother official sent through the ruling: "From now on Herb can't okay anything!"

Practice saying "No" where you can clearly see a "No" is called for. "Buy a chance book on this raffle? Lend me ten dollars? Do my work for me while I go to the ball game?" No!

Say "No" as gracefully as you can, but say it. It will save you a lot of heartaches. And a lot of needless expense. It will bolster the quality of aggressiveness which you need in selling yourself, because the world has instant respect for the man who can say "No."

[10]

How Kinship
Sells You Success

Someone has defined a friend as one who becomes related to you *by blood* where no such relationship actually exists. Indeed, true friendship is a *sheer miracle,* and no one can tell another how to make a friend or where to find one.

But *kinship,* viewed psyhcologically, need involve no miracles, and it's the next best thing to friendship.

In the world of business and society how many close kin have you? Not friends, just kin. Kin, the kind of people with whom you feel safe and who feel safe with you? Who are easy for you to approach, to chat with, to talk business with, to sell?

If you are as missing in kin as you are in friends, prepare now to do something about it for kin are easily made, and though the making of such relationships can be called strictly artificial, there is nothing artificial or unworthy about kinship.

As a member of the human race you already have in you all the basic elements of human kinship. Kinship means nothing more or less than getting into the same psychological climate with the people you meet in your daily rounds.

> No one likes to deal with strangers.
> No one likes to buy from strangers.
> No one likes to hire a stranger.

151

Often a personnel man is impressed by the qualifications of a prospective employee but the applicant fails to establish warmth, humanness, and familiarity. What should the employing individual do? He simply can't force himself to give out a good job to a cold fish—a stranger. Sometimes he will work for hours trying to make the stranger-prospect into a true member of the company family. He may try to get a laugh. Or a loose statement that suggests heart, imagination, or a sense of humor. He wants to find a link that can let him say to himself: "This man belongs!"

But it's too much to expect outsiders to convert you into a familiar. Kinship is up to yourself. If you don't carry it with you naturally, you have to create it.

Many an employer is easily sold on an applicant who merely *looks* like himself.

In a vast majority of cases husband and wife look enough alike to be mistaken for brother and sister. Think of it, on an important decision like marriage, which might be considered the ultimate example of two people selling themselves to each other, *both* must be shown *kinship* before they'll take the fatal plunge!

I once hired a young copywriter because his teeth were *as white as paper*. I like white teeth, everybody likes white teeth, and everybody once had white teeth. The copywriter wasn't very impressive personally or even as a writer.

But I felt safe with him, I trusted him and was willing to bet he would make good simply because he had white teeth. A ridiculous reason? Not at all! Anything that creates kinship is worthwhile.

The fact that my white-toothed friend is now owner of a large advertising agency, with a personal income of more than $50,000 a year, is incidental to my point.

By selling himself to me through made-kinship, he got a fair job, he got extra coaching and tutelage, he had an older man to defend and excuse his shortcomings and help him build confidence and skill. Building kinship is not an end, but a means to the happy end of seeing hundreds of newly made kin going out of their way to help you, improve you and put you in the path of fortune.

Now, I am not trying to suggest that you have to have teeth as white as paper to sell yourself via kinship. But some outstanding personal asset you do have will positively click with some or many persons. It may be clear eyes, clean skin, athletic build, a genuine smile, a respectful look or any of a score of fine points you have either cultivated or inherited. Never let any faculty or characteristic which can link you warmly with others go to waste.

Nor need the "fine point" be a rare physiological asset. I know a salesman who makes a hit nearly everywhere he goes by his use of slang. Buyers who like to keep up on modern jargon love the sight of him. Again, I am not recommending that you become a slangster. When you find yourself clicking with any asset, you are entitled to work it to a fare-thee-well. Observation should tell you which of your assets go over best.

If you're a salesman, wouldn't you like every buyer you call on to be a warm, familiar friend? Wouldn't it be great to be able to talk turkey with every prospect, be given all the time you need for your sales story, always be welcome?

If you're a lawyer, wouldn't you like every judge whose courtroom you enter to greet you with a warm smile and handle you with special forbearance and understanding?

If you're a teacher, wouldn't it be great if all your pupils not only respected you, but actually *liked* you? Whatever you are, you have a choice:

You can be stranger or kin!

The First Key to Real Kinship

The first key to real kinship is the magic word: SAME.

SAME is the connecting principle which makes all men brothers.

The next man you meet has many things about *him* that are exactly the same as *many things about you.*

Sometimes the sameness doesn't meet the eye; it turns up by accident. A young salesman was turned down by a buyer six times in a row. The reason: This buyer said he had to buy from another competitive salesman because that man helped his company get needed material in World War II when material was scarce.

On the sixth rebuff, our young friend, figuring he had nothing to lose, and again hearing the same alibi, blurted out: "Well, I helped you just as much by allowing myself *to be shot at in Korea!*"

The buyer came alive. He relented with: "Me, too; they shot at me in World War II!" The *same* came out! They were both veterans, though of different times, they were comrades in arms, and now comrades in business. On that very visit the young salesman established kinship and walked out with a nice order.

SAME has an almost uncountable number of facets:

The same school—it's an undeniable link.

The same lodge—it's traditional that one lodge brother does help another in a business way.

The same church—it brings a feeling of safety, security.

The same neighborhood—mention instantly brings up visions of the same enjoyments, the same problems.

The same nationality—cannot be discounted.

The same hobby—you're his kind of a man!

Even when you pass a stranger on the road driving the same car as you, the same model and, better still, the same colors, you simply cannot resist the feeling of kinship that instantly wells up inside you.

The Second Key: BE YOURSELF!

Don't try to be educated if you are not. Don't try to be sophisticated if you are naive. Remember, you want *kinship*. Can you fool a sister or brother in your own blood family by posing? Never! And it's just as difficult to fool outsiders.

Be always pure in the sentiments and emotions you show to others. Let all your expressed feelings be your very own.

Here is a good test:

Before expecting others to "buy" you, how about taking a fling at "buying" yourself? Have you made yourself into a desirable package in your own eyes? This brings us again to the basic principle for developing kinship: *forsake shame!* Drop your guard which futilely tries to protect you from the silly feelings of guilt and false shame that afflict nearly all human beings. Nor rely on recourse to convention to save you from the scars and scratches which you fear the world will inflict on you if you try to be your real self. Self-exposure of the body may be a crime, but self-exposure of the heart and the emotions is a magnet that draws all people to you.

Once you convince yourself you are a legitimate member of the universal human family, whose members all feel alike and respond alike, you will recognize that the greatest safety of all lies in just being yourself.

A good way to do this is: *relax!* However, it is much easier to say "relax" than it is to relax. We all like to be conventional, we all like to make good, and we are inclined to feel most of the time, as if we are under a *test*.

There are several good devices for relaxing. One is to think of a person you know and see frequently, who is definitely relaxed all the time. Perhaps he is funny, says outlandish things. Perhaps he makes hundreds of mistakes and cheerfully laughs them all off. When you feel too tense, too tight, think of him as photographically as you can. Make believe he is actually in front of you. How would he act in this situation you now face? What kind of an impression would he make? Would he be nervous, straining to show his very best side? Not at all. He would probably be a human being first and let the chips fall where they may.

If you cannot relax when the occasion calls for relaxing, it is well to be on the lookout for happenings, little accidentals in the situation itself, which have the power to relax you.

Troy Donahue, a young Hollywood star, tells how he got his start in the movies. He was being given a screen test, the tension was great, he knew he was being too stiff, too unnatural. Failure seemed so close he could even taste it. But the director suddenly called a halt, having found out the cameramen had run out of film, making the first test valueless. In the ensuing skirmish of excuses, bawlings out, and the rush for new film,

Troy reasoned thus: "If these professionals can make stupid mistakes like other mortals, and get into trouble even as you or I, why can't I behave like a human being, loose and casual, not as if my life depended on the outcome?" When the men got the new film and proceeded with the test, Troy was more casual and relaxed than a veteran star, and his sponsors saw in him the quality of kinship that makes box-office draw.

If appearing in front of an audience, look at all the faces for one that will remind you of a funny friend or a past incident which was full of human looseness and recklessness. In your case, *more relaxing may come from the outside than from the inside.*

It is one of the travesties of life that we all think we think alike, and speak accordingly, when no two individuals ever think exactly alike. No "rational" communication between people is ever transferred accurately or satisfactorily.

The same misconception pertains to feeling. When we feel, we each believe that we feel differently, specially— in some vague, touchy, personal way that no one else feels. Actually *we all feel alike!* And the deeper, more personal, more private the feeling, the more we resemble all other mortals in that very same feeling.

To make new kin at will, shed your personal, private shame and speak your innermost feelings outloud! The head of a great corporation, a multi-millionaire, once confided in me that when a bad thunder and lightning storm comes up, he runs and hides under the bed, if a bed is handy!

I loved that man in an instant, not because I ever run under the bed (it's always too dusty there) but because in other circumstances I do things equally as ridiculous and preposterous.

Mark Twain once said: "Man is the only animal who can blush, or who needs to." A blush is a sign that you have been trying to hide or guard some shame and you are suddenly exposed. If you were willing to bring the hidden matter out in the open, you would not need to blush about it. Nor would you hurt yourself by doing so. Rather you would make all around you understand and appreciate you better.

Be yourself by showing *a sense of humor*. What? You haven't any? Don't tell me that; all you need to do is shed shame *by exposing the deep-down private feelings* you have on any subject. People will laugh, and *you* will laugh, the instant you are brave enough to speak your feelings outloud. The laughter you produce is your passport to enduring kinship.

When a baby giggles in the cradle and makes untoward noises, when a tumbling puppy plays on the lawn, when a pompous individual slips on the ice, we all simply *have* to laugh! For shame and convention are being cast to the four winds and human kinship is instantaneous.

Pompous, sanctimonious individuals are clearly out to sell themselves, and they think their pomposity impresses people. Actually it only estranges. When Al Smith called it the "raddio," he made more friends by mispronouncing one simple word than he could have made with all the fancy language in all the libraries of the world.

The Third Key: ILLUSTRATE

I have said that when we think, we all think unalike. Words are our chief medium for transferring thoughts and if we rely totally on words and their rubbery meanings, we can't achieve much kinship.

In fact, words keep more people apart than they bring together because they mean so many different things to so many different people. If you find you are not "getting across" with certain people, try the following experiments in your conversations or personal selling.

Appeal to the "good old days." Modern stuff scares most people away. "Sulphur and molasses," "Halloween," "red flannel underwear," "horses and buggies," draw them to you.

Specialize in human subjects. "Show," "picnic," "puppy love," "elopement," "weddings," "funerals" and a thousand similar subjects are surefire. The heart is stronger than the mind as a welding agent for uniting people.

Sparkling comparisons. "A heart as big as Texas"; "like an elephant trying to make a meal out of a single peanut"; they can be cock-eyed: "As sweet as castor oil;" or in reverse like Sam Goldwyn's: "You roll off my back like a duck."

Gossip. Not too much about people, but the latest gossip in the trade or the activity in which you are engaged will intrigue every listener. Talk big and the man is lost to you; talk small and he comes right back. *Examples.* A simple human illustration may help to get the message across perfectly. Translate your meaning by any kind of an example you can fetch up. The picture of a cross conveys a lot more meaning than the word "cross."

Bartlett's Familiar Quotations. Buy a copy of this great book and never let it stray from your possession. The great thoughts of great men are here stated with such concentrated clarity you will instantly recognize the *streak of universality* which draws all of us into the same family.

Let Bartlett emphasize to you how important it is to cultivate a universal streak in your dealings with your fellow man.

Remain an individual and you speak from far away; become universal and you speak from close up.

The Fourth Key: THE HELPING ATTITUDE

You can't possibly help everyone you meet, you can't truly help more than a very small percentage, but you can always carry in your heart the *desire and willingness to help all!*

Don't try to put this attitude into words—you will scare people away. But *feel* willing to help and *be* willing to help.

On meeting anyone for the first time, present him *silently* with your full stock of sympathy, consideration, attention. *Give away* these spiritual treasures without any hope of return. Instead of trying to gauge the personality of the man, instead of trying to find his faults or weaknesses, or discovering in him quickly the things you do not like, blind yourself to these things. Mentally transfer to him your sympathy, consideration and attention.

Just *feel* sympathetic and though he might announce he does not want sympathy (he really does), he will feel the touch of your heart in your handshake. Look at things from *his* point of view (consideration) and he will immediately conclude you are a man in a million.

John, the last of the Twelve Apostles to die, when old and infirm was often carried on a stretcher to the services of the early Christians. His friends would always call on John for a short sermon. But on each request, all John would say was: "My little children, be kind to one another!" That was all. One message, the same thought and words, was John's only sermon. One day a young man accosted St. John and blurted out: "Why do you always say this same thing to us? You knew Christ. You lived and worked and preached with him. Why do you not tell us more about Christ whom you knew so well?" And John quietly answered the young man: "If Christ were alive and asked to speak to you, I am sure that the thing He would be most likely to say to you would be this: 'My little children, be kind to one another!' "

Those who knew Albert Einstein personally were not nearly so much impressed by his tremendous knowledge, as by his visible overflowing kindness. When a stranger succeeded in catching him alone, Einstein never fell back on the trite "What can I do for you?" expression. Often he said openly: "I am going to do something for you and it is this—" and proceeded to detail the practical help which his keen mind reported the stranger most needed.

Bill Kittredge, late director of design for the Lakeside Press, was a formidable figure in the graphic arts, and in the printing trade enjoyed a rough, tough reputation as a man who got things done superbly but executed his fine works as absolute monarch of the job. But a thousand artists whom Bill helped on their way to success will testify that in person, Bill was as soft-hearted as a child. When he saw an artist that needed help, he again, like Einstein, cast aside the worn-out phrase "What can I do for you?" and proceeded to show his willingness to help. He gave the man an art job, or helped him get a job somewhere else at a salary. He analyzed the man's special abilities and immediately started to fit his abilities into the places where they were most needed. He gave this impression to many a struggling young artist, now famous: "I am going to be your agent. I want no commission except the right to work for you and your success in life. I am going to help you make some money in the next week!"

That's how definite and clear was the willing kinship of Bill Kittredge. It is anomalous that he was known to many outsiders as an exacting master whose demands seemed impossible to fill; and to a legion of "insiders" who still revere him as the finest kind of a friend any man could have.

Arthur Godfrey, after what could have been a series of fatal setbacks, came back strong, and his radio and TV network announced: "Godfrey's time is again ALL SOLD OUT." Although bigger stars with higher ratings have great difficulty in getting enough sponsors, Godfrey is always quickly bought up: The common explanation is that Arthur Godfrey is a great personal salesman and moves merchandise off the dealers' shelves.

A fair segment of the public does not like Godfrey's type of entertainment and many of your own friends have told you this. But he still sells merchandise! Why? Because he is human, familiar, and fairly oozes with kinship for all mankind.

If you watch him closely in action, you will notice one little BIG gift he lavishes on his fellow actors, on his guests, and sometimes—right out in public view—on the stage hands and incidental people who work with him—THE GIFT OF ATTENTION. Often a guest will make an unrehearsed personal remark that needs probing. Godfrey probes the remark right down to its last ounce of humanness. Sometimes a remark is made which no one but Godfrey hears. He pays attention. He gives the incident or the utterance a noble hearing. Unconsciously, we all notice this penchant of the man, this desire *to hear everyone out*. It makes him a real kin, a cousin in intimate emotion. We may not like his entertainment, and say so, but his grand gift of attention to one and all, instills in us a belief that what he says about the products he advertises is *safe and honest*. Anyone who will pay attention to all people is a good man to ride the river with.

How many feminine hearts have been won by young men who lavished attention and attentiveness on their sweethearts! Rushing around to open car doors, driving miles to keep a date, making a thousand telephone calls, sitting down, standing up, noticing every little chance to pay a sweet compliment—oh, how grand is the attentiveness of courtship! And how conclusively does it prove that the "courter" belongs in the familiar wedlock!

Give your complete attention to the person you want to sell. Drink in everything he says and does in your presence and he will mentally clasp you to his bosom. For even his own wife, children, parents, sisters or brothers never give him such *complete* attention.

Don't be trying to think of what you will say when he gets through talking; simply *listen.* Listen, and between the lines of his language he will tell you how to draw him out, he will give you the shape and size of the key that will unlock his heart, he will give up sacred, special membership in his private super-family.

Think of it! By not saying a single word, by merely giving your personal attention unstintingly, you can sell yourself much faster and more surely than by spouting out the contents of six dictionaries in a torrent of non-communication.

To prove you are listening, on occasion make bold enough to take written notes on what the man is saying. This can be a supreme compliment if not overdone.

To prove you are following the man's words, ask an occasional "cleanup" question. If a subtle and deep talker gets only nods of approval from you, he may begin to suspect all his pearls of wisdom are going over your head.

So do not let his performance be an uninterrupted monologue. Break in and mention some odd thing he said just two minutes ago to prove you have been really listening.

LET THE FAMILIARITY COME FROM THE OTHER

Don't be the first to claim familiarity with another. That's the big mistake most "get-aheaders" make. Let him be the first to put the two of you on a "first-name" basis.

Salesman Joe likes the first-name basis and he says: "Certain people may wait forever before they'll call you by your first name, thus making it impossible for you to address them in kind. With such people, you have to be coy and try to bring the first-name exchange about without showing your hand. I manage to give such a man a sample or a memo and simply sign it 'Joe.' Nothing else. If I meet a really big man in passing, I say 'Hello, Oscar!' but never stop for further conversation. Sometimes I give a man a magazine or newspaper clipping that he should be concerned with, and use nothing but absolute silence. Here the silence brings about a suggestion of rich camaraderie without any words to spoil it. I consider all prospects, whether twice or three times my age, first-name people and not mere 'Sirs' or 'Misters.' The main thing is to carry the first-name-attitude-of-mind around with you at all times."

Don't be a clown. No one wants a clown for kin.

Never exert any claim to friendship. A claimed friend is a near enemy.

Don't "Mister" or "Sir" the man to death. If he has red blood in him, these terms used too often may congeal his blood.

Don't be always on guard. Try to make time in reaching the status where your guard is always down and you have no fear of making a tactical error in his presence. This state is perfect confirmation of kinship achieved.

Wait long enough, listen attentively enough, and he will drop the name of a friend of his who is also a friend of YOURS. Or the name of a school, a club, a game or activity that makes the common meeting ground.

And the next man you call on may know you far more intimately than you can suspect. He may actually be a childhood playmate or a schoolmate whom you have long since forgotten. But for some reason, he has not forgotten you.

Just yesterday, I was making a call on a man of great power and importance. Gaining his office, I shook hands and sat down hoping for an opening. It came. The man said: "The last time I met you was 45 years ago! We played a game of billiards!"

[11]

How to Make
"Connections"

INDIVIDUALS with the defeatist attitude are always chanting:
"It's not what you know, it's WHO you know!"

That chant gives them a lot of pleasure and, they think,
nicely explains their own failure to get ahead.

But I say: *It is neither what you know nor who you know* but
rather:

WHAT YOU KNOW × WHO YOU KNOW

You may be sure you know a lot. Try to sell your knowledge
or ability without any outside help and you are taking the
HARD way. Make the right connections and then multiply
your ability by the number and kind of people who can bring
that ability to flower, and success is an inch away!

You insist you know your line, your subject, your trade,
your profession. How did you get your skill and knowledge?

Along the line someone helped you learn. Teachers, associates, former employers. Are they dead? Have they evaporated?
You knew them once. What's to prevent your resurrecting
them?

You have probably moved your place of residence several
times in your life. You have had several friendly neighbors in

163

the past, warm, human contacts as rich as any you can ever hope to make in the future.

How long since you've called up or visited a former neighbor? Maybe that old neighbor is now an influential man, maybe your contact with him can mean a lot to your future success. But whether it does or not, see him, talk to him. The main thing is to get into the habit of maintaining and renewing all old contacts and connections, in order to equip yourself with fresh skill in making new ones.

How silly to say, "I know so few people!" You know as many as the next fellow, as many as you want to know.

When the head of a great department store organization, Frank V., changed his job and his life work and moved over into the electronics field, followers of the man's career were astonished. Why should Frank, who had made his success in merchandising, take on such a different kind of job seemingly unallied to all his experience?

But Frank's main experience had not been department store merchandising but actually the doing of thousands of warm favors, large and small, for people he had met along his way to success. He did more than merely *remember people;* he thought about them constantly, their hopes, their problems. Though he physically may have been far removed, his imagination guided him into sending them help when most needed, thus making his all-generous personality practically ubiquitous!

The day he moved into his new job, Frank's employers threw a "little" luncheon for him in the big city hotel. ONE THOUSAND GUESTS ATTENDED, coming from hundreds of miles cross country. In no uncertain terms they made it clear to Frank and his new associates that he was to get *all their business* in the electronics field or any other field he cared to enter!

Frank was once bluntly asked how he could make so many more friends than other men who had the same opportunity. Frank said: "To borrow a line from Keats, I view each new person I meet as a 'new planet swimming into my ken.' He is a whole universe to observe and wonder at and to get to know better. I never view him as a contact which may someday be of use to me, but rather as a dignified human being whom I may be able to serve."

So Frank's friend-making system is quite simple. Do not look on contacts as *your* contacts, but always view the relationship this way: *you* are *their* contact. This attitude is more than mere Christian spirit or brotherly love. It's philosophy is: "I am the world's service man without pay."

Here we see how "imagination of the heart" pays off in terms of connections. Frank's personal work in one line quickly carried over to another line, thus proving his versatility in any kind of a business operation. Such a man could be elected Senator or President because the people behind him had been sold, via their hearts, on his all-around ability.

A well-know lecturer had a spell of sickness and had to forsake public speaking for a few years. Well again, and needing income, his plaint was: "My phone never rings, my mail box is always empty, everyone has forgotten me." He was ready to work at his old activities but apparently there was no work.

One day a friend said to him: "Perhaps it isn't that they have forgotten you; could it be that you have forgotten them? How many phone calls, how many letters have you sent to your old contacts since you've been out of the running?"

The lecturer woke up! He wrote several letters. Made some calls. Suddenly he found there was a greater demand for good lecturers than ever before, and one agent booked him solid for a year!

Start now to build up contacts as the permament foundation of your "new career." List the connections you have made in the past. You wouldn't throw away good money which you made 20 years ago and still have! Don't ignore your old contacts.

Write down a list of the names of everyone you know and have known and also those you feel know you or know of you, though you have never met them personally. Be thorough. Let the list be as "long drawn out" as it will, and indeed it will be so long, you will be astonished no end!

Stare at the list, and you prove to yourself you have the power to make connections. What you have done once, you can do again. Glance over the old connections and ask yourself, "HOW DID I MAKE THEM?" Write the answer in a word or two behind as many names as you can.

Here you have disclosed ways and means of making all the new connections you desire.

You go about expanding the number and quality of your connections very much like a salesman prospecting for new customers. Concede that the best connections are not handed to you—you have to find them for yourself.

Take stock of your potential right now.

The people you like naturally, though your paths have not crossed intimately. They probably like you the same way, naturally. Give them more time, more of yourself, at least a frequent letter. Contacts are not easy to make so take advantage of the ones that come naturally, always treating the relationship unselfishly.

Consider the many people who have "stood up for you" when you were in trouble, or who have taken your side in an argument. Strange as it may seem, if you will examine your own experience, you will be able to recall the names of several persons who have "sided" with you. These are choice and rich connections, for they are people who evidently think the way you do and like you for the same reason.

Your list of connections need not include any "big shots." Big shots are a little hard to crack. If you come into physical proximity with a so-called big shot, do not fawn on the man, or defer to him, or bend over forwards to gain his good will. Do not "soup" around, but remain a little remote, and they will pay much more attention to you because in this regard you are so different from the common throng.

When you were very young, you always tried to use your father's or your family's connections. Now that you have grown up and are on your own, conscious of your own youthful strength and resourcefulness, you may deliberately disregard these connections. But they are just as useful now as they once were.

Sell something, though selling is not your business. This selling may be connected with your hobby or avocation or a community cause, but whatever it is, it is most practical to continuously have something to sell. This forces you, willy-nilly, into contact with others. Among such contacts you will ultimately find many new "connections."

Because you are at present stagnated by a lowly occupation or job, you are never excused from the duty of circulating and seeking out new contacts. Sam, the barber, gives away free combs with his name on them at Christmas. Sam occasionally takes a $10 ad in the church program. These efforts may be crude but Sam is at least trying. But what can Bill, the office clerk, do? Why cannot he give away free combs or something else with his name on it, copying Sam the barber? Why could not Bill, without any business to advertise, make a big splurge and take a $10 space in the church program? What seems like an uninspired idea for one man, becomes a sensational promotion for another!

In this tough business of selling yourself, the age-old business slogan, "You gotta spend money to make money!" applies just as well as in any other field. Make a special appropriation from your spending budget and call it your "Acquaintance Account." Merely having a definite amount of money to spend on finding and cementing new friends and acquaintances will suggest many new ideas to you.

Occasionally you may publish a little essay or article. It is not difficult or expensive to get the magazine which published it to make reprints. Then send it to your "Acquaintance List." It keeps people from forgetting you.

One advertising manager who, among his other duties, edits a house organ for company employees and consistently writes inspirational articles over his own name, mails the magazine each month to his "Acquaintance List." He has received worldwide acclaim not only for his magazine and its modern make-up but also for his articles which are often picked up and reprinted by other publications. When one receives the "Phoenix Flame" from Harry Higdon of the Phoenix Metal Cap Company, it's the next best thing to a hearty personal greeting from an old friend.

A publicity man who sends out hundreds of publicity re-leases for his various clients regularly directs certain of the releases to go to his list of personal connections. Now a pub-licity release in itself is a very plain thing, mimeographed on plain paper and usually without any letterhead. But in the lower left-hand corner it says: "Released by—" with the public-ity man's name. It is his way of letting old friends know about some of the work he is doing and often to get additional public-ity from these same connections.

No matter how restricted your line of work, or how small the sphere in which you operate, if you will study what you are doing you will find some way, every once in a while, to tell your old friends about it.

This is a most practical answer to the question former associ-ates and acquaintances ask: "What's he doing now?"

If it's Christmastime, send Christmas cards to the whole list! A little expenditure of energy, a little extra expense, and it's done if you will only tackle the job with "connection self-education" in mind. It's cheap and unworthy only to send cards to those who send cards to you. Send them to all your old contacts.

Doctors, dentists, lawyers and other professional people feel it is unethical to advertise, yet they admit the need for self-promotion in their careers. No ethics forbids them from sending cards to old friends, present clients and former clients, even to people with whom they have had a falling-out.

No ethics forbids their going to wakes, to funerals, visiting the sick, inquiring about their friend's children and relatives, and occasionally giving a little advice without charge.

You don't make connections sitting on your fanny in the office or lolling on a couch at home. Circulate!

Ray H. is a man who loves to meet people, remember their names and their special abilities or fame. In a conversation with Ray you will probably find that he has just had personal ses-sions with the biggest names and personalities in town, from which circles stem his long list of powerful connections. Ray's secret is simple. He spends even more time on "nobodies" than with big shots. But he gives every "nobody" the same kind of

concentrated attention and courtesy he has for important people. It's as Sylvia Beach says of the famous Irish genius James
Joyce: "He treated people invariably as his equals whether they
were writers, children, waiters, princesses or charladies." If
Joyce arrived somewhere in a taxi, he would not get out until
the driver had finished what he was saying.

Dave Harrington, top executive of the Reuben H. Donnelley
telephone book concern and direct mail house, has probably
attended ten thousand meetings in his lifetime. Large or small,
you always see Dave at any industry meeting, smiling, shaking
hands, working to contribute to the success of the affair. He
has so many contacts he could never possibly count them. And
every contact has contributed something to his success.

You are too inclined to believe that the making of contacts
is the most difficult part of selling yourself. Actually, it's the
easiest! For it doesn't depend too much on psychology, the will
of others, personal finesse, or any deep or delicate faculty.

Just move your body around! Circulate!

When introduced to a new person, catch his name. You'll
never be able to remember it until you hear it pronounced correctly, and until you have pronounced it silently several times
so that it is engraved on your memory.

And don't be satisfied merely with the name. Get some personal facts about the man's work, his friends that are your
friends, his special qualities; his hobbies and interests. These
personal facts will cinch his name in your memory and his
name will sometime in the future deliver all the personal facts
with it.

What to do when you cannot remember a man's name and
you know you should? Don't fight it, give him a hearty greeting
in warm terms and the name generally comes to you at once.

When the name is stuck in your brain and will not come
out, associate the person with a past event in which both of you
participated intimately. Mention it. Recall some high spots of
the event, glow a bit with a sincere touch of mutual joy. Often,
the person whose name you cannot remember will exclaim:
"What a man! What a memory!" It seems that if you forget a
name, you will inevitably be able to recall an event.

If you are at a public gathering, do not remain long in company of the man whose name you cannot remember. Other friends will approach and expect you to introduce him to your embarrassment and his.

Wouldn't it be more honest to ask the man outright to state his name since you cannot recall it? More honest yes, but not very expedient. You and he may have been real thick in the dim past and such an admission would be catastrophic. I am thinking of a person I know who asked a supposed stranger for his name. "John, don't you know your own cousin?" cried the unrecognized one.

Take your time in meeting a new person or several new persons. You have more time than you think, whether confusion or hustle and bustle are causing you to gloss over these many new contacts. Take your time and be personal with each.

10 TIPS ON CONTACT-MAKING

1. Put the other man in your debt.

Foolish people try to squeeze the value out of a new connection as soon as they make it. They ask for help, favors, seem to insist that because they know the man, right away he must do something for them. A mistake!

Right away *you* try to do something for him. Put the man in your debt as fast as you can.

You can be extra polite, you can be especially kind, if you cannot think instantly of a more practical favor. But with the right attitude of mind you will think of many things, some little, some big, that you can do. Everyone needs help of some kind; a lift in your car, an umbrella in the rain, a book he should read.

Leo McGivena, noted copywriter and advertising agent of New York, has to my knowledge given away thousands of books to friends and contacts. A book is a great gift. McGivena just doesn't give any book but he spends a whale of a lot of time selecting just the right book to fit the receiver. Such a gift is a tremendous compliment, and is never forgotten.

2. Meet them in the flush of victory.

Joe X is a mediocre golfer, but a great golfing enthusiast. His friends often wonder how Joe happens to be buddies with so many big-name golfers since he is out of their class definitely.

Joe explains: "Why, I catch them in the flush of victory! I like to see the big pros play and when a certain man wins a big match, I am the first to congratulate him, talk to him about the special shot that he pulled off, or some other feat that struck me as phenomenal. Maybe a few weeks later I write him a personal letter (golfers don't get much fan mail) and when he's playing in my territory I go and see him again *before* he gets into his next match."

It's easy. In the flush of victory, a golfer, a bowler, a winner of a lawsuit, a manipulator of stocks—anybody—is the most approachable man in the world.

3. How to use your best connections.

Your very best connections should rarely be asked for any favor, large or small. Perhaps they may supply material for legitimate name-dropping or anecdotes to illustrate a point. Save them for an emergency, and if the emergency never happens, so much the better!

Never ask a person who owes you a big favor to pay you back with a small one. He may be glad to do it, of course; but in this way you are foolishly forfeiting a valuable reciprocity.

4. Stand by them in defeat or disgrace.

A man who has been struck with sudden ignominy, defeat or disgrace is approachable, too. Go to him, ask him to take a walk with you in public, let him know you are not ashamed to be seen with him by anybody under the sun.

He will never forget your kindness and your nerve.

Later, when he recovers, you will be at the top of his list of personal friends.

A powerful businessman was sentenced to jail on a technicality too serious to be forgiven. Most of his friends deserted him, pretending they had only known him slightly and hence were ready to wipe him off their list. But one friend went to see him the day before the sentence started and offered to take care of his outside business affairs while he was temporarily incarcerated. The convicted one was so grateful, though he had declined this offer of help, that six months later he set up this one friend in a thriving business of his own.

An unknown author wrote a very well-known publisher a simple letter of good cheer on the day the publisher had received a suspended sentence for a violation of the law. In the hour of the big man's disgrace this was the only friendly letter he had received from anybody. And, naturally, the author who had acted solely from an impulse of the heart, found he had made a powerful friend and sponsor in his chosen line of work.

Many of the things we consider a "disgrace" for others actually have happened to us. Every living person, rich or poor, is subject to temporary defeat and to the imaginary disgrace that goes with the defeat if it reaches the public ear. This is the time to give your friends the gift of your physical presence; not your sympathy but rather encouragement or practical help.

They will never forget your help offered at a time when most needed. They will become lifetime connections who will never forget or desert you.

5. Give ability top priority.

If you have the power to select associates, always search for the best talent. Surrounded by highly skillful assistants with reputations of their own, fame will come to you automatically and your own production become more brilliant. And the connections of your skillful assistants, which they have earned in their past jobs, are now yours free.

Men of small caliber are often afraid to hire as an assistant a person who already has a good reputation for ability. The fear instinct suggests: "Look out! He may know more than you and you may suffer by comparison."

I have nothing but scorn for this type of individual and feel sure he will never sell himself in any good way or reach satisfactory success at any time in his career.

All big men in business, whether in top jobs or minor ones,

realize that talent is the best connection of all! Each person of talent has a coterie of friends and followers who back him up in his job with talent of their own. They may be suppliers of material or services. They may be able to suggest a new source of supply, a new method of production. The man of talent may be said to be a working organization in himself. Tom Ball, an old-time Chicago printer, as long as 35 years ago had 25 top artist-designers working for him and his thriving institution. Every one of these designers now enjoys a world-wide reputation and, though Tom has long since departed, the fame of his associates stands as a shining testimonial to one of the greatest printers of all time!

6. Every letter is a liaison.

You cannot write too many. A letter needs no excuse. Every letter is a contact. It would take a phenomenal lot of work and expense to meet the president of United States Steel Company in person. But to meet him through a letter only takes four cents.

Never write a letter to a big man asking for something for yourself.

Make your letter one of praise, of suggestion, of question if you wish, but never of supplication; a big man has no time for letters asking for charity.

No letter need have a "very good reason" behind it; the mere fact that you have written it and sent it justifies it completely. A quick examination of your many human duties of gratitude, of congratulation, of sympathy, of acknowledgment, of introduction, of recommendation, of service to others will reveal countless letter-writing opportunities, every one of which is an open invitation to a new and solid contact.

7. Learn from others.

You know a gate-crasher or two. A young man in my town has jumped his income from $5,000 a year to $25,000 by his gate-crashing methods in selling insurance.

He loves to sit by the hour and tell me of his tricks for getting in to see the "hard-to see" big shot and selling him on the first call. Every good contact-maker will tell you, if you ask him, the special devices he uses for getting by receptionists, secretaries and other assistants.

Social "gate-crashing" or "social climbing" are activities at which many people crave help and suggestions. Usual avenues chosen are organizational work in associations and clubs, volunteer work in charity, Red Cross and similar programs. In this regard it should be carefully noted that the solicitation of donations to a charitable cause is not in itself an efficient way of making friends. But if you are creative and inclined toward showmanship, you may have original ideas for parties and get-togethers that may aid the cause to a bigger extent and take away all the sting of trying to browbeat your "victims" into donations. This may be the easiest way of gaining prominence in a desirable social atmosphere—with an idea.

In this same climate, you should always be conscious of a universal trait of human nature, a surefire principle for going places in the social whirl. I call it the "matchmaker's complex," and this does not mean primarily the matrimonial matchmaker. Every man and woman is by nature a matchmaker; they like to have the right person meet the right person, they enjoy the management of seeing that the right person fits into the right need in whatever cause or program is involved. Cater to this matchmaker's complex, especially as you find in the well-known person's heart. Ask him for help. It is indeed hard for anyone to resist this kind of a plea, which may result in your meeting a whole new list of good connections.

Ask "the man who knows and has met everybody" just how he makes his rich contacts. Wonder of wonders, he will probably tell you! For contact-making, in the face of great difficulties, is such a fascinating art that the experts love to describe their techniques to others.

8. Make your approach unselfish.

Let the man see, *through the clear-cut message you have sent him in advance,* that this interview will not be lopsided with your selfishness. Put yourself in his shoes. A busy man is hounded to death by strangers who want to take something away from him.

Years ago, when the late John Swigart, paper merchant, was outselling nearly all of his competitors, I was asked if I had ever met him. No, I had not, though my business activities crossed lines with his in various places. I was told he was a hard man to meet, a harder man to open up, and a still harder man to turn into a "connection." Just to take a dare, and knowing I personally wanted nothing from Swigart, I made an appointment through one of his own representatives who had sold me considerable quantities of printing paper. The interview wheeled around a *suggestion,* not a *request.* "Why don't you do something for the paper industry," I suggested, "something to translate the part your company plays in it? Put in an up-to-date display room showing the best samples of printing on all your papers, the wide variety of uses, then make the room available to every user of paper and printing?"

It was done. John Swigart and I became good friends. And I had made a new connection based on mutual regard for each other's unselfishness.

Mrs. Theron Wright, head of the Moser Secretarial School, though a busy executive, insists on personally interviewing certain prospective students to her school. These are usually girls from wealthy families bearing well-known names. Mrs. Wright not only bears down on selling these girls into taking secretarial courses but generally succeeds in inducing them to bring along former schoolmates from other well-known families. Consequently the caliber of the Moser students and the quality of the secretaries the school graduates is of the highest. "One good connection always leads to a chain of other good connections," says Mrs. Theron Wright.

Your basic attitude toward any interview should begin with the question: "Whose interview is it? Who is interviewing whom?" If you made the appointment, it is certainly your interview, regardless of the wealth, power or reputation of the man you are meeting. Know what you are there for. Package up your objective in your mind's eye so clearly that you can see yourself walking out of the interview taking this package with you. All

men applaud the salesman who knows exactly what he is trying
to sell, especially when it is an invisible, intangible service or
idea. And no man thinks much of an interviewer who allows
the party of the second part to steal the interview away from the
salesman, by changing the subject, holding the floor and doing
all the talking.

You are in this spot, this interview, to sell something. Sell it
by first selling yourself and insisting on interviewer's rights. Or
let your interviewee know you are going to exercise all your
rights and sell yourself thus by your aggressiveness, your leadership, your showmanship. Regard every such interview simply
as an informal speech. You are the speaker—the other person is
the audience. Hold the floor till the real reason for this interview is finally resolved, and your audience—in this case your
auditor—will give you his complete respect and attention.

9. Try to make your visit brief.

A few minutes with a busy man is enough. A pleasant short
contact is much better than a very long boring one. You can
always follow him up by mail, or through his assistants. Don't
kill a contact by staying too long.

And any contact with a *subordinate* is important. Ignore no
one along the way, whatever his position. A smart office assistant
may be able to tell you more about the inside workings of a
given firm than the boss himself. The secretary, the information clerk, the switchboard operator can aid you in making
many a connection. Never hesitate to make a good connection
with *them*.

And in social life always remember that any contact is a good
contact! The man you ignore at a social party may be the most
influential man in the room. If he isn't, he at least has *some* influence which, if he gets to like you, he may throw into your
path to help you on your way to success.

10. Cultivate naturalness.

Comport yourself in the presence of the new individual as
if the connection has been made. Don't assume too much but

take the meeting of personalities for granted. Keep steady, keep your voice steady. Don't fawn, don't be a hypocrite.

Avoid the "dead fish" type of handshake; shake hands with warmth and just the right measure of strength. When introducing one person to another, try the "toastmaster's" type of introduction—give a little of the background of each person and not merely their bare names.

Start "confronting" people in your own neighborhood. Etiquette says a woman should speak to a man first—but not in your own neighborhood. Introductions are positively not required to speak up at once to a person whose face you have seen frequently. When working in your own yard or meeting on a bus or in a railroad station, "neighborhood" faces are the property of the person who believes in good approach.

Keep This Truth Foremost in Your Mind

You make all your valuable connections by selling yourself to each new contact. The rules for selling yourself to others apply strictly. And contacts, combined with your personal abilities, will do much to *guarantee your success in life.*

[12]

How Dependability
Sells You to People

THAT DEPENDABILITY sells you to others is an old, old story. It is the first lesson they teach you in school.

Yes, in many ways, it is the *only* lesson taught at school which has a direct connection with life in the business world and the snarled trails that you will have to follow outside school in your search for success.

Many items of advice that I give you in this book you may challenge and dispute. In the many lectures I have given on the topic of selling oneself, the reaction I have noticed most often from serious students is that sometimes my advice is self-contradictory. And it is, when the essentials for self-selling are taken one by one rather than all together.

To sell yourself, you must be an expressionist, an individual who takes the ball, gets himself across by words, words, words; by acting, acting, acting; by initiative, audacity, aggressiveness. But sometimes to sell yourself, you must be a *diplomat,* remaining silent, pulling strings, and keeping your aims secret. My defense is that you must have the ability to empoly both ends of the seeming contradiction, only never exerting opposite qualities at the same time.

But when it comes to dependability, YOU MUST BE DE-PENDABLE ALL THE TIME. To try to be anything else, for any motive whatsoever, would be sneakery and deception, and very poor strategy, indeed.

To recite all the rules for achieving dependability would require going back to everything we were taught at grammar school, everything we were subject to in the business world from the first day we started to work. Better to present a few examples of the "Do's" and "Don'ts," the "Why's" and the "How's." Strangely, but inexorably, all hints and tips for creating dependability are closely related to one another. Read a few accounts or case histories and you will remember many more from your own experience.

1. Avoid the label: undependable.

The label "Undependable" is the worst term that can be applied to a man in business. You can suffer to be called "slow" and still be successful. And many highly successful men have been termed "stupid" by those who knew them well, and their very lack of brain power or brain brilliance did not keep them from success.

But few people who have proven themselves undependable have ever gotten very far.

2. Be accurate.

I am thinking right here of an energetic, vibrant and quite intelligent man who is assistant manager in his department. He meets people very well; he catches on quickly; he's good looking and always well dressed.

But on the subject of accuracy, the man is an *outright slob.*

Gifted with rich word-power, he blurts out everything that comes into his head, and his head is crowded with a million "facts" that aren't true.

He insists he has a great memory, and in a way that memory is something to marvel at, for he remembers a small fraction of facts, incidents and business items. In other words, he maintains a tiny connection with everything that has happened or is happening, and when pressed for answers he actually *makes up* the rest of the event to suit himself.

He has been caught so often in his glaring inaccuracies that nobody will go near him when they want solid information. Meanwhile, this fellow is ravenous for promotion and a raise in salary. He cannot understand he is chained down for good by his own undependability.

There is a hardware merchant in the Beverly Hills section of Chicago, named William Sommers. He has had his store directly across from the neighborhood railroad station for some forty years. Mr. Sommers pride and joy is his big clock on the front of his store facing the station. To anyone's knowledge who has lived in this neighborhood, or passed through, this clock has never given anything but *the right time* through all the years.

No, sir, not a minute off, perhaps not a second off! Commuters set their watches by it, direct their personal movements by it. Mr. Sommers has never tried to enter into competition with the railroad or other stores and their clocks. He has simply seen to it that his own clock has always given the right time. Here we have an example of one man using an inanimate device to achieve many great personal benefits. Sommers has prospered because consumers for miles around believe that the merchandise he sells is as dependable as the Sommers clock, which has never failed them. They think, too, that the kind of man who would give such remarkable and accurate service to them at no cost must be a fair and honest man in any kind of a business transaction. And—most important—a CAPABLE man, because so few owners of public clocks seem able to keep their clocks dependable and accurate.

The corollary is obvious: if you display any public instrument or thing that reaches the public, you can sell or unsell yourself by either the accuracy or inaccuracy in that device. It does not have to be a clock. It might be a thermometer, or a sample, a business card, an advertisement, or an ordinary sign. Take care—do it *right*.

Be accurate. Never guess—be absolutely sure or don't say it!

And never be afraid to say those beautiful words "I don't know." The great leaders of business, politics, religion and society have to say "I don't know" several times each day.

If you don't know, and you must give an answer, say "I don't know." This statement in itself is a badge of dependability, because it implies that you do not want to steer another wrong, waste everyone's time, and cause loss and complications by guessing or frabricating.

You cannot do a cross-word puzzle without a dictionary; so every office and home should have a good dictionary to help supply your facts on words and things when you need them. You cannot consult the dictionary too often; though reaching for the dictionary for every little reason is a bother. But bother or not, it is probably true that you have never consulted the dictionary for any reason without coming away with at least one new fact!

A compact encyclopedia in one or two volumes should always be handy. When you come upon a new fact, pertinent to your work and your career, seize it firmly, nail it down, repeat it several times. It is a good practice to keep a record of pertinent facts in much the same way that you record mathematical figures pertaining to your bank account or income tax.

If you still have any of your old high school or college textbooks, consult them every once in a while. Here is material you once knew, but have not kept fresh in mind. Review it, remember it, and you may find an opportunity to put it to use.

Be proud to be known as a "factual man." Never guess. If you have the slightest doubt about a supposed "fact," check and recheck it before you give it out.

3. Measure and weigh.

The fastest way to become accurate is to *measure* and *weigh*. When you're subjective (relying on your own feelings only), you can go haywire quickly. When you're objective (relying on facts presented by scales, rulers and instruments that can't talk), you don't get off the track easily.

They say "the man who never made a mistake never lived." But Everett Byron Eckland, great industrial designer with whom the author was associated for a quarter of a century, to my knowledge never made a mistake in *measurements*. In his career he designed over 400 coin-operated machines which worked automatically and served the public, young and old, all sizes, under all conditions.

The walls of Eckland's studio bore a thousand cryptic marks that looked like hieroglyphics but were an endless variety of different measurements, heights and widths, and depths of familiar things both human and inanimate.

I once asked Eckland: "What are the measurements of the average man's HAT?"

He stepped over to the hatrack with his ruler.

He said then:

"My hat measures so and so. Your hat measures so and so. The average man's hat will fall within these measurements": (he announced them).

Now, I'll ask you, attentive reader: what, approximately, are the measurements of a man's hat, give or take an inch of length, width and height? If you answer by guessing before you take a ruler to a hat, you may be astounded by your own gross inaccuracy!

4. To be dependable, tend to your knitting.

Joey O'R. is an experienced salesman. He's been at the game long enough to know how to sell his own line well. But, married and with six kids, he's always strapped for money. So, he accepts part time work, and will take on any job he can during his spare time, trying to bring extra dough for rent and groceries. He puts in at least an average of three hours a day, including Saturdays and Sundays at this extra work, which is in no way related to his main income.

So he does make extra money and his family survives.

But Joey is making a mistake. He is not tending to his knitting. His big opportunity for getting into the real money is in his basic job of salesman of a line he really knows. His spare hours belong to that occupation and that alone. He is entitled to a little play and leisure, and you can't call him lazy, because he gets none of these benefits. It's work, work, work—extra work—every chance he gets.

If he used every spare hour he picked up to advance himself at his basic calling, to make investigations, to talk to users, to analyze the market, to make unusual visits and experiments connected with his own specialty, he wouldn't make extra money for a while, but the kids and wife would eat and live much better in the near future.

His boss knows he's a hard worker. His boss praises his energy and his drive to bring more bacon home. But he has forfeited his future for the present. He has failed to sell his boss on his *dependability* for too often he has left his knitting incomplete, and hurried away to do other jobs.

When promotions are in the making, Joey is definitely out of luck.

You Can Be Truly Dependable and Still Fail to Sell Yourself!

The world of business is full of dependable people. But they are like the precious gems on the floor of the ocean, they are for the most part unseen and unknown because they put no value on the art of selling oneself!

Every great city, loaded with bureacrats and political appointees of the drone variety, has in each of its departments at least ONE DEPENDABLE MAN. The department could not function unless he were there. Little work would ever be done unless he did it or worried about its being done.

The politicians leave him strictly alone. When major elections are won or lost, many of his fellows are fired overnight, but his job is never touched, his position is sacrosanct. The powers that be know they would be inflicting a serious wound on themselves, were they to release him.

But his name is never published; no one outside the inner circle could recognize him on sight. His salary is insignificant, worthless politicians get all the real promotions right under his nose.

I salute this man, in whatever government job he operates; yet I cannot admire his lack of good sense and practical opportunism. Almost indispensable, he knows nothing about the need for making his indispensability known to a large number of people who count. *He will not stoop to sell himself.* His dependability alone fails to sell him; he won't add anything to it.

5. *Dependability, unexploited, can be a millstone around your neck.*

You can be *too* dependable, if you despise the need for publishing the quality and volume of your work-contributions. This is a fault, almost universal, of truly dependable people. They refuse to sell themselves; they think it is a sign of weakness to point to their accomplishments. They are unobtrusive; they are always quiet, and generally silent. They let others take credit for their deeds; they are anchors and leaning posts for the unreliable loudmouths who want to get ahead by stealing from a good man's pure labor.

If you know you are dependable, do not take umbrage in false modesty, or foolhardy unselfishness. Make your dependability pay off; announce it; publish it; put it into the public eye. You are SURE you are doing good work? Then contrive to make your superiors, and the stranger-public at large, conscious of this good work. You know you can back up what you say? Then, for goodness sake, say it outloud, and every once in a while *shout it to the heavens.*

6. *Self-Confidence*

Dependability is the inclination of *others* to depend on *you.*

But what should *you* depend on? Impersonal methods, unspeaking facts—or *yourself?*

Self-confidence is complete dependence on yourself. What you don't know, you know where to find out. What you can't do, you know how to get done. But what you believe in first and foremost is your ability to *deliver.* And all the fears and obstacles in the world won't stop you from delivering.

There's no trick or special secret about selling yourself by means of your own self-confidence. Simply *have* it, and you automatically inspire the confidence of others in you; self-confidence sells everybody on *your ability!*

The magic word-wand which swiftly delivers self-confidence to you is: BLUFF.

Bluff yourself first. Your fears of the obstacles in front of you will bluff *you*—if you let them. Your fear of your own smallness, your own incapacity will scare all confidence out of you—if you let it. If you don't bluff yourself, and if you don't bluff your difficulties, you will be forever tied down with fear of your work and despair in your future. Say "Bluff" when you're trembling, say "Bluff" when you doubt, bluff everything negative you ever face!

But you can't bluff forever without something in back of you. That necessary something is *ability*. Ability, skill, knowledge, all-around personal power come primarily from worthy experience. But experience is not just letting time go by, waiting for the years to give your seniority and a claim to an experienced lifetime.

The fastest way to get ability is through study and *practice*. Practice laughs at years and delivers experience in hours, days, that it might take others years to secure.

While you practice, study, concentrate, experiment. Watch for errors and mistakes and correct them quickly in *practice*.

While you are practicing you can make all the mistakes you want, and no harm is done.

But never keep on practicing mistakes. Change, correct, improve, improvise, experiment, with an infinite number of variations. Don't be ashamed of your practice. If people find out you are intensifying in your study and practice of some particular work or activity, they are already taking the first step in "buying" you, for practically everyone will place a bet on the man who practices.

The best way to incorporate dependability in your own person, is to make good on all your own private resolutions. If you go "on the wagon," or on a diet, for a given term of time—keep your word to yourself, demonstrate an iron will-power to *yourself*, and this possession of will power will ever after get through to all who know you or meet you. It comes out in your voice, in your convictions, in all your positive actions. In your whole life, more things than dependability are needed for you to sell yourself to others and to make good in your career or in business, but remember you are always in danger of unselling yourself and forfeiting many hard-won gains through a sudden exposure of undependability.

7. Pick quality for your first ally!

Two quotations apply here:

"Who shoots at the midday sun, though he be sure he shall never hit the mark, yet as sure is he he shall shoot higher than he who aims but at a bush."—Sidney.

"It is a funny thing about life—if you refuse to accept anything but the best you very often get it."—Somerset Maugham.

Jack Aspley, head of the Dartnell Corporation, has spent a lifetime in sales instruction and business education. If his philosophy had to be put into two words, they would probably be: "Sell Quality!"

The tip is deep and rich. When you pick a job, be sure of the quality of the firm and its products. When cultivating friends, select people of quality. Put quality into your ideals, put quality into each day's work, have a mania for quality, make a fetish out of it, and very soon you yourself will be known as a "quality person."

8. Be a craftsman in something and demand craftsmanship in all things you buy and use.

Torkel Korling often takes *three hours* to make a single photograph, but that photo is better than 300 made by noncraftsmen.

R. Hunter Middleton, type designer, took *five years* on a short piece of calligraphy he was doing gratuitously for a friend.

Frank Reilly, who even 30 years ago, was famous as the highest priced lettering artist in the world, once answered my question: "How does one become a good lettering craftsman?" with: "Draw the Caslon alphabet a thousand times!"

Very likely you can't spend the years in becoming a scrupulous craftsman. O.K. You can still, if you set your mind to it, become an *appreciator of craftsmanship overnight.*

One evening a clergyman visited my home and I wanted to make a real impression on him. I talked of religion and some

extensive studies I had made in the field. He wasn't interested.
I talked books, literature and art and couldn't get a rise. He saw
my billiard table, wanted to play, and I beat him disgracefully.
He said I was lucky.

Still wanting to sell him, now especially since I saw what a
tough customer he was, I showed him a few books from my
typographic library, gems of the printing art by noble men
who had put their souls and their ideas into their work—master
craftsmen all. He was so impressed, he stayed till midnight.
Craftsmanship sold him on me, where all else failed!

9. *Keep your promises.*

If you are free enough to make a promise, you should be
dependable enough to keep it. Fulfill your contracts and don't
try to back out of them. If you're a promise-breaker or a
promise-forgetter, you are quickly advertised to all and sundry
as an undependable person. The grapevine is hard and long;
people who never had any relations with you are told—and
what is worse *believe*—that you cannot be relied on.

The *call to be prompt* is a form of contract. The habitually
tardy person, holding up the start of a meeting or a party, or
interrupting its progress is never regarded as dependable.

Rube Goldberg, the cartoonist, suffered from a disease which
he called "On-time-itis." He could never allow himself to be
one minute late for any kind of meeting. He took announcements literally, and always appeared *before* the time announced.
Inevitably, he was always the first guest at any party—and the
most welcome! Everyone loves the prompt person and regards
him as supremely dependable.

Meet every deadline, miss none! A deadline is another com-
mitment which often is more stringent than an actual promise.
A deadline is much more than a date or a day or an hour or a
tick of the clock. It is really an announcement that you will
have a job completed before this point in time is reached.
Newspapermen can't be stragglers, procrastinators with their
work. When the forms are ready to close, their stories must be
done with enough time left to set the words into type.

Simple way to be a deadline-conqueror: do every job as if you were a newspaper reporter and had to have it in before the time promised.

Do not let your promptness depend on the whims or failings of others. If your commuter train tends to be late, rather than relying on it to get you there when promised, take an earlier train which may get you there a half an hour too soon. If attending a social gathering, do not be afraid to be first there. Often the host and hostess get nervous when no one shows up on time, thinking they have made a mistake in their announcement. It is a welcome relief to see you appear first and start the party officially!

The management of time and the keeping of appointments is a worry of nearly everyone in a business or profession. Know one thing for certain: *you cannot fool the time of day*. Better to make too few appointments and handle them properly than too many and mess them all up.

Write all your appointments down on paper, each on a big sheet 8½ x 11, in large handwriting, Lay them down on a desk or table and stare at them. Commit those appointments to your subconscious, as you sometimes do when you go to bed at night, knowing you must wake up early in the morning. Figure people. Figure distances. Figure weather. Figure travel interruptions such as railroad crossings, detours, parades, storms. Figure the unimaginable interference, such as a "last-minute" long distance phone call which may delay you ten or fifteen minutes.

Time-conscious people always have a margin to compensate for the time lost when others let down on their promises. The man who is always on time *by always being ahead of time* is known to everyone as a supremely dependable man.

A young plastering contractor has caught on grandly in the use of time as a most effective device for selling himself to his own employees. John, the contractor, gets up very early each morning, and appears on the sites of his several jobs to see that his crews, reporting later, will have all the materials and equipment they need for proceeding with their work. If it is winter, he starts a fire to thaw out the frozen sand. If a piece of equipment needs adjustment or repair, he takes care of it. He does much of the menial labor which his skilled union labor might rebel at. And the biggest impression of all he makes this way; after preparing the way for his help to proceed with their work, he disappears for a while from the site! They all know he has been there already, seeing what has been done for them. But he does not flaunt his physical presence as a sanctimonious example. He waits till regular work has started to come back on the jobs.

Everyone is disgusted when a man falls down on his promise. Perhaps you can break a promise with a friend and get away with it, but a stranger judges you by the first experience. If you have promised to meet him at a definite time, be there on time. Punctuality is synonymous with dependability. Be there a little ahead of time and your dependability will be safe.

If you are selling merchandise or an intangible, always manage to deliver a little more than you originally promised to deliver. Do not expend all your promises in the attempt to make the sale in the first place. Hold back one or two little things, little extras, which you can throw in at the time of delivery without calling special attention to the extras.

10. Thoroughness.

You don't get ahead by winning raffles or daily doubles at the racetrack. You don't sell anybody by your so-called "luck", for everyone knows there is no such thing as steady or habitual luck. Hence, luck can't make you dependable in the eyes of others.

But thoroughness can. Resolve to be a true mechanic in your work. Every pure mechanic says this as he faces a job: "There are a thousand ways for this job to go wrong. I must think of every monkey wrench that could spoil it and prevent any misfire from happening. I must be *thorough* as well as energetic and skillful."

Every thing you do or plan has a relationship with some other vital part of any project. Think of these possible relationships!

Think of the consequences. There is no sense in calling a detour off the main highway for safety purposes if on the new detour road you are going to cause a dozen accidents worse than the possible accident on the main highway.

11. Pay your debts.

J. Ogden Armour, meat packing magnate, ran into financial difficulties in the last depression and, when he died, left many debts unpaid. His wife worried over these debts and over the possible blot to the name of "Armour." When a little later she made a lucky strike in some oil properties, Mrs. Armour *paid off all her dead husband's debts with her own money!*

She had no legal obligation to do so and certainly no personal obligation in conscience. But the gods of Quality and Dependability guided her to this noble sacrifice and certainly sold her to the financial and industrial world as ONE OF THE GRANDEST WIDOWS IN ALL HISTORY!

Money is a great test of sincerity—and of dependability. If they mark you down as a "slow-pay" type of individual, your dependability in all other fields is thrown into question.

One of the most dependable home builders I know, manages to get his buildings built in two-thirds the time of the average builder. His buildings are solid, dependable, full of extra value—and his competitors know it. But their biggest question about the man is: How does he get his quality work done so fast, how can he get each sub-contractor to hurry on his jobs and give this one builder decided preference over competitors who often have to wait weeks for a subcontractor to move in with his workmen, when the new home or structure is ready for them?

A successful builder not only does good work, but he must perforce *do it fast,* in order to shorten the time his capital is tied up in the project and hasten its turnover. Two crops of new buildings erected in the same year are much more profitable than a single crop.

My friend, the speedster, recently revealed his secret to me. "I pay all the sub-contractors cash in advance," he confessed.

"They have to buy materials, they have to meet payrolls and they like cash. Having it in advance—and I don't know a single one of my competitors who gives them this kind of cash—they have to favor me and move their gangs in the day I am ready for them."

Now, you may say: it's all right to pay out cash this way, if you had it, but you don't have it. But when you contract for any kind of a service or article of merchandise, you must pay eventually, sooner or later you do get the cash. Why not get it sooner or scale down your operations so that you have SOME cash always on hand to help you command better service, better prices, better deals?

Cash is always king, and the cash-man is always king among his fellow mortals. You sell yourself with cash, and if your cash is rightly managed it will help you sell your way to speedy success.

If you feel you need to establish credit for some future emergency, open a charge account with the biggest and most reputable department store in your town, the store to which purchases may on occasion be returned without a battle.

If you bank your money, it is well to have more than one banking account, should you need banking references in some future emergency.

12. At all costs build a good memory.

Almost every successful man in history, with very few exceptions, has been noted for his excellent memory.

In old age, memory generally fails a man. But if you're young and still lack a good memory, you are already an old man in the opinion of others, and therefore undependable.

Care about your memory. Treat it as something precious.

The real key to a memory is this: PAY ATTENTION. CARE ABOUT PAYING ATTENTION. Pay attention to everything you see, hear or hear of. You can command your own attention. You can force yourself to pay attention; it's just a matter of the will insisting on attention. Your memory power has no load limit. Your memory can be trained to take in everything and *recall* everything at will.

In the McCarthy-Army hearings on television the whole nation was astounded at the ability of *total recall* shown by the young lawyer, Roy Cohn. Most viewers called him a sheer genius simply because of his remarkable memory.

But there are hundreds of thousands of people who have the ability at ultimate total recall and they are not geniuses. Don't ask yourself to be a genius before you can believe you have a good memory.

I know a bum who can recite the Declaration of Independence by heart. I know a schoolboy dunce who passed a most complicated personal examination in higher chemistry by memorizing 15,000 words, whose meaning he did not know, but whose possession got him by a most difficult hurdle.

Simply care about the matter to be retained, pay attention with your whole heart, soul and mind, and you, too, will be a phenomenal rememberer!

Quit marvelling at the memory of others and decide to have one of your own, just as good as theirs. It čan be done.

And here's a simple device to prove it. If you are troubled by mislayed articles, if you put things down while you work and can't find them a minute later though you are sure they are nearby, try this. As you lay the article down, *make an extra impression on your mind,* and tell yourself *where* you are putting it.

Just one little extra impression is enough to prove you have the makings of a great memory. Do the same with every piece of true information you come upon. Just don't accept the information *once:* make that extra impression on yourself and let the fact come in *twice.* The trivial amount of added *attention* you are thus forcing on yourself will take care of your memory of it!

The best extra impression of all is a handwritten note made at the time the item to be remembered comes up. The people who make no notes and rely solely on memory find that their memories often slip up. Those who deliberately "distrust" their memories by making notes, find that the "extra impression" of the note, makes their memories extraordinarily keen and alert.

A vital note for something to be done when you get to your

office should be put into a place in your money pocket or person where you simply have to bump into it several times before you get there. If the note has bulk and size, it will be hard to miss. For instance, a memo written on the cover of a small box placed in your pocket has to be self-reminding by its very clumsiness.

With a good memory, you impress everybody you know and meet. You sell yourself to them as a keen, smart individual. You convince them you are wholly dependable.

This chapter could go on and on. A treatise on dependability is, in effect, a complete course in education and character development and there isn't enough room in this book or in a thousand books to tell the reader how to become completely educated.

But let me throw in quickly a few practical suggestions for building and increasing dependability, and especially the kind of dependability that others see and recognize—the stuff that helps you sell yourself to them:

To get at the heart of any matter: Ask these questions first silently, and then outloud, so others can see how you want to operate:

> Why consider?
> Where does it fit?
> When can it be completed?
> How will it be done?
> How much will it cost?
> Of what kind?
> Under what circumstances?
> Guaranteed by?
> Recorded by?
> On what valid basis?
> Reason or emotion?
> Logic or fallacy?
> Proof or guess?
> Childish or mature?
> Personal or impersonal?

Most meetings, conferences and committee get-togethers are

rife with confusion, duplications and minds working at cross-purposes.

In such a morass of bad thinking and talking, you can always score if you are bold enough to interrupt the meeting when it reaches its deepest slough and ask these two questions: "What are we trying to do here?" and, "How are we going to do it?"

The first question, "What are we trying to do?" should not be difficult to answer in the middle of any conference, however muddled, if you have been taking significant notes up to this point in the discussion. Even though your own statement of the intent of the meeting may be slightly incomplete, someone will usually help supply what you have missed and the salient question will be answered in full and with complete satisfaction to all.

Now, as for the second question. Again, if you have been taking notes, you are in a position to consult your own notes and at least state some of the ways and means already offered. Number these One, Two, and so on. Your conferees will now supply a few more how-to's. The meeting gets more sense and point at once. The chairman is grateful. All others are impressed at your adherence to basic logic.

AIM AT PROFESSIONAL STATUS

Your ability, reliability and dependability will increase *if you want them to increase.* They will increase so fast, you will be unable to recognize your own amazing progress.

Then you will reach a point of seeming stagnation where improvement apparently stops.

This is the time to decide *to make a radical personal change.* Leave your old haunts, your old companions, and get into the sphere where the pitching is faster, the skill is sensational, the individuals have class to burn.

You can be a pro, if you want to be a pro. The pros are approachable. You can watch them. You can bring your body near their bodies. Believe it or not, you can talk to them—they are human beings like you, and so disciplined in human relations, they are committed to be decent and sociable with any stranger who is sincere, studious, and stamped with the aura of wanting to get ahead.

They themselves got ahead by wanting to get ahead. They, too, got ahead by moving in faster company. Whether that pro is a famous athlete, or a tycoon of business, he owes you the debt of allowing you into some kind of association with him. You don't need to "sell yourself" to him. Just be bold enough to walk into close proximity with him.

But when it becomes known to your own friends and to the public at large that you, already a dependable person, are now associating with the best in the field, you will have re-sold yourself to them and to the world as a dependable and successful entity.

How do you get close to the "top gun"? If you are in the same area, and have never been introduced to him, just walk by him saying nothing. Do not look at him or try to catch his eye. Should he by chance smile or nod at you, acknowledge this slight recognition without trying to build onto it at the moment.

If he sits across the hall from you, and should you catch his eye, smile with an understanding smile (but no nod). This smile can be, or not be, a smile of personal recognition. But it can often register deeply.

If the "top gun" has made a good speech, or turned in a phenomenal performance at some game, such as a hole in one at golf or a 300 score at bowling, you can now approach him with complete confidence that he will heartily receive your congratulations. For no man at such a time can be anything but warmly human and accessible. Your congratulations can be overly-effusive, too, with great safety, because usual congratulations to anybody for any achievement are mild and soft-spoken. Make your congratulations as thrilling as you can, and the man will be more grateful to you than to many of his intimate cronies. He certainly will remember you.

When you are trying to get on good speaking terms with the top gun, always bide your time, conceal your eagerness. Make a program or a project out of moving into faster company. Do it slowly and carefully. Strategy may sometimes dictate that you yourself play a "little hard to get."

We have seen that selling one's self is no snap. A lifetime of labor and application goes into the project. How foolish, then, is it to step into a pitfall that can undo so much labor in a minute! One must always be on guard to prevent himself from unselling himself.

You believe in the importance of selling yourself to others. Be sure you believe in the importance of not unselling yourself once you have people's notice, respect, and good will.

Tell a lie, break a promise, and poof! out the window goes the regard of your public.

Do sloppy work, disregard neatness and accuracy, and this same hard-won regard is immediately lost.

It is much easier to earn a bad reputation than a good one. And one mean negative trait can easily offset a dozen fine qualities that are worthy of universal acclaim. I hired a painter, Jack, to paint my house. He came highly recommended. And indeed he was a marvelous painter, neat, thorough, professional. But he was always short of money, and every second day as the job proceeded he complained of being broke, even though I had paid him good amounts from the start. All of Jack's fine work was buried and lost in his one great failing. He had the financial "shorts." Though friends who saw his work wanted to hire him and asked my opinion, I had to tell them of Jack's big drawback. All of his skill and admirable work could not sell against this drawback.

If you have a skill or an ability that appeals to the public, by all means display it anytime you are invited to do so. The public loves skill and instantly "buys" its possessor. But be careful never to make a public demonstration of your lack of skill.

You have often observed the guest panelist on the television show, "What's My Line?" This guest has already won a great reputation in another field. He has probably sold himself to millions and is definitely a success. Yet how often does this guest mumble and fumble his way through his part in "What's My Line?", exposing his lack of detective ability, his lack of wit, and sometimes his stark lack of intelligence! To make it worse, the guest publicly admits he cannot even ask a pertinent question and passes. What a mistake! To discolor a hard-won reputation in one field, and often to forfeit it in a single appearance, is not the better part of wisdom.

Every public appearance is dangerous. I have watched doctors bowling in their once-a-week "night off" bowling leagues. Having fun, sure, but for any well-posted observer laying their medical reputation on the line, at a ridiculously cheap price. "Who of these men would I allow to slice open my belly?" asks the observer who knows bowling, and can see the hideous mistakes the doctors are making.

If you must play games for relaxation, it is far better to pick a semi-private game like golf, where only your playing companions can notice your ineptness and, if you lack experience in the game, can make allowances for your unimportant failures.

[13]

How to Use Finesse
in Selling Yourself
and Speeding to Success

ALL SELLING of self is a form of salesmanship.

They call it the "selling game" which tips us off to the hard fact that the clever finesser usually wins the game.

The invisible side of good selling clearly resembles a game of checkers, chess or cards. You play your hand with all leverage and skill; you take advantage when your opponent drops his guard or makes a mistake; you find your "ace" and show it when it means most; you keep a poker face always, especially hiding weakness, disappointment or despair.

A good salesman is always a diplomat and finesse is another word for diplomacy.

THE VISIBLE FINESSER

He lays his cards on the table face up and they are beautiful cards. He is always doing things for people, stroking them the right way, doing a hundred favors large and small. He is out to please.

He is a master at the art of praise.

The late Peggy Joyce, in my opinion, was history's most skillful praiser. Peggy could be divorced from one millionaire today and have her choice of six millionaires tomorrow. How did she do it? She *practiced* every minute of the day on all the men she met; bellhops, cab drivers, policemen, and what have you.

She reduced praise to this simple definition: "Praise consists in telling a person to his face something about him which is favorable and true."

To his face! Praise behind his back may never be heard by him. Have enough nerve to face the man and praise him in the open!

"Something about him." Something personal, something he owns or is, something for which he and he alone can take credit.

"Favorable and True." Not *only* favorable, for flattery is not praise, since the flatterer often says things the receiver knows are untrue. The praise must be *true,* and the more *special* and *exact* it is, the more powerful.

How do you find things to say to people's faces which are personal, favorable, true and very, very special? Only by practice!

You cannot practice until you make the first start. Make that start no matter how crude or clumsy it is. If it is visible, direct, special, favorable and true, it cannot be clumsy! The more praising you do, the more skill you acquire. You can quickly make the buyer's head swim with superior praise-salesmanship and lower his buying resistance to the zero point.

My friend Milt is the best greeter I know. He sees you coming from any distance, up to 150 feet. Outdoors or inside a big building like a bowling alley, he always sees you first. Furthermore, and this is the delicious part of it, the instant he spots you, you somehow know it, and become alert and eager to receive his exuberant greeting. He just doesn't smile, he uses words—clear, clean-cut words slightly on the exaggerative side, but always fresh, original and vibrant. You feel like a new man after you get a greeting from Milt; you laugh a little, giggle with glee, doubt whether he means what he says—but always enjoy it.

And though he greets everyone in this same merry way, he is no professional greeter, certainly no politician. He's not a "pro-

fessional" in the sense that he greets with an ulterior purpose of
making friends or winning votes. He simply puts a ton of spirit
into the simple act of meeting and recognizing another human
being, and no one knows exactly why he bears down so hard in
his greetings or what he gets out of all the excess energy he ex-
pends on them.

Is he sincere or hypocritical? Is he so possessed of overwhelm-
ing good will toward men *that he has to do it?* Is greeting a
sport? Or is he just making fun of the people he greets and
laughing up his sleeve at them?

I've talked these questions over with him for Milt is the kind
of a fellow with whom you can talk cold turkey. He knows the
question mark of *hypocrite* is always hovering over his shoulders like a left-handed halo, and yet he's willing to face and
meet the charge head on.

He confesses: "I don't think I'm a hypocrite in this matter,
but supposing I am, we'll say, a little bit over-sincere." He con-
tinues: "Wouldn't you rather receive a peppy, inspiring highly
personal greeting from a semi-stranger than a sour, dead,
mumbled 'Hello' from your very best friend?"

Hemingway could just as easily have made Milt the hero of
The Old Man and the Sea. He is just as unknown as the old
fisherman, with only one small boy as his follower and fan.
(After all Milt has one follower, too—me!) And the art of greeting a fellow human as if he were a living person and deserving
of a warm and live salute can be considered an even more noble
art than the gory game of trapping and fighting monsters of the
sea. If more people took it up—saw it not only as an opportunity but as a burning duty to humanity—the whole world
would soon be rocking with lilting gaiety and gladness, every
day would be as hysterically happy as Christmas. Though all
the new excitement came from a source we may concede to be
artificial stimulation, in the end the new found joy and laughter would be sincere. Hatred and evil would have a harder time
creeping into men's hearts.

My son knows Milt and a few years ago, while he was doing
a bitter stretch on the front lines in Korea, I one day asked myself, what could I possibly write him to cheer him up, give him

a real boost and morale and make home seem a few thousand miles closer. The answer came in a flash: I advised him that any time he was feeling low or in the dumps, he should think about Milt, imagine himself meeting Milt and getting one of those incomparable greetings, and then he simply couldn't remain blue for very long. He told me he followed the advice and it carried him through many a black watch and helped him return home with his physical and mental health.

Ernest Hemingway's book, *The Old Man and the Sea,* received almost as many different reviews as there are book reviewers. The critics all praise the work, but seem to understand the point of the story in many different ways. I think they all missed the point, and the real point of the book is one which Hemingway himself has always been trying to make, and it is there despite the critics. There are many forms of sport, and skill and human activities—and THERE ARE CHAMPIONS IN ALL THESE FIELDS. Sometimes the champ is an unknown who will never have the label of "greatness" pinned on him; nonetheless, he is just as great a champion (like the old fisherman in Hemingway's yarn).

The Invisible Finesser

He avoids mentioning the unfavorable truth. He is never the bearer of bad news.

He has only one thing in mind—his goal. He watches for the opening, he picks up whatever free percentage is lying around, he seldom tips his mit.

Don't say what you think till you're sure it's what he thinks.

If what you secretly think is the opposite to what all others think and it is patent that your thinking will start a row or tend to label you as a "troublemaker," smile and keep quiet, especially if the point at issue is a minor one. Some advertising writers want to fight if a single word of their copy is altered. If the client insists on the correction, why fight a battle you cannot win, especially when the opposition may be RIGHT? Save your life struggles for the time when your life is really at stake.

A big business executive admits that he has on more than one occasion received a public "dressing down" in which the entire organization has been called to an open meeting to hear the executive criticized for selling too hard or being too eager in his activities for making profit for his company. "It's a form of discipline, not humiliation," he says, "when the owners of a company criticize a man for being too zealous in his job. But it is a real compliment to be bawled out in public, and before lesser employees, for working too hard in the company interest. It is better to be known as man who does too much than too little."

Play politics but maintain entire control over all your political maneuvers. When you have to "join 'em," join 'em; but still retain your own individuality, your right to success, your ability to sell yourself and yourself only!

Always strive to cultivate the ability to "let-go." It is much easier to drop a grudge, to learn to like the fellow you despise, than you now imagine. Seldom is the question of character at stake. All strong characters know how to forgive, how to overlook slurs and insults. The offender will surely regard you as a bigger man, once he perceives this "let-go" ability in you.

If others insist on helping you to success, always accept and applaud their help.

A common ordinary man, dressed in overalls, is considering buying a lawnmower at the big outdoor hardware emporium. The lawnmower is expensive, the buyer undecided. The salesman asks what kind of grass is in the lawn.

"Oh, nothing special!"

"Take the mower out in the parkway and try it on our *Blue Merrion* sod!" suggests the salesman, inferring if it works nicely on expensive grass it's certainly good enough for any old grass. The gesture is exceedingly rich because the mower, after being used to cut grass of any variety, probably could not be sold as new to anyone else.

Suppose your superior in business has devised a plan which you, as a junior executive with more experience and perhaps better judgment in the field in question, cannot in conscience endorse. Should you keep your mouth shut or be overtly honest and tell your boss what you think of his cherished brain child?

I would say: play it safe, if there is real danger here, and use finesse. For instance, you can fail to show *enthusiasm* for the plan. And enthusiasm is homage no one ever is required to pay. If you ordinarily are enthusiastic and here and now you show no enthusiasm, you are, by using no words at all, cleverly hinting that you do not O.K. the plan. Neither can you be expected to supply great initiative or to add extra ideas to the plan.

Do not attempt to correct the bad points of the plan—let others, less diplomatic, attempt to do that. Never be the bearer of bad news, let someone else be the first to spill the beans.

Jack Kilgallen, uncle of Dorothy, TV star, is a great real estate salesman in Oak Lawn and Evergreen Park, Illinois. He does not mind whether his diplomacy-finesse is visible or invisible, just so it makes the sale. When offering a vacant lot to a buyer, he insists that the man "bring the family with him." Once on the site of their prospective dream home, he finds the surveyor's stakes and makes mama and papa and two of the children stand on each corner of the plot so all can then and there visualize the legal boundaries of the lot. He achieves a warm, earthy appreciation and feeling for the ground. They generally buy after having "felt" their lot so intimately. And a good show always pleases!

When Bill Treadwell, vice president of a mammoth advertising agency, writes a book (and he has written several), he manages to put the names of as many people as he knows or has met in the book. The names are always used in a context that is highly favorable, and no one could possibly object to seeing his name in a Bill Treadwell book. In fact, any individual on finding his name has worked its way into a BOUND BOOK has a hard time refraining from buying that very same book!

COURTESY

Courtesy is Visible Finesse and it is beautiful. It perfectly oils all relations between human beings on earth and proves that man can be "just a little lower than angels."

But courtesy does not consist merely in saying "Thank You," "Pardon me," and "Pleased to make your acquaintance." Courtesy comes from the heart and the mind, not the mouth.

A Christian Brother has said: "The less a man needs to say 'pardon me,' the more of a gentleman he is."

When you need to say, "Pardon me," it means you have made a mistake or a slip of some kind. If you keep on making the same error over and over, you will certainly be a "pardon me" man.

Why bump into people, why stand stupidly in their way, just to say "Pardon me." Don't be a blocker, standing in aisles and doorways and preventing others from getting by you.

Don't stand with your back to anybody, or between people who can't see each other.

Another wise man has said: "A lady is a woman who gives a man a chance to be a gentleman." Which seems to suggest any man given the opportunity, and given a hint in the right way, should see the courtesy light and act accordingly.

And courtesy doesn't come from a book on etiquette either. Rather it is best learned by memorizing these three words:

LOVE ALL PEOPLE!

If you love them all, the next representative of the human race you meet won't annoy you too much. You may not like him, but by loving people in general, you will try to treat him with the courtesy you owe to the whole human race.

Because you like to be comfortable, you will want to see others comfortable, too.

Because you like honor, you will acknowledge that others like it too and hence, at every chance, you will honor all men you can without regard to their importance or significance. *Wanting* to be courteous, you *will* be courteous, and the more often you are courteous the more your skill in courtesy will grow. You will remember people's names and their conversation. You will remember the names of their children. You will remember their confidences, their troubles, and their worries.

Naturally you will sell yourself to them in the most diplomatic way, and turn them not only into friends but also *boosters*. And the more boosters you have, the greater the odds on your ultimate success.

If you are not courteous by nature, and if good friends have informed you of your lack, decide to do something about it. You know a lot more about courtesy than you suspect. Force yourself to act courteously even though you feel like a hypocrite. Your latent talent in the art will amaze you. People will exclaim and enthuse about the example you set.

Little acts of courtesy—tiny acts, not sizable favors demanding reciprocity—are often spectacular. Ask the visitor in your office to reach something to you. Get a guest in your home to do some trivial work such as moving a chair or getting something out of the ice box, and he will feel at home instantly.

Love all people and you'll be kind to all people. If you are kind, you are courteous unconsciously and this is the most delicious variety of courtesy.

Practice courtesy by increasing your kindness to your wife, children, and all the family. Here you will find a double payoff, a new kind of happiness in your home life, and greatly increased skill in the world outside.

And never fight discourtesy with discourtesy of your own. You may allow yourself to be disturbed internally by another's mistreatment, but don't let your rancor show on the surface. Maintain external calm and politeness and it will win.

Courtesy marks you as "a man who has been around" and surely establishes you as "a man who is going somewhere."

Did you ever notice that every big business executive usually has a big leather sofa in his office? It is placed to one side of the room, definitely removed from the desk and chair area.

When the executive wants to be especially nice to a visitor, whether the visitor is an old friend or a caller with a request which the executive knows he must refuse, he diplomatically moves the caller over to the sofa. In this informal area, dissociated for the time being from sordid "business," the executive puts on his warmest courtesy and his most effective diplomacy.

Consideration as an art or science rises far above good courtesy as a form of diplomacy that wins people to you, to your product, or your cause.

Consideration is the finesse of putting yourself in the other's shoes, of going with your entire mind into his entire body. Sometimes he detects your doing it—that's visible finesse, but still he likes it. Sometimes he does not suspect it's happening—that's invisible finesse and just as enjoyable!

Sell yourself to others in the same way others have sold themselves to you.

Take a person who has made good in your eyes. Who has your total respect and admiration. Whom you definitely consider a big shot. Just what has he done to make such an impression on you? Since you have "bought" him, you know him. Carefully analyze his good qualities, point by point, and write them down. Also put down on paper the finesse, or smart execution, he uses in getting these good points across to others. Look over your notes, then ask yourself: "What has he got that I cannot have?"

You don't need to *copy* his tactics—that would be bad. But you can *aim* at his self-selling methods and in working them your own way, you will undoubtedly come up with some fresh, effective methods of your own.

You will find that nearly everyone who has sold himself to you has been adept at the art of consideration for others. And not only consideration of *heart*, but *mechanical* consideration as well.

When another rattles off a message so fast you cannot take it down; gives you a phone number or address in such an indistinct or mixed-up fashion that you have to ask him to repeat himself several times; gives instructions that are incomplete and full of road-blocks; writes you a letter asking for something free and doesn't enclose a stamped self-addressed return envelope; assumes you know everything about the company you are working for on your first day; and does a hundred and one other things that leave you thwarted and hamstrung though you are eager to help and have the ability to help—well, that man definitely proves to you that he is not a *mechanic* in his relations with others and, by his lack of mechanical consideration, is *unselling* himself!

The first rule of selling a thing, an idea or a personality is: SERVE THE BUYER IN THE WAY YOU WOULD WANT TO BE SERVED IF YOU WERE THE BUYER.

I am thinking of a girl who is top secretary for an industrial magnate. She takes the boss's dictation, yes; but to call her a stenographer would be grossly inadequate. For she is really a master engineer of all his business moves. She remembers. She has the facts. She calls attention to his omissions. In quiet and very indirect ways she makes suggestions for things to be done, and they never bear the label "suggestion." The man leans on his secretary far more than he would care to admit, but he admits his dependence to this extent: He pays her $10,000 a year salary and knows she is worth three times the amount.

Perhaps the ideal secretary is more an exemplar in the field of efficiency than an outstanding example of mechanical consideration. But how does anyone become efficient at anything? Mechanical consideration is the first avenue to efficiency. By putting yourself in the others man's shoes and doing the things that make work and life easier for him you are doing your own job with supreme efficiency. The good mechanic in the mechanical trades is the man who thinks of a thousand ways in which a job can go wrong and then sets out to prevent mistakes and accidents and inefficiencies. When all the wrong things in a job are blocked out and prevented, perfection is the result.

Therefore, we must insist that there is a tremendous chasm between courtesy and consideration. The courteous driver in the lane nearest the sidewalk may stop his car and wave to a group of little children to cross the street in front of him. This is sheer courtesy, but it can be a stupid thing without mechanical consideration, for he may be blocking the vision of the car driver behind him in the center lane, and this driver not seeing the children may become involved in a catastrophic accident.

OPEN UP YOUR EYES TO PERCENTAGE

Open up your eyes to the thousands of different ways in which you can finesse your way into people's esteem!

Look and think.

Every situation is loaded with *free percentage*.

Find the percentage. When you are playing cards, you hope for good cards. In business relations and human relations the good cards are dealt to you every time, if you will only recognize them.

A silverware salesman had made an appointment to call at a certain home one evening. On arrival he found the whole family there, but to his dismay saw at once that they were intently admiring a bright new red rug which had just been laid down on the floor. "How can I overcome the competition of that bright red rug," the salesman asked himself, "when clearly it is showier, flashier and more shiny than my silverware?" But searching for percentage, he had an inspiration. One by one he began to lay dozens of pieces of his silverware right on the bright red rug! The rug made a perfect background for his merchandise and the sale was made in jig time.

When the cruiser *Indianapolis* was sunk in the closing days of World War II, the crew had about 10 minutes' warning of the disaster after the torpedo hit. Most of the men had time to strap on life preservers before they hit the water and get a good distance away from the ship before it blew up and sank. Yet of the big crew only a comparatively small number saved their lives. These were percentage men, the type that studies any dire situation to learn quickly where the percentage lies. If many men are involved in such a situation, instinctively the percentage men get together to fight against the odds.

In the case of this sea disaster a few survivors told the story of group percentage. How the strong young sailors tried to swim to a shore that did not exist, and were destroyed by sunstroke by day or freezing cold at night, or by sharks, or exhaustion. How the small group of percentage men, sticking together, quickly decided to remain near the spot of the sinking. Grabbed wreckage to support their bodies. Treaded water at night to keep warm. Woke up tired buddies who might doze off and sink. Covered up in daytime to shield themselves against the blazing sun, AND STAYED ON THE SCENE, knowing that when rescue came, it would come there FIRST—which is exactly how it happened!

The percentage player always sells himself to the people who count, the informed observers who know percentage themselves. In the sinking of the *Indianapolis* this type of sailor had been observed and certified by similar types long before the fatal day of the sinking. In any business office or organization the same kind of individuals are selling themselves consistently without fanfare or acclaim, day by day. And when a crisis arises, such as a big job to be filled or a heavy assignment to be allocated, they are the ones chosen.

At a game or contest, athletic or perhaps intellectual, you have often seen the so-called "better man" lose. The less flashy individual comes out winner by employing the percentage of mathematics, of tradtion, of experience, or of plain common sense.

1. *Your percentage in company suggestion system.*

Your company has put in a suggestion system and is asking all employees to contribute suggestions for company betterment, offering a special reward for good suggestions.

To most workers, the plea of the company for suggestions is a pain in the neck. At first flush it may seem that way to you, but open up your eyes and *consider*.

Your percentage is the fact that most employees will *not respond*. Now, if you respond, you instantly make yourself a little different, a little superior. That is, if you send in merely one suggestion. But suppose you make up your mind that in a given month you, and you alone, will offer *MORE SUGGESTIONS than all other employees combined*.

What's to prevent you? You have the zeal, the knowledge and the imagination. It's a matter of forcing yourself. Think of what a standout you will be when the suggestion jury, generally composed of top executives, discovers that one employee

is so anxious about company welfare he outdoes all others in his
thinking for invention and improvement.

2. *Your percentage in the deadline.*

Everybody hates deadlines, considers them something to be
feared and ignored. A deadline is full of powerful, friendly percentage, and is your friend! For the shorter the time for com-
pleting a difficult project simply means there will be fewer
people objecting to ways and means. Straight thinking and efficiency are honored above all. And by your insisting the deadline will be met in the last inning, your passion draws to you
powerful support from both the big people and the little people
involved in the project. And such a last-minute drive usually
succeeds!

When all is said and done, diplomacy is getting the right
thing done, done on time and with maximum efficiency. Doing
the thing is always visible and a good job done on time sells
you to all concerned as a person of power, a successful figure.

The "maximum efficiency" which you use is seldom visible
to the public; few can appreciate true finesse.

As chairman of special events for the Treasury Bond Drives
in the last war, I induced the building trade unions of Illinois
to pay for the erection of "the largest home front war display in
the history of the world." The display called for the hanging of
4,500 model airplanes from the ceiling of the Union Station in
Chicago. A dozen or more mural paintings of huge size. All
design and artwork to be free, the union only to pay for the material and construction. Scheduled for Labor Day, a few months
away. Finding that all the material was war-rationed, I tried to
explain to the union officials that the completion of the project
would have to be delayed. *But they finessed me with the deadline.* "Listen," they said, "you and you only are responsible.
You talked us into this. We will take no excuses, no alibis. We
want the job done by Labor Day."

Finessed by a deadline, I decided to do a little finessing of my
own. I started the contractor on the construction, the designers
on the designs, and without any authority (other than a little

guts) I promised the necessary priorities for the lumber, the steel cable, all the other scarce material which was strictly rationed. Then I proceeded to send a stream of telegrams, long distance calls, letters to Secretaries Knox and Morgenthau, to Maury Materlink in charge of government priorities. The rationing was full of RED TAPE, and red tape is an enemy of any deadline. I kept the construction men going, secured all material without *any legal permission on paper,* merely insisting "this is a government job which must be completed by Labor Day." A week before Labor Day the priorities finally came through from Washington. The whole job was then almost done (without priorities and in spite of red tape) and Labor got its magnificent war display completely finished *one day ahead of time.*

The deadline is your enemy if you keep it to yourself—your friend if you share it with others and use its power to force them to work for you.

In selling yourself to others on your way to success, always keep your objective clearly in mind. Your objective, which is success in definite form, is more important than time or any kind of interference, animate or inanimate. If you can visualize your objective sharply, keep its picture always before your eyes, it will suggest the ways and means for its own accomplishment. It will do a large part of the finessing for you!

Free percentage is all around you. Sometimes the use of these free assets requires work on your part. You can take the job which few people crave, "chairman of the meeting." Or you can agree to write up the decisions and sense of the meeting, a thing someone should do or the total usefulness of meeting be lost. You can agree to write a letter for the boss's signature, knowing he does not want to write it himself. Or make a speech or a personal appearance representing him. His lack of desire to do what he personally ought to do is your free percentage. In a business office, your job may not be selling, but you may be able to secure a real order from the outside. Do it, though it requires work, and especially because it is not work required of you.

If you are alert to find percentages that involve a little extra work, you will concomitantly acquire skill at spotting percentage where no work is involved. In most cases, when attending a banquet or a business conference, the choice of a seat is up to you. Never be afraid to take a chair that is in the foreground— the background is for the timid who hesitate at being too "prominent." He who fears prominence must be afraid to sell himself.

Section Five

DEPARTMENT
OF THE EXTERIOR

Here we emphasize this precept: When it comes to selling yourself, the OTHER GUY in some ways is more important than you!

For, in the end, the decision on whether you have successfully sold yourself rests with him.

Therefore, and first:

He must be made aware of your existence on earth. This is PUBLICITY that capitalizes on SHOWMANSHIP.

Second:

He must be induced to acknowledge that you are ALIVE and that you, as a living person, are attractive and pleasing to him. This is PERSONALITY.

Third:

When you realize that you have become stronger than others and can influence them for their good, you must begin to exert this influence on all people, especially those in your own business or social circle. This is LEADERSHIP.

Fourth:

Since you meet with people MORE OFTEN than you consciously perform nearly all other human acts, and—

Since the impression you leave with them can make or break your success in the long run,

It is obvious that you must chart your future with HUMAN RELATIONS uppermost in your mind!

[14]

How to Develop and Use Personal Showmanship

MANY have the mistaken idea that to be a showman you have to be in show business. They connect the idea of showman with figures like P. T. Barnum, Flo Ziegfeld and then exclaim: "Not for me!" Of course, there is much to be learned from the great stars of show business, basic characteristics and formulae that any individual, not in the entertainment world, can apply to his private career. "Success can be had from studying success; the ability of another, when dissected, is partly yours."

Barnum liked freaks. Ziegfeld was lavish. Ted Lewis' trademark is a battered stove-pipe hat. Cecil DeMille, the Bible.

Other celebrated people, not in show business, have exercised great showmanship by latching on to a specialty. Clarence Darrow, suspenders. Winston Churchill, the perpetual cigar.

Napoleon was the great showman of war. "Give 'em action!" was his theory of showmanship and for 15 years he gave the world action it can never forget.

When Charles Augustus Lindbergh flew the Atlantic solo, he performed the greatest single act of showmanship in history. But Lindbergh was, and still is, the last person you would call a "show-off" or an actor. A quiet, unassuming young man can overnight become a great showman and perhaps, like Lindbergh, make a million dollars out of the ensuing publicity.

A fair conclusion is: anyone, however obscure and modest, can develop and use showmanship and help sell himself thereby. Showmanship does not demand great genius or sensational gifts. It does demand a willingness on your part to do some *acting*. You do not have to be an "actor" to take up acting. Remember that Demosthenes, famed for the "hard sell" he put into his oratory, listed the three essentials of great oratory as: first, acting; second, acting; third, acting.

Acting in the world of show business is "putting on an act," engaging in pretense at being someone you are not. Acting in the serious job of selling yourself is no make-believe art but a hard-boiled, effective instrumentality to make people aware of you, pay attention to you, give you their respect and deference.

There is a difference between finding or creating something with which to make a show for the "show's sake" and turning what might be a drastic crisis or an outstanding performance (done for another reason) into a show. Lindbergh's solo flight might have been a simple though spectacular act of daring, with no showmanship intended. But Lindbergh offered no objection when the American Ambassador in Paris received him with glorious honors and proceeded to make a great show out of the deed.

When Roosevelt was laid low in the prime of life with infantile paralysis, friends and foes alike predicted his political career was finished. F.D.R. certainly did not want a wheel chair as a showmanship label, but he did not recoil at it when it was forced on him. You have plenty of obstacles and handicaps at selling yourself, especially at selling yourself in a big way. Set out to use the odd or spectacular things that happen to you, either favorable or unfavorable—it makes little difference whether it is an asset or a setback as long as it contains the material for a show.

Showmanship for self-selling usually appears quietly; it registers without disclosing its presence; no brass bands or flagrant *hoopla* are necessary. When your spectators don't consider you a showman, *and meanwhile you truly are,* your showmanship is all the more potent for not being visible. Some tips? Sure!

1. Any act of self-transference makes you a showman.

Go back and glance over a few of the preceding chapters. Make a speech and you're a showman. Write a letter and you're a showman. Write *anything,* and you're a showman. Anything you do to transfer part of yourself to a multiple audience plants you right in the middle of a stage in which you are the main actor. Don't think you have to inject color, oddity, drama into the action; the action all by itself makes the showmanship. Give us the *act,* and some color, some special accent will appear.

Homer Capehart, U.S. Senator from Indiana, before entering politics, was limited in business experience mostly to selling popcorn machines and juke boxes. Neither of these products falls in the "prestige" category, but "Cape" didn't mind that. He made some money out of his juke boxes and felt he could now indulge his secret ambition to become a national political figure.

Wendell Willkie was a dark horse candidate for the Presidency of the United States. Of course, Willkie was much better known than Capehart at the time; but that was an asset, not a drawback. Homer had a big Indiana farm and decided to throw a mammoth party for Willkie. Where better than on the farm —back to grass roots, back to the land and the tremendous farmer bloc of the voting population than can often make a man Senator merely by endorsing him unanimously. Willkie liked the idea. The party was held in the open field and hundreds of thousands of voters travelled many, many miles to attend. It gave further limelight to Willkie, of course—and afterwards he did receive the Republican nomination for President.

But more important to our "showman" friend, it put Capehart into the national limelight. His national reputation was made overnight and eventually helped make him Senator from Indiana.

Consider this: just one "show" did it all. Is there a show you can put on? Have you a simple, but fresh, idea for using a "show" to aid you in your secret ambition? Then by all means start it going. It may fail as a means of helping you attain your secret objective but it cannot miss in making you known as a man who believes in selling himself to others on his way to success.

2. Don't put the acknowledged showman on a pedestal.

At the age of seventeen I wrote short stories for a movie magazine and got to know many of the early stars personally. I found Francis X. Bushman, Gloria Swanson, Charley Chaplin, Mary Pickford and all the big name actors to be gloriously human and easy to talk to. They did not seem to look down on me because I was younger or because they were famous. In fact, they seemed to *look up to me* when I acted casually towards them, not showing any signs of hero-worship.

The fact that a person is a showman simply means he is more a human being like yourself; the greater the actor, the more human he is. And the more human you are, the more makings you have for showmanship. It takes a little nerve to feel like this, sure. But how fast are you going to travel the road of selling yourself if you don't show a little nerve here and there along the way?

Mentally, it is possible for anyone to transplant himself in the hero roll, and thus consider all heroes his equals. To paraphrase another saying: "There—but for reluctance to sell myself—go I."

3. Try stealing a few scenes.

I was having a late supper at the Blackstone Hotel with Edward Arnold who had just finished the picture *The Life of Diamond Jim Brady*. Arnold wasn't very hungry so he ordered a plain American cheese sandwich on white. I glanced at the menu and saw an item: "Helen Jepson Salad." Now I hadn't heard of Helen Jepson and did not know what would be in the Helen Jepson salad but ordered it anyhow. Three waiters carted in big trays and, with great flourishes and gestures, began to mix the salad. The eyes of the other diners were focussed on Arnold, the great eater, with awed interest and several of the curious sent over notes asking: "What is Mr. Arnold ordering tonight?" The waiters carried back the answer: "Mr. Arnold is eating American cheese on white but that guy with him is having a Helen Jepson salad!"

At nearly every party or social gathering, someone tries to steal the show. This is the instinct of showmanship that is in all of us. If you see a small chance to come into prominence by doing something a little irregular or daring, don't hesitate. The scene belongs to the one who has the bravery to take it. It's very good practice in the art of showmanship because the practice revolves around little things, inconsequential matters that will not make or break you. If you fail, nothing is lost. If you win, you find what real showmanship tastes like.

I know a man who cannot sing a note of music but, strangely, remembers the WORDS to thousands of old songs. He loves to get people (who incidentally recall the music but not words) singing at social gatherings by supplying the words and boldly attempting to lead a few of the songs. The company soon forgets he cannot sing but never ceases to marvel at his extraordinary memory.

A stamp collector brings a few special stamps with him when attending a party, on the chance that someone there will be interested in looking at them and hearing their history—thus furnishing a good spot of conversation and perhaps a chance for "stopping the show."

Do not search yourself for "big gifts." Find the little odd things—and there must be many—that distinguish you from other people. Then proceed to find the showmanship possibilities that are in every little odd thing.

4. Be unconventional.

My friend, John Kelly of Chicago (now deceased), won *two* Congressional Medals of Honor in World War I. One day the King of England was decorating Kelly with a high English honor and in pinning the medal on his chest said: "My boy, I'm proud of you!" The conventional response would be to smile lightly or nod in deference. Not Kelly. He told the King: "I feel pretty good myself!" Every newspaper in the world ran the story.

They were discussing a new convention building for Chicago and, as a long-time civic leader, I wanted to put in my two cents. At the preliminary meeting I proposed a 150-story building on the site of the old Chicago courthouse. No one seemed to give the idea any attention; perhaps they thought I was kidding when I suggested the tallest building in the world for Chicago.

Six months later a much larger meeting was planned. Things were getting hot. The public wanted action. The biggest men in town were coming to the meeting, the noted architects, the Mayor's and Governor's Committee.

Talking with Harry Reutlinger, the managing editor of the *Chicago American,* before the meeting, I told him I was going to hurl my 150-story idea at them again.

"Jim, don't do it," said Harry. "They'll laugh you out of town."

So, wanting to see a laugh this size, I proposed it again. Next day the representative of one of the largest insurance companies in America came into my office, saying his company had *a couple of BILLION dollars lying idle,* and wanting me to submit a formal proposal.

Later still, the idea received an even bigger compliment. Frank Lloyd Wright, most unconventional of the architects and one of the world's great showmen, proposed a 500-story building—one mile high—for Chicago!

Please do not tell me that it is hard to be unconventional and still "be yourself." I can see no conflict whatsoever, because all of us, deep down in our hearts, have twinges of rebellion at social convention. There is the fellow who always keeps his hat on, if etiquette permits, when other men take theirs off. They think he is baldheaded; but when challenged, he shows a luxurious head of hair. If you like to wear a hat indoors and there's no law against it, go ahead, regardless of the rest of the company. There's a millionaire who, when his work carries him into the neighborhood and he happens to be dressed roughly, likes to eat in skidrow restaurants. Many times he has been asked in advance if he could pay for the meal. And on other occasions he has been noticed by astonished friends going in or coming out of the restaurants. His explanation: "I like to eat with bums and remind myself now and then that I am not really a bum."

A businessman saves and files every personal letter he ever received, makes a carbon of the answers, and saves the answers. He can always astonish an old friend, or group of old friends, with warm personal data they themselves may have forgotten.

Try to make the acquaintance of a few people who talk radically and think the same way. An acquaintance was telling me about his plan for an 18-hole standard length golf course, steam-heated and all under glass, for a northern climate so that the public could play golf all winter long. "Why, the man is balmy!" anyone will say who hears the story. But is IMAGINA-TION, no matter how wild, ever to be condemned completely? No one can learn much from "status quo" people and too much of their company may turn you into a "status quo" man yourself.

5. Circulate.

You can hardly be a showman unless you manage to be *seen*. You don't have to go around looking for the spotlight or be always trying to cut capers in public. The head of the world's largest directory business attends every meeting in his trade. He isn't especially anxious to get on committees or make speeches; but no meeting is too small or incidental for him to miss. *He goes everywhere.* He has made himself into a showman of shining brilliance merely by being prodigal with his body. Think of it! Your body alone, without any dramatic power, can still be a dramatic instrument.

6. On occasion, make a nuisance of yourself.

A journeyman mechanic, member of a labor union, wants me to tell him how to become a business agent of the union.

My advice: "Make a nuisance of yourself! Get up at every meeting and talk as long as you can. Do not buck the powers that be, do not be radical or urge any radical changes. Just get up and talk, talk, talk—it is your right if you talk about union matters.

"The heads of the union won't like you, because you are wasting *their* time, time in which *they* want to talk; for they have got where they are through the simple device of hogging the floor. They may threaten you, boo you, try to knock you down. *But keep it up. Talk at every meeting for a year* and they will finally come to you and offer to make you assistant business manager of the union at a salary twice what you make as a mere journeyman."

If you belong to a club, society or organization of any kind, you are familiar with the character who gets up at every meeting and puts in his "two cents." He is laughed at, ridiculed, and often told to "sit down and shut up." But at heart we all know the only way to get rid of this showman nuisance is to elect him to some office. Ultimately he gets the job he wants.

Grade up in the spots, places, and meetings you are attending now. If you are hanging around taverns and bowling alleys, try going over your head and being seen at art or science museums, or at a high-toned lecture or two. These places are not as boring as you assume; indeed, they can be a great relief from the humdrum quality of your ordinary haunts.

The more you circulate, the more you are tempted to go over your head in the events you attend. Do not say: "Where will I get the time?" If you like your new high-toned type of circulation, you will magically find the time for it. Nearly everyone has the time to do the thing he really likes doing.

George M. Cohan, the famous actor and producer, who received a Congressional medal for "Over There" of World War I fame, was a writer and producer of Broadway shows. Not all his shows were universal hits, and as he proceeded in his career, he was seldom free from scathing reviews from the professional critics. Most men of the theatre consider it heresy to take issue with a critic who has the power of the press and a huge following of possible ticket buyers behind him. But not Cohan. George decided to publish and distribute a little weekly newspaper of his own, devoted exclusively to criticizing the critics who had criticized him. He pulled no punches in his "reviews" of the critical reviews and this tended to infuriate his critics. But his little newspaper received tremendous circulation and concentrated attention from the critics themselves. They just could not get Cohan off their minds and consequently gave him more space and mentioned his name oftener than that of any other producer on Broadway. Cohan called it: "A million dollars' worth of publicity for practically nothing!"

One of the finest forms of showmanship is *setting a good example* and the person who sets a good public example is directly making a nuisance of himself by silently preaching that others should do likewise. Clear off an open prairie (not adjoining your house), level the ground, cut the grass regularly and you become a public nuisance. People may toss you their jibes (and 99 out of a hundred will say: "When you get through, come over and do my yard for me") but your altruistic citizenship and community spirit will ultimately sway them. Some may help you on your project, others may start similar projects elsewhere. I can think of no man anywhere in the whole world who can honestly say: "There is no chance for me to practice 'good example showmanship.' "

7. Come out of your shell.

I have a friend, a retired school teacher, who has an amazing gift. She can read that monstrous book, James Joyce's *Finnegans Wake,* aloud as if it were written in simple third-grade English. You would have to look into *Finnegans Wake* to know what a feat this is.

For more than 60 books have been published on the subject: "How to Read *Finnegans Wake*." These books are not helpful to most educated readers, for the original seems like nothing but a great hodge-podge of hieroglyphics, with unending sentences, some words three lines long, all of the huge book surrealistic and mystifying.

I have told my friend I can put her on the lecture circuit at a sure $1,000 an appearance, that she would be a sensation demonstrating her rare ability. But she says "No." She cannot brook the thought of getting up before a crowd, she cannot imagine herself even having her *picture taken,* let alone having it published in a newspaper. She likes money but she doesn't want to sell herself or be "sold" by anyone else.

Here we see the whole world deprived of enjoying a marvelous gift, and a great author deprived of still more greatness by an unknown who has it in her power to interpret this greatness.

For I have a record of a reading from *Finnegans Wake* by James Joyce in person, and Joyce himself could not possibly translate his writing to the public in the way this school teacher can. But she remains obstinate; *she refuses to come out of her shell.*

If you have something you can do a little bit better than those around you, for goodness sake decide to come out of your shell! It is wrong, *absolutely wrong,* to take your gift to the grave without letting others share it and enjoy it! No one is going to deride you as an "extrovert" or "exhibitionist." No one is going to envy you or hate you.

Your punishment for refusing to show your gift to the world should be *scorn,* but still you are clever enough to avoid this scorn by *hiding.* It is not right, it is not moral, it is not manly! Come out of your shell! Some part of you is crying for expression, for fame, for success. Show it, release it! The rewards of showmanship are more glorious than you can imagine—joy beyond measure, self-justification with honor, happiness that approaches heaven on earth!

8. When occasion justifies, BE LAVISH.

Samuel Insull, financial wizard of the twenties, anxious to ingratiate himself with the huge Catholic population of Chicago, built an "L" extension to Mundelein, Illinois, where the International Eucharistic Congress was being held. The extension cost ONE MILLION DOLLARS. It carried Catholics to the Congress, and WAS IN USE FOR ONLY ONE DAY!

Once I okayed a party check for a one-night party at the Waldorf-Astoria Hotel. It was a good party—the *New York Herald Tribune,* in a main editorial, likened it to the Tournament on the Field of the Cloth of Gold held by Henry the Eighth of England and Francis the First of France. Was this money squandered? *No, we wrote up $3,000,000.00 in orders at that one party.*

Doubtless you, as a comparative "unknown" now, cannot operate on a big or lavish scale; but sooner or later than you expect, you may be made chairman of some big event, party, or program. If the funds are there, keep showmanship foremost in mind, not to waste money because it is not your own, but to please all people participating because they expect showmanship at affairs of this kind. If you can turn the event into a historic one, long after they forget what it cost and who paid for it, they will remember *you were the one who ran it!*

9. Be original.

Get some new twist into your showmanship. Most unsuccessful events are weak imitations of other affairs that were very successful. Don't copy—get something new. Tell yourself:

FIRST—*Think Big!*

Example: A Christmas office party that had the theme: "Christmas in Russia."

Example: A convention that had the theme: "Trip to Hell."

SECOND—*Think Small!*

Example: Hostess gave cigarette holders to 100 guests attending famous social gathering.

Example: At the Chicago Centennial Exposition in the '30's more men's walking sticks were sold than any other item—about 1,500,000!

10. Get the crowd.

No show without people.

In what way was Tex Rickard, the great prizefight promoter, so colorful? They called him a great showman, but he personally did no peculiar stunts. He was talked about because he always *got the crowd to come to the show.*

A printed announcement won't bring them. If a small event, phone or call on each prospective guest personally. Have others call, too. Get them one by one.

11. Improvise

Not all showmanship is planned. Sometimes it just happens, and usually it is in the form of an unwanted accident.

Once we had planned a great sales drive and my sales manager broke a leg the evening before the drive was to start. I hurried to visit him in his bedroom at home where he had landed after having the leg set at a hospital. He was broken-hearted. "Now we'll have to call the drive off!" he lamented. "Off nothing," I exclaimed, "We'll run it right from this bedroom, and all your salesmen will have to send you flowers in the form of orders!" Not one of his men dared to communicate with him unless an order accompanied the communication. And visitors came to see him in his bed of woe—but always with an order! The drive was supremely successful.

Adlai Stevenson, running for President, happened to display a hole in the sole of one shoe, as he relaxed with his feet on his desk. A photographer snapped the shot. Stevenson's alert manager, instead of trying to suppress the photo, encouraged its widespread publication. And Stevenson's familiar "hole in the shoe" did much to offset his "highbrow" manner and vocabulary, which his politician assistants believed unappealing to the hoi polloi.

Form a big committee. The committee has to be there and in itself will make a nice nucleus.

Load the program with big names, star attractions—IF YOU CAN.

If you cannot, promise a fight, a controversy, a "FREE-FOR-ALL" as bait. Or a big PROBLEM

Drown 'em with publicity in advance

Sell the tickets in advance, if possible. They can't back out if their money is down

Some printing must be used. A genuinely engraved invitation is not as expensive as you think, and it is absolute surefire!

Work hard, efficiently, mechanically to get the crowd to

come to the show. All the work you put into bringing them is the SHOW ITSELF. The actual performance is but the finishing touch.

12. *Tie your showmanship in with the surefire.*

Do not try to be too original in your showmanship, especially if you lack experience. An amateur performance can boomerang.

Stick to the things that you know people like, the ideas that have gone over before and can stand new slants, new presentation. Charles Laughton can put on a great evening's show by merely *reading* gems of literature, great pieces that other men, long dead, have written.

Currently, a young actor named Hal Holbrook has tied in with Mark Twain. Twain is surefire, loved and revered by the whole populace. Holbrook comes out dressed like Mark Twain, looking like Mark Twain, talking like Mark Twain, actually, as some reviewers indicate, being MORE "Mark Twain" than Mark himself ever was in person. Then he simply retails the best of Twain's wit and humor in the same way the famous humorist gave many lectures while alive. Holbrook is a good actor, capable of handling other roles, but his career has been immeasurably advanced by his portrayal of Twain.

SOME PROVEN FORMS OF SUREFIRE:

A party	Sentiment in a telegram
A picnic	Gifts or surprises
Patriotism—flag	Prizes
Girl in a white dress	A gamble
A baby	Mystery
Education	Animals
Self-Help: "How to Do It"	Taking pictures
Size—volume	Music—a march
Motion	Inspiration
Urge to build	News
Urge to decorate	A cane
Christian precepts	Guests' names in print

Learn to read your own emotions outloud and you have the key to all surefire principles that win universal response. For if you are able to state with absolute confidence the (usually) unconventional cause of your own actions or reactions, you can then be satisfied with the same explanations of the actions of others under the same circumstances.

Are you making a market survey? Try to find the person who gives you radical, unconventional answers, as opposed to the answers of most people which are the conventional reports the instigators of the survey seem to want. But if it is your own survey, it will do you the most good to get the emotional truth, which often will supply the ideas for improving your service or increasing your profits.

When making a survey of others, it is best not to inform them that you are engaged in a survey. Just chat on the subjects without asking opinions. You'll get truer opinions by not asking for them. All you need do is keep pointing the conversation toward the topics to be covered.

[15]

How to Carry Out
A Publicity Program
to Sell Yourself

PUBLICITY's relationship to success is indeed wondrous. An unacclaimed performer makes one TV appearance and he's a star overnight. *Life* magazine does a picture story of a man and his business and he gets more orders in two days than he can fill in a whole year. An article in *Reader's Digest* sometimes creates a whole new industry from scratch.

You can call this big-time publicity if you wish. But wait before you start insisting it is not for you. Much publicity is artificially made by the experts, but raw amateurs have also scored at the art.

The rumour went out that Senator Jack Kennedy spent at least $1,000,000 in his public relations campaign to secure the Democratic nomination for President. Whether the rumor was true or not, the point is this: if you want to attain a given objective by selling yourself to others, you have to expend money, time, and most of all, a good part of yourself in the campaign.

And the bigger the objective, the greater the expenditure.

Editors and producers are ready to listen to and consider any story that is interesting and different. They do not haggle over whether it comes from a professional or amateur source; perhaps they may be inclined to favor the amateur source knowing it is not so all-out commercial. Now take the steps that will move you into the public spotlight.

12 Steps and a One-Word Formula for Publicity

1. Be your own press agent!

Don't go around trying to find a good press agent—decide to be your own.

When you notice another man getting into the public eye, getting himself talked about, and you see his name in print every way you turn, you're inclined to say: "He must have a good press agent!" He HAS. And he has the best—himself! At the start he does his own publicity, pushes himself forward, and he's not ashamed to stoop to the practical devices that create publicity.

You have to toot your own horn, because if you don't, no one else will. Later on, perhaps, after you have mastered publicity by practicing it personally, a "Man Friday" or a "Girl Friday", associated with you in your work may become fascinated by the game you are playing and decide to help you out by handling details. But at first the details are entirely up to you!

Are you the kind of a "raw amateur" who lacks the heart for publicity, and who would willingly forfeit all that publicity can do in helping you sell yourself on the way to success?

A certain school teacher I know has a phobia against having her picture taken. She certainly is not bad looking; in fact, her face shows true character and real intelligence. But she "loathes" publicity and is afraid "her picture might get into the paper." Once she entered a newspaper contest where the prize was $1,000 cash. She felt sure she had a good chance of winning but a day later suddenly realized that if she won, the newspaper would insist on printing her picture. So she wrote the editor telling him to cancel her entry.

Now this type of publicity-timidity is not as uncommon as

you may think. Hundreds of thousands of Americans are still
"in their shell." They know the value of selling themselves to
others. They admit that to sell oneself is the quickest way to
success. They are even willing to attempt to master things they
are afraid of such as public-speaking. But the thought of engineering cold-blooded publicity in their own behalf stops them
cold in their tracks.

We should all be honest enough with ourselves to confess
that public speaking is a form of publicity, writing is a form of
publicity. Showmanship is publicity. Personality is publicity.
Accuracy and dependability in a given craft are an approach to
greatness, and *greatness is the greatest publicity of all!*

When you walk into the publicity limelight, publicity helps
you make good by forcing you to make good!

So, though the following suggestions may seem to apply to
professionals, they are all important to amateurs and new-
comers.

2. *Let no day pass without engineering, or trying to engineer,
   a stroke of publicity for yourself.*

Keep a publicity calendar. Take one of those daily appointment books and devote it entirely to what you do for yourself
in the way of publicity. *Each day do at least one thing.* If an
idea for publicity comes into your head, make a note of it. Fill
the book with things planned, with ideas, new twists, old
devices, big things and little things.

A letter to the newspaper, an article for your company's house
organ, a suggestion to your town council, some unexpected
remarks at a business or industry conference—anything!

You'll be amazed at what the smallest piece of publicity, self-
engineered, does for you and your attitude toward publicity.
Friends will comment. They may kid you a bit, but the kidding
will make you feel good. Your appetite for more publicity will
grow. Your skill will move into high very quickly.

You may make an attempt or two without results. But the
very fact that you *tried* will satisfy. Pretty soon your hits will
outnumber your misses. Make at least one fresh publicity bid
each day!

3. Order two dozen glossy prints 8″ × 10″.

Select your best photo (or have a new one made) and order at least two dozen glossy prints 8″ × 10″. Self-conscious about it? Well, don't be. Don't mind who knows what you are doing, just get the photos and send them out with an announcement, a bit of news, the next publicity attempt. *Have* them and you'll *use* them!

But *get* them in your pocket at once.

If you have a favorite newspaper columnist you intend to send frequent news bits to, send him one of your photos early in the game. Not with the hope that he will print the photo, but to allow him to get a good look at your phiz, the next best thing to meeting you in person.

If you send a story to your union or fraternal magazine, an accompanying photo is always in order. If you are giving a speech, the program chairman will often ask for one of your photos.

4. Write your own write-ups.

If you're creating a special event to make publicity, write it up yourself! You know more about it than anyone. You have the facts. No one can do this kind of writing as well as you.

If something happened today that is newsworthy, write the story briefly and succinctly. Best to have *your* name appear only *once*.

If you are giving a speech, and the program chairman asks for your biography, *write it yourself*. Shed all false modesty and self-consciousness. Make your biography *plus*. Put down all your accomplishments. This write-up will eventually land in the hands of the toastmaster who introduces you. He will be happy, indeed, to have your biography all prepared. The audience will never know you wrote it yourself.

It is well to have a number of copies of a less pretentious biography always at hand. This write-up will include the high points of your personal history, experience and connections—in a style quite like that used in *Who's Who*, namely, with few adjectives and many facts. You never know when you will be called on to furnish this kind of a biography—the main point is to get it done and ready, and properly placed in your "sell yourself" file.

5. Meet editors face to face.

Perhaps you surmise that publicity seekers just sit around and wait for reporters to come to them? They don't. You certainly can call up an editor of a trade journal and arrange to meet him in his office. Or if the two of you are at a convention, you can make an appointment to have a chat with him.

Editors like this approach, probably because it is so rarely used. They are pleased to get your ideas and they will sincerely respect your knowledge of subjects in your own, and their, industry. They will find a story in the talk you have with them. Their feeling of friendship for you will last a long time.

Editors of small town, community, neighborhood newspapers, and editors of the metropolitan section of the big-city Sunday newspapers are constantly on the lookout for human interest. For the most part they are tied to their desks. If you drop in on them in person, they are complimented.

So, too, with the top editors of the very largest big city newspapers (specifically the managing editor.) He usually has time for a visit from any sane, respectable citizen. Muster up the nerve to call at his office when planning an event, especially one aimed at community welfare, and he should welcome you heartily.

If you are calling on an editor in a small town, an outline of your story or project should be submitted. Very often this outline will appear in the paper as written because of the lack of writer help.

But in a large city, the managing editor usually prefers a quick oral description of the project out of which he mentally constructs his own idea of the story and how to direct you to the writer best suited to do it.

The big point here: *show your nerve!* If you have the nerve to want favorable publicity for yourself, you should have the nerve to meet the editors face to face. Try it and see what happens.

6. *Write lots of letters.*

Get a nice-looking engraved letterhead and put the expensive stationery to work. Write general letters, personal letters, "Voice of the People" letters—take a little chunk of your heart and spread it over the paper.

Of letters you write which you consider particularly significant, have several copies made and see that they are sent to prominent men who should be interested in the point you make.

Write letters of protest when your principles, your industry, your property is hurt by something appearing in print.

Always be respectful in your letters and avoid all misstatements of fact but always let the receiver see you are a man of principle.

7. *Be a "public greeter."*

Say "Hello" first. Put life and heartiness into every personal greeting. Never be downed by the cold fish who never says "Hello" or "Good morning" until he is first greeted by you. If you wait for the other person to say "Hello" first, it may never happen.

If you're acting as host, or serving on a committee, and the crowd is too big to greet every one in person with a handshake, *then be a glancer.* Catch their eye, and call out their names in greeting across the intervening space. This is a magical device which never fails to establish you as a livewire and a considerate person.

Jimmy Roosevelt and I were working on a premiere in the Hollywood Roosevelt Hotel. More than five thousand people showed up the first evening, trying to crowd into a space that could comfortably hold only eight hundred. They all wanted to shake hands with the President's son.

Jimmy tried to do it, too, for there was never a Roosevelt

afraid of a crowd. But after a half hour of handshaking, it was apparent he could never reach them all.

"Time for a warm speech instead," I was thinking, just as Roosevelt came to me and said: "Please ask for attention, Jim, I am going to shake hands with all these people by means of a short speech." And not to neglect a single soul, he made four speeches in all—in two ballrooms, in the main corridor, in the lobby itself where a good part of the crowd had overflowed.

Sometimes an event takes a turn you had not planned. When it does, throw away your plans; use your wit and go with the next turn.

8. Be a giver.

Giving gets you publicity. Giving gets you "word-of-mouth" favors immensely more valuable than the cost of your gifts. Some people are always attacking the good reputation of others by saying: "He's tight!" Never let these words be said of you. Grab the check *more* than your share of the time. The stingy man gets bad publicity; the generous man gets worlds of good publicity.

Lyn Durant, Chicago manufacturer, who makes a habit of giving an occasional visitor a fine personal present, very often, not knowing and never having met the man's wife, gives his friend a present for his *wife*, too. Hundreds of women all over America, who have never met Lyn Durant, are singing his praises to thousands of friends every day.

Martin Kennelly, before entering politics, was for many years director of the Red Cross in Chicago. Kennelly quietly sold himself to hundreds of thousands of people by personally accepting every invitation he received to attend a meeting or event. And he did not merely make an appearance and leave the next minute. It was his practice to stay at the affair for at least a half hour or longer. Though an extremely busy man he always seemed to have plenty of time to meet and talk with his friends, whether a small meeting in someone's basement or a large one in a public hall.

Martin's big impression on people came from his prodigality

with his body, his physical presence. A natural result of this popularity was his subsequent election as Mayor of Chicago.

9. Do a little publishing.

John Averill, typographic artist regularly publishes a little "house organ" which he prints in his own home. It goes to hundreds of friends and business acquaintances. It is replete with juicy morsels about Averill's home life, his family, his pet dog, cat, or bird. It is very like a personal visit, multiplied hundreds of times over.

You send out Christmas cards. Print up a card for a special occasion (not Christmas) and send it out to everyone you know. It might be a special day of celebration for your nationality, it might be the birthday of a great man you respect. Such a little act of publishing will get you much more publicity than at Christmas when everyone is receiving Christmas cards.

Be personal in the things you publish—people love the man who reveals he's human in print.

10. Do a lot of little things.

(1) *Just being seen in public is publicity.* Your body is a gift. Go to wakes, funerals—as politicians do. Appear once in a while at unimportant affairs, places where the "big shots" would never deign to go. The effect is tremendous.

(2) *Keep a neat house, especially a neat yard.* A well trimmed lawn is an advertisement of your own neatness, your ability, your regard for your neighbors and the entire community in which you live.

(3) *Get on committees.* If you're chairman, act like a chairman and be always available. If you're the least important member, work harder at your job than the chairman.

(4) *Get talked about.* George M. Cohan's chant was: "I don't care what they say about me just so long as they mention my name." A better slogan: "I don't care what they say about me so long as they RESPECT me." The guiding principle here is this: regard all publicity as fine, rich, worthy. Do not stoop to

"cheap" publicity like a public plug in a meeting where the plug absolutely does not fit.

"Cheap publicity" may be defined as extremely selfish publicity instantly detectible by all, such as an out-of-place plug for one's product or store. In fact, every dragged-in-by-the-ears plug for a commercial reason is in immediate danger of being looked on as cheap publicity unless—and this is real publicity—the fine machiavellian hand behind it all is cleverly, and completely, concealed.

(5) *Have an idea for your story.* Give your best consideration to this point: You have ideas. Strangely, most of your ideas call for some kind of public notice or publicity. Unless you are versed in publicity and do not fear it, you will have to abandon many a good idea.

One day, in thinking of my own childhood, I remembered how well I could spin an old-fashioned spear top, keep it going for hours without rewinding. Because topspinning seemed a lost art, I decided to hold a "Top-spinning party for grown-ups" in my own home, and invited contemporaries of mine whom I knew could spin a top with old-fashioned skill. *Life* magazine heard of the party and sent photographers out to cover it. The story ran and reached millions. The day after that issue of *Life* appeared, a man walked into my office and said to me: "If you're good enough to get in *Life,* you're good enough to handle my account." Over the ensuing years he paid me approximately $80,000 in service fees. All because of a ridiculous story which happened to be true!

Procedure for interesting a picture magazine in a publicity project is simple. If you do not know the photo assignment man at the magazine, ask the switchboard girl for his name. When you get him on the phone, give him your idea, and the chances are he will decide then and there whether he is interested or not. But the idea should be unusual, original, and based on fact. For example, your saying, "We are going to hold a Gay Nineties Party," will not excite him. But an announcement like: "Next Sunday, at such and such a place, ten fathers (parents) are formally going to dispense their teen-age sons from the Fourth Commandment" will draw replies like, "Who are they?"

"What organization?" "What kind of a ceremony?"—and, "Let us query our home office to see what they think of this event."

11. Let others sell you.

As you proceed in your self-publicity campaign, boosters will suddenly appear. Some stranger admires you for a speech. An other likes a bit of your writing. Still another falls in love with your "imagination." They become your unappointed assistants and begin to work as hard in your behalf as you yourself. Thank them. Encourage them. Acknowledge the part they play in your success.

Express your gratitude for their encouragement orally or in your letters. When a booster asks you, "What can I do to help you in this cause you are espousing?", have a suggestion for a practical job he can perform right away. Let him know that whatever boosting he does for you need not be submitted for your O.K. or editing. When you see his heart is in the right spot, let him be a full-fledged ambassador in his own methods of operating.

12. Live, breathe, and think publicity.

Never let it slip your mind, never let yourself fall into the doldrums where you try for no further publicity.

The suggestions above are not new. But thinking about your career, about your success, will bring up many new publicity moves that are ingenious, daring, fresh.

Do not be afraid to try out your own special ideas; they may seem wild as conceived, but you will soon learn how to tone them down and make them work. In personal publicity, *your own ideas are always best.*

Now I am going to shock you with my one-word formula for publicity. This is the formula that reveals the proper content of your publicity material, the core of each story, the miraculous element that makes editors sit up and cheer.

The one word is: *RIDICULOUS.*

Many stories are printed because they are sensational, such as crimes, fights, accidents.

Other stories are printed because they deal with important facts, such as Presidential elections, heavy rainfall, the World Series.

But you have no crimes to peddle and you do not consider yourself a very important person. Nobody is seeking you out to publish things about you.

So you have to make up the story out of what you are and what you have *that the editors might want.*

In regard to such made-up material, they are constantly on the alert for what is *ridiculous*. It need not be *news*. But it must be *human interest*. And the chiefly interesting part of the human animal is his ridiculous side.

But I want to condition you for this one-word formula before going any farther into it.

Self-promoters who have the wrong perspective on publicity always want their publicity to be 100 per cent favorable. Veterans of many publicity skirmishes know that 100 per cent favorable publicity is not only impossible, it's worthless. People positively will not read an article composed totally of unstinted praise for you. It is too dull, too dry. Were it printed, it would get no circulation.

Editors demand stuff that nearly everybody will read. If the story is about you, you should be satisfied if it is only *60 per cent favorable.* The rest of the story possibly will be ridiculous, but this is the part that attracts and holds readers.

And after they get through reading the entire piece, *they,* rather than considering the thing ridiculous, are impressed with your warmth, your vitality, your personality. They remember you *favorably* because you spoke to them from the pages of their favorite periodical, and you spoke so humanly they had to like you, to "buy" you as an important personage.

When contemplating a new publicity project, ask yourself what there is about you, your background or experience that is odd, contradictory, irregular, funny. Incorporate it into your story even though you wince. This is the stuff that will make the story see the light of day.

If you can't take unfavorable publicity, you don't belong in the game. Don McNeill of the famous radio Breakfast Club interviewed Mr. W. When invited to the interview, Mr. W. knew he had millions of listeners over his big network, and also was fairly certain that the subject of the interview would be treated in a belittling fashion. And it happened that way! But McNeill got many letters of protest, and one woman listener in a far-away town wrote him a scorching letter criticising him for his treatment of his guest. McNeill, to show his bigness, advertised his reading of the letter in advance and then one morning, again to millions, read the letter, bared his soul, and sought to apologize. The unfavorable publicity turned into an immense and enduring boost for the cause Mr. W. was espousing, and gained a legion of unseen friends.

[16]

How to Merchandise
Your Personality

MANY INDIVIDUALS have a fatalistic attitude toward personality. They say: "Personality? I have none!" and let it go at that. They see personality in others. They like it, succumb to its magic. But they can't imagine themselves shining in a social gathering, sparking a business conference, lighting up a strange crowd at a moment's notice.

If you feel this way about yourself, don't despair. It's a natural feeling and almost universal. I agree with those who say one cannot re-make his personality; but I insist you have a personality right now, and regardless of what you think of it, *it's a good one!*

All your feelings, all your thoughts, all you habits and eccentricities are your personality. Your meditations and introspections. Your likes and your wishes. Everything inside you is your personality. To make it clean-cut, singular, and interesting, all you need do is get some of it *outside* you. No reform is necessary; simply reveal to those outside you a small part of the stuff that you constantly reveal to yourself inwardly.

1. Try being a sport.

A stranger announces: "I was spoiled in my childhood. I had everything. Steaks for breakfast, flashy clothes, plenty of spending money." I inquire: "What were you, the son of a million-aire?" "Worse than that," he replies, *my father was a sport!"*

Try being a sport—you will never be known as a "person-ality" if you are a cheapskate. When tempted to grab a dinner check, do so. Don't say: "It isn't my turn," or "I wouldn't give these cheapstakes here the satisfaction." Act richly! No need to make a bankrupting habit of it, but do it at least once in a while. Being tempted to do it shows it's in your "inward" per-sonality. Bring it out in the open, and your personality is con-firmed.

Lyn Durant of United Manufacturing, Sherm Billingsley of the Stork Club, Ray Moloney of Bally, and many successful business leaders have a habit of giving a very expensive present to an occasional visitor.

These men are sports, sure, but their personality instinct tells them that it's delightful to turn a business visit into a social visit. It isn't so much their generosity that gets them favorable mention and social fame, as it is their *sporting blood.*

All people love a sport because they understand him. They, too, have the same kind of sporting blood but hesitate to spill any of it.

You don't need to be well-fixed to be a sport. Buy a few ice cream bars for the kids, and that makes you a sport in *their* eyes.

Santa Claus is the greatest personality of all to the young-sters because he is a *sport.*

The main idea is this: practice at being a sport in a small way, and your personality will "out" at very little cost to you. Then you are prepared, when the occasion pops up, to *give away parts of yourself,* whether they be money, time, or energy, in a way that wins popular attention and applause.

2. Bring your feelings up to the surface.

The sport's son, referred to above, loves to philosophize on the subject of personality. He told me about a surefire trick for readying up his personality for an evening "in company."

As he dresses, he begins to recall every funny and amusing thing that ever happened in his lifetime. He smiles, he giggles, he chortles over the funny memories. He looks in the mirror and he can even see new light come into his eyes; his very skin changes and becomes alive.

He's going to enjoy the company and the company is going to enjoy him, because all the gayety, all the good times of his past are now visible in his face, his carriage, his words!

3. Easy rules:

(a) *Don't do what you want to do;* rather *want to do* what the other fellow wants, though you detest it (as you contemplate it.) When you embrace the disliked activity, when you force yourself into *pretending* it is your first desire, lo! a miracle, and you suddenly love it.

(b) *Keep awake.* Be a real part of the proceedings. Let everyone see that you are subservient to the main thing, the party, the game, the meeting, the event. Don't try to alter it to your liking. Don't introduce new ideas to make it better. Just go along and give even the most trite theme your full-hearted support.

(c) *Listen. Give your ears!* Listen to tripe and to great stuff with equal eagerness. A perfect listener never makes an enemy.

The rewards of such popularity? You'll be a wanted personality. You just can't be left out of any social or business affair. The regard of others will turn into real AFFECTION, soothing balm for your ego, and an iron-clad guarantee of your continuing good nature.

4. Know your own temperament.

No one has a COMPLETE personality; many good points are always lacking. Get the help of others to supply what you cannot. If you're holding a party, try to get a "clown," the so-called "life of the party." A sharp conversationalist, a good singer, or any other type with a specialty. You'll get the credit for having supplied these entertainers, and your friends will attribute to you all of their good points.

5. *Treat every person as a SPECIAL person.*

Most people know they are not important but they do believe they are *special*. Do your best to remember their special wishes and preference. It is an immense compliment to remember that an individual drinks his coffee straight black, or with cream and without sugar, or any other special way. These small traits of individuals are not hard to recall if you set out to remember them. When you respect an individual wish you respect the owner of the wish. And you very well know that the people who respect you are definite personalities in your own mind. The desire to please makes you a pleasant person.

6. *Reverse your perverse inclinations.*

If something tempts you to be sarcastic, STOP. At the last instant turn your intended sarcasm into a bit of clever praise.

If you find yourself wanting to teach, STOP. Turn the teaching temptation into a humble question, asking the other fellow to wise YOU up on a matter he knows something about. Everyone wants to teach, few want to be the student sitting at the feet of the master. The popular person lets the other do all the informal teaching.

If prompted to duck a certain person because of his dullness, SHIFT, AND HURRY TO CONFRONT HIM. Others may raise their eyebrows and say of you: "What can he possibly see interesting in that person?" but will add: "Boy, what a personality!"

7. *Show your spirit.*

Separate the definition of spirit into these two halves:
First, spirit is what you put into it!
Second, spirit is what you put into THEM!
As I write these lines, I have just received a spirit-compli-

ment. A young man sends word to me that he still remembers *two eggs I fried for him five years ago.* It wasn't the eggs, their freshness or their taste that he remembers, but the *way* I fried them. *I fried them with spirit!* The eggs belong in the past, but the spirit stays on forever!

Put everything you've got into what you're doing, serious work, play, conversation, the most prosaic act you can imagine. It's worth ALL of your spirit. Concentrate! Summon up all of your life force; knead it into an intense concentrated package of spirit. Show your spirit, and they'll say you have personality to burn.

But be sure to get the spirit across and *into* those present. Vibrate. You can say "Hello!" and it can be nothing but a hollow echo in the air. You can say "Hello!" with spirit and it can be a beautiful poem with the best part of the sender going through space into the best part of the receiver. A good many people have spirit but it is entirely internal; no one knows they have it because it stays inside.

Get it out and across. VIBRATE! A strong personality enters a room and you can feel the whole room vibrate with the new presence. This is what is called a "dynamic personality."

You can be dynamic, too, if you will experiment just a little in vibrating, in speeding up the wave length of your feelings. *Feel* with enough spirit and you are "heard" without speaking.

Regard your soul as a distinct machine in its own right; switch it on, make it vibrate, move, tumble, gyrate. Don't give it the right to set its own pace—you *command* it to speed up, deliver more horsepower, more dynes of energy.

You have as much spirit as the next man. The much-acclaimed "outstanding" personality has merely pushed his soul a little harder than you.

Examples of spirit: The way Dinah Shore throws the country a kiss on TV. M-mm-mm!

The drive with which Judy Garland executed some of her great recordings.

The way a lion roars and thus becomes king of the jungle though the elephant is bigger, stronger, and smarter.

8. Enthuse, naturally or artificially, but ENTHUSE!

Enthusiasm is the divine spark that proves man is born in God's image. It requires that you assert your kinship with God. Enthusiasm literally means *God in us*.

Now you may not be enthusiastic by nature, but that doesn't mean you have to deprive your personality of the irresistible force of enthusiasm. You can resort to a few legitimate tricks to create enthusiasm artificially.

(a) Exaggerate a little. Describe the thing as bigger than it first seems, and it will be bigger. (But use this device only as a rare artificial stimulant.)

(b) Listen to the sound of your own voice as you describe it on its exaggerated scale. Take your eyes off your listener and listen to yourself. Do your words seem weak, toneless, unexcited? Then you're not delivering enough enthusiasm. Talk a little louder, a little faster, and with more emotion. Give your emotion as much chance as your intelligence!

(c) Study children and enthusiastic people of all kinds. A kid wants a knife, a gun, or a bike—something dangerous. Reason says don't give it to him, but the child's enthusiasm pushes reason aside and he ends up with what he asks for enthusiastically.

When you enthuse, you *rave*. Associate with enthusiastic people and you see they are all very good *ravers*, and their raving will infect you, too.

Some associates you can't pick, they are forced on you; others you can seek out, and when you have this freedom, bypass the staid, unexcited poker faces and romp with the lovable, irresponsible enthusiasts!

When we were kids, we were all enthusiastic when we wanted something bad enough. And the "no's" we got never made any difference. But as we grew older we received so many "no's" to our pleas, the very number and weight of the refusals carried the day and drove a great deal of our enthusiasm out of us.

Return to the childish credo that *No is no answer*. Laugh at every No. It has no right, no meaning; and enthusiasm can override it every time.

Be a booster and specialize in the good things of life. For every person who admires a negative critic, there are a thousand who love a positive enthusiast, prize his acquaintance and honor his personality.

9. Get personal.

Ben Silberman, Detroit bookseller, is known to bookmen all over the world, for his unorthodox methods of selling books. He talks to a customer who has come in for a certain book in this fashion: "Before I sell you this book, tell me a little about yourself. Why are you buying it? What do you most want out of life? What books have you already read that you can enthuse over?" Ben wants to pinpoint your personality for his own guidance in rendering you tailor-made service.

He never gives you that simple-minded, frustrating and maddening question you get from the average book clerk: "Can I help you?" Yet you know instantly that all his questions, deeply rich and personal, are saying just that. He *wants* to help you and you *know* it.

Often he will positively refuse to sell you the book you came in to get. Competition calls him a cockeyed salesman, a nut. But Ben includes in his endless list of friends some of the finest men in the world of books. We salute him as an outstanding personality, a richly *personal* person.

10. The more serious your standing, the LESS seriously you should take yourself.

A bishop who jokes with an altar boy is immediately termed a man of personality. An employer who often kids with his employees is a beloved personality. A parent who frequently acts more like a kid than a real kid in his children's presence, sells himself to his children forever.

11. Be plausible

Fred Mills, a former boss of the author, had a magic personality. His great knack was *plausability*. When he wanted you to

do something a little difficult or a little obnoxious, he'd never
order you to do it. But he would proceed to give such a plausible explanation of the need for the thing, ease of doing it, and
the great benefits that were bound to ensue, that you would be
fighting to get started at the job before he had finished with his
plausible outline.

Be plausible. Don't use too many words, and never resort to
"reasons why" if you would be a personality man. People on
the average dislike *reasons*, because people are primarily emotional. Dwell on the objective, its beauty, its richness; skip the
means and methods in between. There's always a little shock
in this trick, but you love the plausible man who shocks you
pleasantly.

A great preacher once opened up his sermon thus: "Man's
first duty in life is to save his immortal soul and any man who
doesn't do it is a damned fool!"

A young salesman of classified advertising made a suggestion
to his superiors to drop out the column rules between the ads,
thus making the page cleaner, roomier, more legible. They
said. "Ridiculous, it can't be done." Without permission, the
youth went to the foreman of the composing room and coaxed
him into drawing a proof of an old classified page without any
column rules. On presentation to the superiors, they had to
admit to the salesman's claims. There is nothing so plausible
as an accomplished fact.

12. Contribute some life to the "party."

James Russel Conlin of Chicago, known throughout the land
as the "Treasury Tenor" (for his work in World War II), is
one of the first people I'll invite to any party I give. He's a sure
personality simply because he's bound to be the life of the
party. He clowns a little bit, he approaches everybody, particularly the people he has never met, with reckless savoir faire, and
immediately loosens them up so much, they are laughing and
quickly getting reckless in their own right. Any party moves
into high when Conlin is there!

You have the duty of contributing something real to any

concourse of people in which you find yourself. If everyone held back and remained proper and silent and outside the danger of mistakes, nothing, positively nothing, would ever happen.

Loosen up. Make a minor mistake or two. See how good it makes you feel; see how the others turn to look up to you because you are human!

13. Chuckle, giggle—but don't smirk.

Perhaps I could tell you the best way to stay in a surefire personality groove is to SMILE. But that's too easy to suggest, and too corny. Do the right other things and the smile will not only take care of itself, but it will be a pleasant, natural, irresistible kind of a smile. A forced smile is often mistaken for a smirk.

I asked a well-known home builder for the secret of his personality. He thought over it for a moment. "I guess it's because every time I meet someone I begin to *chuckle*. And maybe I chuckle because I'm glad to see him."

Try it. A chuckle, quiet and low, needs no cause, no defense. It puts you into a marvelous personal mood. Your fault-finding stops, your face lights up, people are attracted to your presence. Perhaps they unconsciously want to discover what you are chuckling about.

But you fill them with unexplained wonder. Your mirth is contagious. Pretty soon they are chuckling, too, and they couldn't for the world tell you what about!

I've had a chance to study this builder close up and dissect him scientifically. Everyone says he has the most outstanding personality in town. But for the life of me, given access to all his possible gifts, his color and his human skill with people, all I can find he has on the ball is a soft, sweet, mirthy CHUCKLE. But that's enough!

14. Much tougher—be everlastingly pleasant.

I ought to skip this "device." It's too difficult, even to be called a device. But it's a way if you can make it. If others have never been able to find you otherwise than pleasant, you have a personality that can't miss.

If you can't be pleasant everlastingly, you can at least try everlastingly and that is a very good substitute.

My neighbor's daughter is that way—always pleasant—and has been since babyhood. She's 21 now and has turned down a score of offers for marriage! (Who wouldn't want to have a wife that was forever pleasant?)

She has an eternal smile on her face and a smile in every word she utters, not merely a telephone girl's kind of voice-smile. She can ask a banal question like, "Are you through with the morning's paper?" and it sounds like a poem by Shelley set to music by Brahms. Like all human beings she has, occasionally, grounds for a justifiable complaint. But the "complaint" comes from her like golden words of praise from the gods! Personality? Hers is heavenly.

Try making your complaints musical. Try making your "No's" sound like enthusiastic "Yes's." Try finding the good in others, not their faults which are so visible any dummy could find them. It takes a pleasant frame of mind to find the good. It takes and it *makes* personality.

15. *Give hearty recognition.*

Personality is this simple: put some warmth, some vibration in every greeting and recognition!

Many a successful merchant will tell you he has built up his business by the hearty, personal and individual way in which he greets his customers. Any customer, on walking into any store, craves recognition. He's serious. He's going to spend some hard-earned money there. A clerk, or a proprietor who makes a big to-do over him will be long-remembered and get his future business in addition!

The first working day of each New Year, Marshall Field, founder of the great Marshall Field Store, would stand in the main entrance of the store to personally meet each customer and warmly thank him or her for the previous year's business. A big job? Field said he always looked forward to it and considered it the most enjoyable day of his year.

Many of the Irish are said to have rich personalities. They seem to be supercharged with electricity and they give it off freely in the presence of others.

You, too, have a natural, normal allotment which you do not realize is there. Find it and use it.

Force yourself to love people, the thought of people; make yourself anticipate meeting with people. Then when you do meet them face to face, be stimulated by *their* presence, *their* electricity, *their* words.

This is the simple device used by all the so-called "dynamic personalities." They first pick up their dynamism from the persons in front of them, combine it with their own, and give off a double charge!

A good example of giving off sparks was furnished by Nikita Khrushchev, head of the USSR, in his recent visit to America. Of course, the visit was a touchy affair diplomatically, and sparks were inherent in the public appearances of the Russian chief. He began acting the moment he stepped off the airplane that brought him here. He continued acting till he got back on it. He ran the gamut of human emotion from anger to good nature and managed to register himself in front of every camera and TV lens in the country.

Let's forget about the possibility that he may not have won many new friends, or that he may have made even more people hate him than before. The man certainly *showed spirit* every minute. Overweight and age 65, at no time did he allow himself to appear tired, or uninterested or *blah*.

It takes something out of you when you give off a lot of electricity but it certainly registers your personality.

Your personality is not actually made person-to-person. Don't wait for the proper moment to find it and turn it on. Personality comes from your own background, from the basic personality lore which you have already discovered and found good, from your willingness to accept and practice at the findings of others and thereby acquire ready skill. If you have this background in your own private world, you'll inevitably shine in company.

[17]

How to Become
a Leader

THE IDEA of leadership cannot be separated from the act of selling yourself to others. Become a leader and many people will *follow* you, many will believe in you and nearly everybody —including all those who do not like you—will "buy" you. Leadership is the great *fait accompli* in selling yourself.

Again, leadership is not merely a way to success; it *is* success. Perhaps not financial success, but definitely leadership is the mark of great personal accomplishment.

You can't be president of a great corporation, or even an executive in a small company, unless you are in some degree a leader. Since promotion and advancement are always on your mind, you had better decide right now to pick up a little extra leadership.

When the national game of baseball was threatened with dissolution on account of scandal and player-collusion with gamblers, the club owners hurriedly began a search for a real "boss."

WANTED: A man who could not only boss the players but the club owners themselves; a man who would re-sell the public on the basic rightness and cleanness of baseball.

The man selected was a *bold, defiant, self-reliant* individual who knew *authority* and knew how to *exercise* it—Judge Kenesaw M. Landis.

Landis, the baseball boss, was impossible to "handle."

Many viewed him as too arbitrary and individual. But by sheer leadership he won the day and carried out his assignment perfectly. He had sold himself as a leader before he was hired. The leadership he delivered to baseball saved the game.

John Llewellyn Lewis, president of the coal miners, has been called a fascist, a show-off, a poor patriot, and a man hard to get along with.

But no one ever called Lewis a non-leader, or a weak self-salesman.

Indeed, an Eastern university, conferring an honorary degree on Lewis, referred to the man as "the greatest labor statesman in America." And the news story of this degree astonished millions of Americans who had previously made up their minds that Mr. Lewis was a "hateful" man.

During his lifetime, almost as many people hated Abraham Lincoln as loved him. Probably more people hated Napoleon than liked him.

That's the miracle of a leader—often he is hated, reviled, feared—but always *he sells himself*.

If you want to be be a leader, and fear neither the dangers nor the benefits that go with leadership, you must be willing to:

(1) *Expend Yourself with Prodigality*
(2) *Give Out Every Ounce of Energy, Mental and Physical, in Your Possession*
(3) *Pay the Price of Envy, Perhaps Hatred, and All the Distresses That Opposition to You and Your Cause Will Bring*

The power a leader wields gives him great comfort. The consciousness of success already achieved thrills him and buttresses his personal confidence and strength. The facts that he *knows* he has sold himself delivers great joy.

You can sell yourself without being a leader; you can be a success without being a leader. But leadership includes both *selling yourself* and *being a success* and does it on probably the highest plane of all.

So—be you today miles away from being a leader, it will pay you to investigate, to sample, to make a journey into the world of leadership.

The "How-To's" of Leadership

1. Inspire others.

Every leader is an inspirationalist. To "inspire" means "to put spirit into." Every leader is constantly saying to his followers: "You can be better than you are." "You can do what you think you cannot do." "Your tomorrow is better than your today!"

Paul Faust, famous merchandiser, used to hold a daily inspirational meeting of his executive staff. At some time during every meeting Paul would suddenly proclaim: "Every man here can make $50,000 a year!" (Later on several of the men present did!)

Another company president keeps telling his key men: "We can be as big as General Motors." That company probably won't reach such size but it is growing with leaps and bounds.

A fine teacher of English constantly repeats this statement to her pupils: "Every boy and girl in this room should write at least ONE BOOK before he or she dies!"

It won't happen. Not to everyone—but to *one* or *two*. For though inspiration "takes" in some degree on everyone, only a few go all the way and believe that what looks like the impossible is truly possible.

But the leadership you want will come out of your own efforts to inspire others. When you try to inspire your fellow man, you are really inspiring *yourself*.

That's the payoff. The inspiration you pass out so freely, awakens the qualities of leadership that are dormant within you.

Some Ways to Inspire, as a leader of groups of individuals. The first way to inspire a group is to make it conscious of its *strength* as a group: The classic story as told by labor union organizers is this: "Here I hold in my hand a small twig or stick. The stick represents a single man in this hall. No matter how strong he is individually and how pure he is in standing up for his rights, he as one individual is easy to break." (Here the twig is broken easily.) "But when I take a bunch of these twigs and hold them together tightly, it is impossible for any power, however strong, to break them. IN UNION THERE IS STRENGTH."

Thus the individual worker, conscious of his own weakness as being just one human being, is inspired with the version of the new strength that will be his when he joins the union.

So the English teacher in talking to one promising student seeks to inspire by delivering *strength*. Says he: "If you can write a paragraph, you can write a book!"

Inspire by paralleling the comparatively small things your listeners have already done with the bigger things others have done. If a man can build a cottage, he can build a skyscraper. This country is full of builders who up to a few years ago had never driven a nail into a board. But the post-war building boom threw the gates wide open. Laymen who could not read a blueprint, office clerks, tailors, salesmen and a motley group of men of no trade jump into building and become successful practically overnight. Here the inspiration came from example. What others have done, especially men of no special training, you too can do.

An essential in all inspiration is the spotlighting of a worthy goal. The new union man sees the goal of shorter hours and more money. The book writer envisages personal fame and bountiful royalties. The political aspirant, a high office. The goal must be worthwhile and the reaching of it must be pointed out as one of the most important things in life.

"It can be done!" is one basic inspiration motive, and strangely, very often the contradictory challenge, "You could never do that!" motivates the individual to go out and accomplish the seemingly impossible.

Through it all, when seeking to inspire, never forget to stress the BIG YOU. "YOU are man enough to take this responsibility!" "You have already demonstrated the ability for a job like this!" "I want YOU with me because I know YOU are not a quitter!" Point out your listener's special gifts, his latent powers. Praise, coupled with an attractive goal, will always inspire him into action.

2. *Feel your own authority.*

Everyone is full of authority whether he knows it or not. If you're a typist, you have authority over your own typewriter, over the paper that goes into it and the kind of work that comes out of it.

If you regard your work *as your own*, as an identical twin to your own personality, then no one, not even the top boss can interfere with the quality of your work. When you make perfection your goal, you automatically give yourself the authority to take you there! And any touch of authority gets you better acquainted with authority.

You have the authority to think for yourself, to think your own thoughts, and to arrive at sound and truthful conclusions.

You have the authority that comes from being a *person*. Your own free will is the greatest authority-gift you possess.

You have the authority to improve yourself in any field of endeavor.

The authority to dream.

The authority to work harder than your associates and fellow workers.

The authority to read, to study, to use your spare time fruitfully.

Don't wait till the day you are promoted to straw boss or head of a small department before getting on speaking terms with authority. Dabble in the authority you now have. Play with it. Swing it around in the small sphere you now command. Get used to it. Then when you do become an executive or a leader, you will never be deficient in authority, nor will you use it wrongly.

Every executive needs the authority to give orders, to make decisions; yes, and often, he has to take the authority to lower his own position and step down and do the work and the details that properly belong to those under him.

You start with your native, natural authority. Feel it. Revel in it. Almost at once you find yourself looking around for causes to lead, campaigns to wage!

Authority is not merely the right to command or give orders. Your first authority comes from your rational nature and your membership in society. You have the right, for instance, to pick up a banana peel so that some other member of society will not come along, slip, and break his leg over it. You have this authority because it involves DUTY.

The exercise of natural authority is thus a transferring of natural duty. Selling is often involved; where people are concerned with authority they generally must see a duty for doing the things they are told to do.

How does George, the factory clerk, maintain discipline over the factory messenger boy?

First, by gaining and holding his respect. He does not ask the boy to do the work that George himself is supposed to do. He is never unreasonable or unfair in the assignments he doles out. He does not threaten. If his "requests" are not complied with quickly, George keeps repeating and reminding till the messenger sees it is easier to do the thing requested than to listen forever to the reminders.

How does the copywriter in the advertising agency get the typists and stenogs in the typing pool to do his special jobs, when he has no direct authority over these workers?

He first mentions to the head of the department that he needs something special in the way of service. Realizing he may be asking too much, he requests the head of the department to allow him to do a little selling. He then turns on his charm, kids the girls, points out his dire need, says it is all "for the good of the ship." He cannot command them to do extra work their jobs do not call for, but by selling them into the consciousness both he and they are true shipmates, he gets the work done. He is not using authority directly, for it does not exist here, but still he proves himself a man of authority by creating a spirit of teamwork in getting what he wants.

3. Keep the common touch.

Leadership and the common touch are synonymous. Franklin D. Roosevelt was a Harvard man with a pronounced Harvard accent but he had the common touch that made him kin to millions of people who never finished high school.

Percy Bysshe Shelley, greatest of all lyric poets, was an intense, fiery defender of the rights of man and while still a youth stirred up the common people of his country to such a pitch that he was called by some the greatest social reformer in history.

The head of a large distributing organization, himself worth millions, finding himself out of pocket money, delights in borrowing a couple of dollars from his youngest salesman. The salesman does not mind the "touch"; he regards the boss as "one of the boys." Always feel and act as if no man is your *inferior*. It is much easier to absorb this idea than to convince yourself no one is your *superior!*

To keep the common touch, *give credit*. Not financial credit, but credit for good work done. Never try to hog all the credit for yourself though you're sure it is your due. Pass it on lavishly; let everyone have as much as you can give, and all the more credit will redound to you. You never lose credit by giving it; the more you give away, the more you have for further distribution.

Lindbergh spoke of himself and his plane as "We." He was giving rich *personal* credit to an inanimate machine!

But all great leaders, who know how to manage the authority that is theirs, generously use the word "we" in referring to any organization, enterprise or campaign. If you are a man of authority, to use the word "I" is to brag. "We" gives you the common touch and makes those you are leading want to give their all to help you succeed in every project.

4. Practice fairness.

To acquire authority quickly, practice fairness. Settle a dispute between your own children with absolute fairness and you simply glow with authority and leadership.

Be fair to your enemy—though you still dislike him—and side with him against your best friends if he is in the right and you know they are wrong.

You won't ever lose friends by being fair. They'll trust you all the more and be more apt to follow you when you lead them into waters and situations they cannot cope with.

A real leader always has to be fair to his followers. The way to be fair is to be a *fair judge*. Imagine yourself on the bench hearing a law case. If you are secretly political, easily prejudiced, and quick to condemn, few will ever acknowledge your leadership.

Be fair in all things—little or big—and people can't help looking up to you for guidance and protection.

One of the best procedures in exemplifying fairness is to first get the facts straight and then analyze them dispassionately. If your first reaction is to favor one particular side, stop right there and try to prove the opposite side is the true one. Leave all emotion out of it. Try folowing the "Ben Franklin System." Ben would run a rule down the center of a blank sheet of paper. On one side he would write all the "Pro's" of the controversy; on the other side all the "Contras." If his analysis of the "Fors" and "Againsts" was dispassionate, the heftier side generally turned out to be the right side, and the fair side.

5. Get the victorious attitude.

Get accustomed to winning and never be a good loser in the sense that losing does not disturb you.

I was once invited to play Willie Hoppe a game of three-cushion billiards. We posed for a photo before the match, the pose being a hand-over-hand pose with a cue, as kids used to pose with a baseball bat in choosing up sides.

Hoppe refused to stand for the picture unless his hand was on top! With nothing to fear from me, he still had to hold on to the *victorious attitude*. "Always bear down" was his philosophy.

To be a leader of men you must first be a leader of yourself.

You must prove to yourself that you can dominate your own person with strictest discipline before you can aspire to dominate others.

You must achieve that supreme *victory over yourself* before you can take others into the battle against the opposition.

For instance, would you rather buy from a salesman who is an ostensible leader, who has the aura of victory about him, than from the man who says: "Business is rotten. I haven't made a sale in a month?"

Learn how to sublimate or transfer the victorious attitude from one sphere to another. For instance, if you have shot a phenomenal game of golf on Sunday, do not spend Monday telling everyone at the office about your sensational shooting and low score. Instead transfer your elation and victorious feeling into your legitimate work. Tackle that tough piece of work you have been dreading and postponing for weeks. The dice are hot and rolling with you—*crowd your luck!*

Sigmund Freud pointed out that man, as an animal, instinctively desires to have as large a family as is possible, say 16 or 17 children. But socialized man, a rational creature, finds that a family of this size is all too rare or too impossible. But the natural drive for reproduction remains. Thus the architect with no children at all seeks to sublimate this instinct by creating "metaphorical" children. His huge and famous buildings become his "babies." His animal reproductive defeats are thus turned into sublimated victories.

Every time you have a victory regard it as precious—not that you have just won a 50 cent bet but that you HAVE COME THROUGH FOR YOURSELF. If it is luck, it is still victory. If it is a hard-fought win, it is victory. But do not let it be a mere "victory item." Do not let the victory end as victory. Keep it as continuous fuel for stocking your leadership engine.

6. Sell many at one time.

You've heard many another person—whether in business, the professions or society—described as "Always selling." Or "Always selling himself." That man is a leader or well on the way to possessing clean-cut leadership. For all leaders are salesmen; they sell person to person, but they sell many people at the same time instead of just one person at a time.

Experienced leaders report that, in the course of building a following, the best plan is to secure one resolute adherent at a time. But how to point out this one particular follower? He has to be sifted out of a larger group by being swayed by some phrase or argument or appeal the leader has made. Nearly all leaders have loud voices or see to it—wherever they are—that they are talking loud enough to be heard by several people. Whether it is a group conversation in a restaurant, or a single conversation in a hotel lobby, the leader's voice is often heard by total strangers and his words drunk in by people they were not apparently aimed at.

The leader likes to talk to the many not the few. At a social gathering, he does not sit in one chair all evening; he moves around, lets himself be seen and heard all over the place. And he never becomes too boring simply because his personality is so distinctive and inspiring.

A Leader Is a Boss

Though the word "boss," commonly used, has an unpleasant stigma to it, we must always remember that a leader is a boss, a man who gives orders, expects them to be obeyed, and sees that his orders *are* obeyed inspite of reluctance or passivity on the part of those receiving the orders.

A leader, therefore, does not necessarily sell himself by being popular, but rather by showing the personal strength and authority that the crowd, small or large, expects from a leader.

You have the qualities of leadership in you already, though you know you are not the bossy type.

If you have a sense of right and wrong, a feeling for what is good for the community or company where you live or work, you already *have enough in you* to show outstanding qualities of leadership.

Some authority comes from the outside but true authority is God-given to every individual. If you can see what is right, and believe in the right strongly enough, God and your own human nature will quickly supply the necessary authority for you to stand up and fight and draw others to you. Most men think they do not want to be leaders. They believe they are not cut out for it. Still they know that without good leadership the right does not always prevail. False leaders block it. Other men, seeing eye to eye with them, are timid about coming to the front.

Leadership is a tool for selling yourself. It is available. It is close by, not far away. You can push yourself into it slowly, or find it thrust upon you by some sudden occasion.

Ray M. was a big boss, owner of a prosperous company, a real leader. He made all decisions personally in the line of production, sales, new products. Suddenly he died. At his wake many of his key employees, along with powerful distributors of the company's products, were wondering who would replace Ray, who would be the new leader? The names of five men were mentioned. Four of the five were well known in the trade, the fifth was only known to a small circle of employees. But this fifth man was much better equipped to know what to do, with the old leader gone, than the other four.

He had never shown any signs of bossiness before, but within a week while the four others were waiting for someone to come along and make or elect them leader, Charlie, the fifth, took the helm of the company, began to make all important decisions without hesitation, giving necessary orders and seeing they were carried out. Naturally, the company heirs and directors elected him leader—that is, PRESIDENT!

Charlie probably is not as personable as the late Ray, not so much a foreground man or a self-salesman, but his dependability, his knowledge, and his fresh display of audacity and authority did sell him far better than publicity or showmanship ever could.

The big point is this: though Charlie had never acted like a boss before, had never exerted authority openly, when the right time came he stepped into the breach and showed his native leadership, which had been inside him for years waiting for the right opportunity. Charlie was not afraid TO BE BOSS!

[18]

How to Chart Your Future

In any grouping of requisites for selling yourself, *promise* must come near the top of the list. "One of our most promising young men" is a phrase used by top echelon executives in referring to young men who are "comers" in the company.

If you can have a phrase like that fastened on *you*, you just can't miss. The big men, convinced you have everything on the ball, are ready to go out of their way to help you, boost you, and often *promote you* ahead of others who top you in seniority.

12 Devices for Becoming "A Man of Promise"

How do you become a Man of Promise? Of course, you must have something on the ball, a little something at least. You must have a variety of good qualities, especially the different "sell-yourself" qualities described elsewhere in this book.

But whether your ability is prodigious or near-mediocre, you must handle whatever ability you have with the idea of building up a picture of future promise for all around you to affirm. What are the neat and easy devices?

1. Be a "tomorrow" man.

Edison and Steinmetz are good examples. They always tied their work and their aspirations into developments for tomorrow. They left "today" and "yesterday" to the other guy.

Talk about the past and people peg you as a fellow who has seen better days. Talk of the present and you run into dispute after dispute. Hitch your wagon, like Henry Ford did his T in Lizzie, to the future—and you are immediately a standout.

Christ talked of salvation to come. Lincoln preached a united nation but only after everyone did a lot of hard work to achieve and cement the union.

Luther wanted *reformed* Christianity, a change in the *status quo.*

Churchill said, "We will fight on the beaches and the streets," but the British did not have to get around to it.

Lenin preached the *five year plan;* the five years ahead seemed like an awful chunk of the future to bite off, but the Russian people bought it.

Ghandi, when independence for India seemed a total impossibility, insisted: "We will settle for nothing else."

Even before these men, and thousands of other dealers-in-the-future like them, could demonstrate even incidental success for their plans and crusades, they had already *sold themselves* to a multitude of followers. For the multitude, strangely, loves the future, loves *that which is not,* but may come into being, infinitely more than it loves the present or past.

So hurry up and hook yourself up with an ideal, a dream, a miracle or achievement for the tomorrow of your life or your business. The famous architect Frank Lloyd Wright, who everyone will agree sold himself better than any modern architect, when long past three score and ten, was still battling for and clearly envisioning dreams that other architects insisted could never come true. But he kept on selling himself with those announced dreams. Such as his "Mile-High" building for Chicago.

"Let's make our company (now small and inglorious) the Number One company in our field!" There's a dandy starter.

Maybe the owner of the outfit will laugh at you when he hears you say it. But keep on saying it, keep on believing it's possible, and that self-same owner will begin by apologizing to you, will labor to explain why it can't be done, but all the while will be looking up to you as to a prophet-on-high, and will soon believe you are his most promising employee.

2. *Chart the future!*

I mean that literally. *Make up some charts.* Everyone loves charts—they are surefire.

(a) Cite your objectives.

(b) State the statistics, the circumstances backed by figures.

(c) Mark down the means you will employ for reaching the separate objectives.

(d) Enumerate the different steps in the plan one by one and in practical sequence.

(e) Justify the whole operation by weighing costs against benefits, recite the gambling percentage *for* you as well as *against* you.

Going through the *motions* seems to be an essential of every executive or department head in any business of average size or larger. You must have a plan—or your status as a man who is still growing—is in jeopardy. Nor do you want to be labelled merely as a "dreamer."

Nobody expects your plan to be achieved immediately, no one will hold a stop watch on you and demand results overnight or even over a year!

That you have a plan, that you believe in it and are enthusiastic about it is enough to earn universal respect and approval.

Every well-sold cause has a map or blueprint of some kind behind it. Every big builder has a "progress chart" hanging in his office which will tell him in an instant the stage of progress his construction has reached. Every good salesmanager has a sales chart of all his operations always before him, identifying the salesmen who are producers and disclosing weak points in the sales operation.

There was a young man who later became known in his own circle as "Charts" McArthur. His friends thought him chart-crazy because he charted practically everything. One day he charted his own experience from the very day he was born, in order to see at a glance what his connections were, what special abilities he had developed over the years. The chart proved to him that he should change jobs. He did. Being put in charge of a small department, he began to develop charts on a grand scale, and practice at the art made his charts something to look at and to mull over with interest, because a good chart always contains sound logic. "Charts" McArthur is now vice-president of his company. Though in his earlier years he used charts pragmatically as a device for selling himself to his superiors, he now demands charts from all his subordinate managers on plans, progress, constitution, and everything worthwhile. He says: "I find I can read a chart ten times as fast as any kind of a report and get a lot more out of it."

3. Insist on respect.

The very fact that you are a dealer in things to come will get you respect. But never be satisfied with transitory respect, or just a little respect. For you—enduring respect, or nothing!

Maintain your *dignity* at all costs. You have dignity because you were born with it; you don't need to earn it. It is not a prize to be won, so don't try to win it; just assume it. Feel it through and through as an indispensable possession. Be proud, immensely proud, of your own name, of the company you work for, of your ideals and aspirations.

When Hays MacFarland, well-known advertising agent, was sales manager of the old *Chicago Examiner* he had a widely discussed rule which he required all of his advertising salesmen to follow. *They must come down every day in a white shirt with a white starched collar and white starched cuffs.*

Nearly all of them rebelled, for starched linen is not only a bother and an extra expense, in many cases it is downright uncomfortable. But MacFarland told them one and all: "This is to command respect. You are a walking advertisement for your newspaper, and this is a newspaper that TAKES CARE."

That was long ago, but I have followed the careers of several of the self-same salesmen and to a man they have been extraordinarily successful. One is salesmanager of a large trade paper. One is owner of a prosperous magazine. Another is salesmanager of a national organization. And so on. Do *they* demand that their own salesmen wear starched collars and cuffs? Certainly not. Times have changed. But the lesson of enforced discipline in making a more-than-neat appearance to command respect has not been forgotten. They are just as strict as their old boss was, but in contemporary matters.

Pride in your appearance may be condemned by some people, if "appearance" is your sole concern. Always keep appearance in its proper perspective. The best rule here is this: always maintain an appearance in dress that is definitely above the average presented by your associates. This is not hard to do, since the average is usually not very high. If you are not inclined by nature to be immaculately neat, you can spend more money for every article of clothing you wear. A $1.00 necktie, a $2.00 shirt and a $40 suit of clothes cannot do anything to help you become a man of promise.

Keep your promises.

Don't make any more promises than necessary, but keep those you do make. A promising man is not necessarily a person who is making promises day in and day out. A promise puts you to a cruel test, but if you do get involved in a clean-cut promise, come through, make good. Never run out on your word or respect will be instantly lost.

4. Get the plus attitude.

A man who is forever carrying around the defeatist attitude, looking for poison, defeat and destruction is never viewed as a fireball, a man on his way to success. Get on the plus side and stay there!

Walter Somers of Chicago for forty years has been known as one of the best Ford salesmen in America. In all his business and human relations Walter is a sparkling example of the plus attitude.

He has converted this plus drive of his into an amazing and unrelenting skill at *approbation.* He has nothing but praise for the high and the low, and his praise is always delicious and special. He praises the mayor and the laundress, the alderman and the street sweeper; he praises his best competition.

"No one but an idiot," says Walter, "would try to rap the

Chevrolet or Plymouth!" When he gets around to praising his own car, he has already built up a mountain of personal promise, and sold himself to the hilt. They buy his Fords, and as they buy, they feel they are getting a beautiful future of motoring pleasure and mechanical satisfaction.

Each pridefully, ever after, refers to his Ford as a "Walter Somers Ford."

On Blue Mondays when you may not be up to par and feel least like conquering the world with a plus attitude, any little trick you have learned in the past for restoring your plus feelings should be called up and used. Clean out that drawer in your desk, all full of junk, and throw all the useless stuff away. The relief is enormous! Tighten your shoe laces—it will pep you up instantly. Wash your hands and let the cold water run on your wrists for a minute—it was a favorite trick of Theodore Roosevelt. You should have a special file of letters of praise you have received over the years: pull it out now and re-read the letters! Dictate a letter of praise to a deserving friend. Dwell for a few moments on that great golf shot you made yesterday— praise yourself! Give someone—anyone, the office boy, the janitor, the window washer—a helping hand. Simply TRY to break the blue mood in any and every way possible, and if you persist, the blues will quickly vanish and you will be a full-fledged plus-man again.

5. Be always fair.

A man can sell himself to you by being your prejudiced friend and can give you the breaks which he denies to others. But if he is guilty of just *one unfair act*, be it in your favor or not, you are not fully ready to believe in his future promise.

It's hard to be fair when a close friend or someone you love dearly is involved.

It's hard to be fair when a vicious opponent or a real enemy is involved.

Fairness may get you into many a tight situation but it has its own rewards. The weak and the strong, the sweet and the bitter, will ultimately cheer you, believe in you, and want you prominently in the foreground for all the future. Case Study: The most common and open study of the need for promise in any person's career can be found in the case of politicians, or potential candidates, aspiring to high office.

These men are extremely careful to establish the public impression of *fairness*. They give a play to all factions and blocs of the population but are never seen as favoring one over the other. They cannot be found out showing discrimination of any kind and when facing an audience or public jury that wants any kind of discrimination, they tread very carefully indeed, even to the point of straddling the issue, but never giving offense to any particular faction.

You are probably not involved in "politics" as the word is applied to voting and elections, but if you hold a good job in a private company, sooner or later you must become involved in company politics. It is a serious mistake to join a particular clique and thereby confess lack of fairness by being *against* any other group inside the organization.

The best plan is to work with all cliques when they are right, and diplomatically avoid any clique when you know it is in the wrong. Preserve fairness and you preserve your promise. By becoming a known member of a petty office or factory clique, you can lose all your fine promise overnight.

Politics in private industry is a real bugaboo—especially for the conscientious worker. There is everywhere considerable talk of loyalty and many executives boldly announce to the world: "Give me a loyal man, I want no other kind," and mean an employee who at all times will be loyal to his superior.

We should understand the different forms of loyalty. Some loyalty is reprehensible; for example, the loyalty of a parasite which lives off the body of another. This is 100 per cent loyalty—but not admirable. I like to break loyalty as it refers to a man working at a job into these three parts:

Your FIRST Loyalty: Loyalty to the Assignment. Do the job in the right way and fight everything that gets in the way.

Your SECOND Loyalty: Loyalty to Yourself. No matter where you work or what your work is, at all costs save your own integrity. Do not say "Yes" when you mean "No"; do not agree openly when you disagree silently. A passion for saving your self-respect will win you the universal respect of others, even that of your political enemies.

Your THIRD Loyalty: Loyalty to Your Company. Many sanctimonious individuals like to pose as being forever, first, last and always loyal to their company: "My company, right or wrong!" This philosophy appeals to some bosses and owners, but not all. The modern business leader with the success of his company at heart, nearly always favors men of integrity who place the doing of the work they are assigned to do in top position of priority, and if company rules or company politics interfere, try to convince the company that it should not prevent a man from doing what he is assigned to do.

Following these three loyalties will not free you from political mix-ups and troubles but will cause all factions and cliques to grade you as a solid company fixture.

6. Let them overrate you.

How often have you heard a speaker being introduced by the toastmaster in flowery, exaggerated terms, and then getting to his feet when the introduction is over, *deny all the good things* that have just been said about him. Folly! For the audience wants to hear a public speaker graded up, wants to believe the forthcoming speech comes from a great mind and a great man. Such a man degrades himself immediately by taking issue with a plus introduction!

When you engage in a scientific program for building an aura of promise around yourself, you may sometimes be called a "genius" or a "person of superior talent." Though in your heart of hearts you know you are just another Joe Blow, never admit you are *not* a genius.

When people refer to you as genius, it simply means you have definitely sold yourself to them by means of *promise.* Don't stoop to unsell them at this point.

A banker friend once gave me the inside story on his appointment as president of a large bank. The appointment was a big surprise, for the man came from an entirely different walk of life, and was never a banker per se. My confidante explained matters this way: "All my life people always accredited me with having a great deal more money than I ever had. When I was in high school, all my classmates were sure I was rich—and I wasn't. But I never disillusioned them.

"Later on the story got out—never denied by me—that I owned an immense amount of real estate. After that, I was supposed to have made a startling coup on the stock market. I did have some money, and I had learned how to handle it and conserve it, and I often wished I was worth one-tenth of the fortune attributed to me.

"How the mistaken idea came into being I didn't know, and truly did not care; for I never set anybody wise to the real facts. I sensed this overestimate of my finances was an asset—and it was exactly that! I now have a big place in the financial world because I always liked to be associated with money, and realized that the high rating others gave to my finances would someday be very useful to me. Anyone can overrate me anytime he wants to!"

If you are overrated in any particular field, you can tell yourself there are really some grounds for this high rating. The public is seldom entirely mistaken.

7. Never let them underrate you.

A gifted young salesman was being drastically underrated in his new job by the bosses.

They talked down to him as if he were a schoolboy, and though he was careful to show no resentment, he resolved some day soon to put the shoe on the other foot.

The day came when the bosses decided to give everyone in the company—including themselves—a very comprehensive intelligence and personal aptitude test—a real lulu costing $75 per person.

My friend, from college and army experience, found himself in very deep waters that suited him to a "T." He scored number one in the entire company and was actually judged better fitted to be a top executive than those already in the spot!

When the news leaked out, he quit his job and his explanation was significant: "I don't want to work for so-called smart men who aren't wise enough to keep themselves sold and allow themselves to be put on the spot needlessly."

8. Be known as an "idea man."

If you are gifted with the ability to produce new, good ideas at will, scatter them around lavishly, and actually *give most of them away* letting the other man take credit, if he will, for them.

But the chances are you are not this type of person; perhaps your biggest regret is your inability to manufacture any idea at all. If so, don't be disheartened.

Here's a cute trick for getting a rep as an idea man. Though you are here seeking to establish *future* promise, now dig into your past for ideas, wild or mild, which you had a long, long time ago. Consult your memory, old notes for possible inventions, recall some advanced theories of your young days.

Certainly you did put a lot of time and thought into those buried efforts of the mind, and a little rehearsing will bring them back quickly. Now look them over in the clear light of the present day.

Times have changed; the years, which at the time you had the ideas were all ahead, have now gone by. There's a good chance that your original creations have been miraculously improved by the passing of time. They are not dead, they are not stale or old. Bring them out, tie them into your business or career, and talk about them again. The chances are people will now give you credit for idea power and imagination you didn't know you possessed.

9. Practice imagination with "heart."

Imagination is a great asset for establishing future promise and selling yourself to others. If you think your imagination is sluggish, awaken it now by combining it with heart.

Think of some people you know who are lonesome, sick, and neglected. Write them a letter, visit them in person. That's IMAGINATION!

Start your imagination working first on acts of personal kindness and you will be astounded at how quickly your imaginative machinery now speeds up in matters of business or personal opportunism.

If you have ever been in business for yourself, you know how difficult it is to get started, to get customers, to begin to make money after you have first opened up your doors. Many an imaginative businessman with a heart has made it a practice to send some kind of an order to a friend on the first day he has opened up for business. On such an occasion it is perfectly all right to send flowers and well wishes; but nothing is a better congratulation or good wish than to *buy something* from the man who has just started in business. Ten dollars worth of business feels a hundred times as good, on that day, as ten dollars worth of flowers.

10. Don't be afraid to go out on a limb.

If you have a subtle idea, or a very complicated plan that is almost impossible to put into words, try putting it into words anyhow and speak it directly to your associates, your superiors, to all and sundry.

Don't do this regularly or else people will conclude you are vague and dreamy—but once in a while it's fine for confirming their belief in your future promise. The thing you have studied deeply is bound to be over their heads; when you reveal it boldly, they may not O.K. the thing, but they will O.K. you!

A company which had long been rich and prosperous was going broke. The owners had lost the money-making spirit and were living softly. Internal politics were rife; waste and mistakes, rampant.

The top executives could see what was happening, but politics and selfishness handcuffed them from doing anything about it.

But one such executive, an independent man who put loyalty to the company above loyalty to the owners, formulated and submitted a plan for saving the sinking ship. The owners insisted the ship was not sinking, that everything would be all right in another few months. This man, having gone to the top, could have quit, saying there was no further place to go. But at the risk of being known as a traitor, he privately called on the president of the bank which held huge mortgages on the property. The banker examined the plan for reform and okayed it. "It goes through," he said, "and you are the one who will operate it."

In a week the owners of the company, who up till then had been supreme lords of the institution, were "put on ice" and told they could not interfere till the loans were paid off. And in six months the company, a great money-maker with a strong driving hand behind it, having cleared out all the deadwood and dissension, got back into the black.

The owners were given back their rights and their power. They had by now learned their lesson. The "traitor" was their unanimous choice for president and operating head.

Never go over your superior's head in a small, petty thing. This destroys your promise by making you yourself small and petty. But when it's a case of "do or die" then it is *your duty to go over his head* whether he likes it or not and regardless of how great the risk to your personal destiny.

11. Pour good suggestions into yourself.

This you must continually repeat to yourself: "I am a promising fellow. I am on the verge of genius, talent, superior intelligence and ability. My biggest years, my greatest achievements are all ahead of me!" The world is generally fault-finding and critical but it loves a man of promise, for in him seems to be wrapped up all the progress and benefits mankind may enjoy in the future.

12. Stay young.

Once the world puts you down as an old man, your promise is all gone. Stay young! The secret formula for perpetual youth is *study*. Keep on studying, one subject or a dozen, let your wonder and curiosity be intrigued and your faculties of observation and deduction improve as time goes by.

René Descartes, genius in philosophy and science, was once

surprised by a stranger who walked unexpectedly into Descartes' room. "What are you doing?" asked the stranger and Descartes replied, "Studying."

"But where are your books?"

Descartes pointed to his own forehead and said, "Here is the only book I need."

Of all forms of study, *independent study* is the best. Go into a new subject all by yourself, without instructor, without books or any other equipment. Figure the thing out with no power other than your own. Of course, many of your findings will duplicate the prior discoveries of others, but what does that matter?

What you learn all by yourself, you learn for good. Furthermore, you develop a Rock-of-Gibraltar type of self-confidence which advertises you to the world as an individual able to cope with any contingency, able to meet any possible challenge, a man of illimitable resources and promise.

Promise alone will sell you. Promise alone can make you successful for, once established, like a great magnet it draws to you the gifts, favors, and cooperation of other men, the acts of humankind sometimes referred to as the "breaks." All successful men are said to be successful because they got the "breaks." But it was the promise which they developed by their own powers and ingenuity which brought them the "breaks."

What Next?

Now THAT you've learned the secrets of selling yourself to people, now that you've decided to be the one man everyone looks to for the answer to that knotty problem, the finesser who is able to handle the toughest customers, now that you're ready to take on all the situations that call for the person who can truly sell himself—*go to it!*

But go to it with a plan. Take each section of this book and devise your own plan of attack to improve yourself in those areas where you need it most. Construct a Self-Selling Chart with which you can plan and plot your progress week by week.

Analyze yourself. List the positive things you're doing to:

1. Pin down your idea of success.
2. Become a livewire.
3. Build a better vocabulary.
4. Be a bright conversationalist.
5. Train yourself as a public speaker.
6. Develop a better writing style.
7. Attempt the audacious approach to things.
8. Chart your future plans.
9. Make those important connections.
10. Use finesse in situations where it can help you most.
11. Develop your "kinship rating."
12. Become a better showman.
13. Carry out your own publicity campaign.
14. Merchandise your personality.
15. Become a leader.

And what aren't you doing? Write down the pluses and the minuses of your program so that you can see where you're improving and where you're not. But most important, be doing something about selling yourself every day. Get in the habit of checking your Self-Selling Chart every night.

The success with which this program is carried out is up to you, of course; but with day-to-day practice you can make your own opportunities for success. Try it and see.

Tomorrow morning, for instance, begin by starting a conversation with somebody whom you've merely nodded to for mornings on end. See if he doesn't perk up and doesn't begin to "buy" you as a first class individual. Tomorrow noon, eat lunch with one of the new fellows at work; find out what interests him, what his ambitions are and before you know it, you'll have sold yourself to another person and have made another friend in the bargain. Tomorrow evening after dinner pull yourself away from TV long enough to write two letters or four postcards to people who only hear from you at Christmas—you'll be amazed at the results.

By putting these secrets to work for you now, you can begin to achieve all the minor successes which are the stepping stones to reaching that big goal you've planned to achieve for so long. With what you know now, the sky's the limit; you can sell yourself to anybody and everybody every day in the year!